CREATING AN INCLUSIVE AND ACCESSIBLE WORKPLACE

HR Initiatives

CREATING AN INCLUSIVE AND ACCESSIBLE WORKPLACE

HR Initiatives

Editors

Anu Singh Lather

Shalini Garg

BLOOMSBURY

LONDON • NEW DELHI • NEW YORK • SYDNEY

First Published, 2014

BLOOMSBURY PUBLISHING INDIA PVT. LTD.
London New Delhi New York Sydney

ISBN: 978-93-84052-20-1

10 9 8 7 6 5 4 3 2 1

Published by Bloomsbury Publishing India Pvt. Ltd.
Vishrut Building, DDA Complex, Building No. 3
Pocket C-6 & 7, Vasant Kunj
New Delhi 110 070

Laser Typeset by FORTUNE GRAPHICS
WZ-911/2, Shankarlal Street, Ring Road, Naraina, New Delhi

Printed at ANVI COMPOSERS, Paschim Vihar, New Delhi

Contents

Preface vii

INVITED PAPERS

1. Association for Rehabilitation under the National Trust Initiative of Marketing (ARUNIM): An Innovative and Inclusive Model Promoting Micro-Enterprise and Entrepreneurship 3
Thilakam Rajendran
2. Gender Discrimination and Sexual Harassment 9
Neena Sinha

REGULAR PAPERS

3. Promoting an Inclusive Workplace: A Study of the Tata Group 15
Anu Singh Lather, Shalini Garg and Sona Vikas
4. Constitutional Imperatives of the Inclusive and Accessible Workplace in India 24
Anuj Vaksha
5. Gendered by Age and not by Knowledge at Professional Working Places: A Case Study For Professional Environment 30
Ramani Swarna
6. An Inclusive Workplace: A Great Place to Work 38
Shruti Sargam
7. Inclusion in Consulting Firms 48
Rupa Mittal
8. The Image of Persons with Disabilities as Portrayed in a Daily Newspaper: A Short Term Content Analysis Study 52
Shalini Garg, Sanchta and Puneet Kumar Gupta
9. Perception of the Employed Sexual Minorities (LGBT) on their Inclusion in the Workplace in Bangalore 66
Justin J. Philip and Bino Thomas
10. Work-Life Balance in Socio-Professional Life: Need, Necessity and Utopia 73
Rajesh S. Pyngavil
11. The Problems of Discrimination Faced by Women at their Workplaces: Experiences and Lessons 84
Bhavya Nain

12. Predictive HR: Paving the Way for an Inclusive and Accessible Workplace 93
Rekha Mishra and Shalini Garg

13. Challenges of Higher Education and its Role in Social Development: A Case Study of India 102
Ashish Kumar

14. Flexi Work: A Welcome HR Initiative in Creating an Inclusive Workplace for Techie Moms – A Case Study 108
Y. Lakshmi Prabha

15. Lifelong Learning for Organizations: Managing Inclusiveness and Growth 115
Vijita S. Aggarwal

16. Empirical Study of Work-Life Balance of Paid Workers in Banking and the Financial Services Sector with Special Reference to Women 122
Pranava Prakash and Somya Bhargava

17. An Inclusive and Accessible Workplace – HR Initiatives at Wipro 131
Manisha Vijayran

18. e-HR: Towards Accessibility and Creating HR Value 140
Puja Sareen

19. Towards Inclusiveness at the Workplace for the Differently Abled: Issues and Challenges 157
Meenakshi Handa and Jyoti Kukreja

20. Gendered CSR: An Initiative Towards Creating an Inclusive Workplace 166
Prachi Jain and Vijita Singh Aggarwal

21. A Study of Employee Wellness Programs in IT Companies in India 177
Gunjan Mathur and Deepali Dabas

22. Opportunities and Challenges in an Inclusive Workplace: With Special Reference to Corporate Leadership 188
Anshu Lochab, Megha Grover and Priyanka Gautam

23. Creating an Inclusive Environment for Expatriates: Challenges and Initiatives 200
Vijita Singh Aggarwal and Shefali

24. Creating the Road for Inclusion of People with Mental Illness 211
G.B. Sitaram and Poonam Khurana

25. Reservations in India: An Inclusive Perspective 218
S. Sanjay Kumar

Author Index 225

Preface

An environment where everyone is treated with dignity and respect, where talents and skills of different groups are valued, and where productivity and customer service improves because the workforce is happier, more motivated and keenly aware of the benefits that inclusion can bring. An inclusive workplace is one where human rights principles of fairness, respect, equality, dignity and autonomy are promoted and are part of the organization's everyday goals and behaviour.

More employers are coming up with solutions to create and promote an inclusive workplace in order to maximise productivity, attract new talent and increase employee commitment. An organization's action on equality and human rights issues can have a significant impact upon their brand reputation, so inclusion makes good business sense. Inclusive workplaces that understand the needs of their employees and make the staff feel valued and respected also have greater success in retaining staff. Having a range of policies and facilities in place to ensure that all employees are able to balance work with other aspects of their lives has a positive impact on job satisfaction, productivity and commitment.

An inclusive workplace is one where human rights principles of fairness, respect, equality, dignity and autonomy are promoted and are part of the organisation's everyday goals and behaviour. In an inclusive workplace:

- There is a welcoming workplace culture where everyone is treated with respect and dignity and everyone feels valued.
- Policies are in place concerning equality and human rights, working conditions, dignity at work, employee welfare and fair recruitment and procurement practices.
- Members of staff at all levels are aware of the inclusive values of the organisation and are actively consulted and involved in policy development.
- The workforce is representative of the local community or customers (if not, under-represented groups are encouraged to apply).
- All employees are encouraged to develop and progress, and any barriers faced by specific groups are identified and action taken to address them.
- Unnecessary hierarchies and occupational segregation, where groups of employees are congregated into certain areas, are discouraged.
- The organisation is aware of any potential tensions within the workplace, and takes action to anticipate and address them.
- Inclusive strategies are fully supported and promoted by senior staff.

This book provides readers with a better understanding of the initiatives taken to ensure an environment where everyone is treated with dignity and respect, where talents and skills of different groups are valued, and where productivity and customer service improves because the workforce is happier, more motivated and more aware of the benefits that inclusion can bring. All the papers were selected for publication through a blind review process.

We take this opportunity to express our sincere thanks to Prof. Anup Beniwal, Hon'ble Vice Chancellor Guru Gobind Singh Indraprastha University for his enduring guidance and motivation. It is with his vision and support for his pupils in the university that we gathered courage to produce such works. We appreciate the efforts of academicians, researchers, and industry practitioners for their valuable contributions in the form of research papers. We also express our gratitude to the publishers for enabling us to release the book in the public domain for further deliberations and contemplation.

Editors

Invited Papers

Association for Rehabilitation under the National Trust Initiative of Marketing (ARUNIM): An Innovative and Inclusive Model Promoting Micro-Enterprise and Entrepreneurship

Thilakam Rajendran

National Trust, Old Rajinder Nagar, New Delhi

Kewword: *ARUNIM, Disability, Workshop, Innovative, Empowerment, Marketing*

ARUNIM is a pioneering and path-breaking innovation for creating livelihoods through entrepreneurship, with a special focus on persons with developmental disabilities.

CHANGING PERCEPTIONS AND CREATING IDENTITIES

From passion to path for self-reliance, Art in form of paintings is everything for S. Pushkala; the young entrepreneur from Bhopal, Madhya Pradesh. Painting was introduced to her by her Parents as a means to explore her ability and engage her. Now over a decade since those humble beginnings, through perseverance and hardwork it is becoming a means of economic achievement.

In the year 2011, Pushkala started exhibiting and selling her Paintings and later that year she joined ARUNIM as its member. This move gave Pushkala and her 'Pushkala Art Center' a concrete base, visibility and growth potential. ARUNIM has over the three years now provided various opportunities at different exhibitions and conferences across cities, promoting and selling Pushkala's Art and products. It was under ARUNIM's mentorship that

Pushkala transformed her Art into value and aesthetic products, thereby creating more market and customer base. ARUNIM is not just an Organisation to Pushkala, it is more of an extended family. In ARUNIM people she has found a social circle to interact on her own, which she longed for . They not just appreciated her work and effort, but gave her a platform to express herself as an independent and confident individual in Public during their AGM 2012 meet. Pushkala's accomplishments clearly establishes the impact of a positive nuturing environment and its importance in everyone's life, normal or challenged. The need to respect every individual and providing a healthy environment for growth can't be undermined.

Today with huge plans and a support structure, Pushkala has left behind the barriers that her challenged intellectual and hormonal imbalances had created. Today she feels not like a specially challenged person, but specially abled creating special products for all out there. She is an inspired woman and is scripting a story sure to inspire others.

BACKGROUND INFORMATION

As on date, there are about 900 NGOs registered under the National Trust. Majority of them have set up sheltered workshops, which focus on vocational training and on making products. However, various formal and informal studies undertaken about the functioning of these workshops revealed that people with disabilities engaged in these workshops did not have sustainable work and income. They were unable to leverage the potential of the real-world markets. There was lack of proper training, access to resources, business skills and marketing expertise. To address these issues of sheltered workshops and to convert them to micro enterprises, ARUNIM was set up by National Trust.

INTRODUCTION

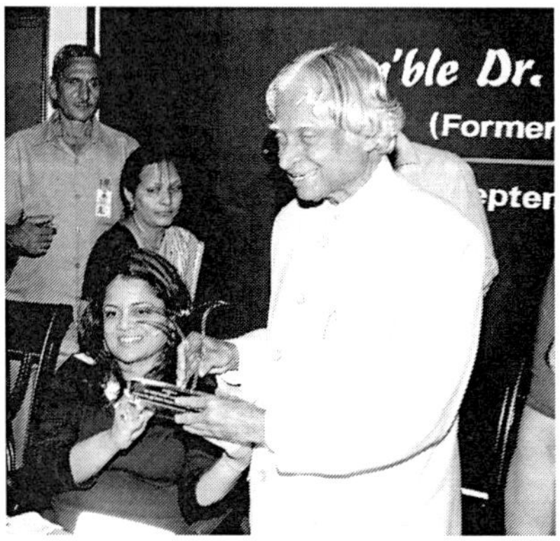

ARUNIM (Association for Rehabilitation under National Trust Initiative of Marketing) is a path breaking initiative of National Trust which is a statutory body under the Ministry of Social Justice and Empowerment. ARUNIM is registered as a non-profit society and was launched by Dr. Abdul Kalam on the 22nd Sep 2008. It is an independent Marketing Federation which works towards Economic Empowerment of persons with moderate to severe disabilities employed in sheltered/supported work environments particularly those covered under the National Trust Act. Its key objective is to facilitate livelihood and capacity building through the promotion of market driven products and services.

VISION

Persons with disabilities are empowered to be active partners in contributing to the growth of the global economy

MISSION

ARUNIM builds an entrepreneurial approach towards economic empowerment and self reliance for Persons with Disabilities and other marginalized groups, with a focus on developmental disabilities.

ARUNIM will enable Persons with Disabilities to say I AM...I CAN!

CORE FOCUS AREA

ARUNIM's mandate is:

- To strive for minimum wages for persons employed in sheltered/supported work environments
- Innovative product designing and entrepreneurship skill development
- Introducing adaptations and mechanization where appropriate and feasible
- Working towards building 'ARUNIM' brand for chosen products
- Standardizing quality
- Marketing products using sound strategies in Packaging, Pricing, Placing and Promotions
- Establishing web based initiatives
- Setting up retail outlets across the country

DETAILS OF THE PROJECT AND ITS BENEFICIARIES

ARUNIM's strategies include building the membership base across the country and networking with financial sectors, Corporate sectors and the various Government bodies and Ministries that promote micro enterprises, and building a brand. Its activities range from **policy level interventions to providing information, training in product design, introducing technology based solutions and marketing opportunities to all its members** and to providing intensive support to sheltered workshops, individual with disabilities, Self Help Groups, which could be inclusive of parents, siblings and persons from other marginalised group, for incubating micro enterprises. ARUNIM works with **250** NGOs, and individual entrepreneurs, as members across 26 states in the country. It reaches out to more than 3,000 persons with disabilities. ARUNIM's training on Micro Enterprise, Design Workshops and Product Evaluation Programmes have been attended by more than **1000 trainers and participants** from across the country since its inception.

MARKETING AND BRANDING

ARUNIM's products are categorized under six business verticals.

1. Life style and Décor
2. Handcrafted Gifts and Souvenirs
3. Food products
4. Festival and celebrations
5. Stationery
6. Printing and Packaging

Currently the marketing channels are:

1. 4 Retail outlets in Delhi through which products are sold.
2. Participating in mainstream Exhibitions and Fairs and creating Corporate campus fairs opportunities
3. Bulk orders through Institutional sales from Govt bodies, Corporate and other organisation.
4. Participating in International Fairs and initiating export orders.

ARUNIM has networked and converged with other Ministries (Textiles, MSME, Environment, Labour & Employment, etc. for mainstreaming persons with disabilities and benefit from their schemes which would enable and include them to be part of the society.

Key Achievements 2008–13

1. Conducted more than 60 Capacity Building trainings in Product Assessment, Product Development and Micro enterprise by involving professionals from premier Design Institutes and Management Institutes This changed the market perception and brought product worthiness! Customers no buy products out of charity but for its own value.

2. ARUNIM launched the E3 (Economic Enterprise and Empowerment) Challenge 2010, a Business Plan Competition as a first ever unique programme for persons with disabilities in partnership with NSDC, NT and UNDP to scale up participation. ARUNIM received 21 business proposals from 8 States and selected 6 projects for incubation and mentoring to

convert them to business models especially focusing on people with developmental disabilities. These 6 projects were given close mentoring in every aspect to convert the sheltered workshops/Vocational units into micro enterprises.

3. A Pilot Project: ARUNIM installed a semi automated paper bag unit for production of paper bags as a pilot project. This has helped our members in mass production of paper bags in competitive rates. The automated paper bag project, has trained 46 people with disabilities and people from marginalised group so far.

4. 128 member NGOs got an opportunity to participate in Exhibitions like Shilpotsav organized by the Ministry of Social Justice and Empowerment in Delhi, Mumbai, Kolkata and Chennai. Members also participated in number of corporate fairs, India International Trade Fair, Blind Relief Association, and International Conferences
5. ARUNIM participated in International fair - 1st China South Asia Fair in Kunming, China. Our traditional Indian handcrafted products were in huge demand.
6. ARUNIM got registered with Fair Trade India

7. ARUNIM has facilitated producer member sales from Rs. 3 lakhs (2008) to Rs. 80 lakhs (till January 2013), which is a sign of improved product quality and market response
8. ARUNIM was recognized in the International platform as one of the Innovative Practices for "Promoting Micro Enterprise & Entrepreneurship for persons with disabilities" by Zero Project. The zero project is the Essl Foundation's project which advocates a new and innovative approach to the rights of persons with disabilities internationally. Its mission is working for a world with zero barriers. More than 71 experts from 30 countries took part in the Zero Project by nominating outstanding and Innovative Practices and a total of round 120 nominations were submitted and only 40 were selected and ARUNIM was one of the three Indians selected. (http://zeroproject.org/)

ARUNIM's Key objective is to create a Marketing Federation and facilitate Entrepreneurs with disabilities to become "Contributors and Job Creators".

REFERENCES

[1] Further information and reading:

[2] http://www.arunim.in

[3] https://www.facebook.com/ArunimIndia

[4] A 'Different' Market, The Hindu - http://www.thehindu.com/todays-paper/tp-national/article3402558.ece - .T6vTjC6JoFM, 10 May 2012

Gender Discrimination and Sexual Harassment

Neena Sinha

University School of Management Studies, Guru Govind Singh Indraprastha University, New Delhi

Keyword: *Women, Discrimination, Work, Gender, Harassment, Sexual, Workplace, Corporate*

INTRODUCTION

Loehr and Sehwartz (2003) evolved the concept of 'Power of Full Engagement' according to which it is 'energy' and not 'time' which is the most precious resource for achieving high performance. A passionate work culture is outcome of composite impact of the individuals forming part of the workforce. Creating an inclusive workplace – where all talent, including women, can thrive and well being of the employees is ensured is the answer. Yet women employees have to deal with gender inequities and sexual harassment at the workplace.

The Tehelka Episode involving alleged sexual assault on a female Journalist by the Editor-in-Chief of the company Mr. Tarun Rajpal and the revelation of a Law Intern accusing a retired Supreme Court Judge of sexual harassment has brought the focus of media and corporate on Sexual harassment at workplace. In the case of a working woman, reporting the crime is all the more difficult because of the apprehension that it would involve, in addition to everything else, the loss of livelihood. In case after case this is what happens: the woman who dares to complain of sexual harassment against her boss loses her job (Karat, 2013). It is well reported how Tehelka tried to mislead people about the incident terming it as banter. Attempts were made by them to conceal the gravity of its Editor-in-Chief's alleged sexual assault. As per the amended Indian Penal Code (IPC) his conduct tantamount to rape but in this era of Twitter and Facebook, the story took no time to go viral. However women are subjected to even other types of social hazards at workplace that go unreported.

Despite the rhetoric of women emancipation there are innumerable instances of discrimination at the work place. Making decisions on the basis of someone's gender, or sex, is gender discrimination. In employment, this includes decisions related to recruitment, remuneration, terminations, career advancement, promotions, leaves, and benefits. In education, this includes decisions related to admissions and grading for the students as well. Irrespective of the work place, be it the Corporate Board Room or the agricultural field it is true that women have to deal with obstacles, low wages , harassment and other form of discrimination. It is often argued that discrimination is not based on gender alone, both men and women can be subjected to discrimination and harassment on the basis of race, caste and a host of other factors yet the fact remains that women are more vulnerable.

Gender discrimination is not an isolated phenomenon. Even in United States of America (USA) companies like Wal Mart and Morgan Stanley have been under scanner for gender inequities and tried in courts. The result of a 2010 Pew Global Attitudes Project survey that examined attitudes about gender around the world has shown that compared to males from other 21 nations Indian male have a strong belief that when jobs are scarce, men "should have more right to a job than women." Ninety five percent of the respondent believes that women should be allowed to occupy jobs outside the home. It has been revealed that Pakistani males (eighty two percent) also endorse the belief of Indian men when it comes to the issue of who should have the preference during the days of job scarcity. Ninety seven American males have no problem if women work outside the home and only fourteen percent opined that if jobs are scarce, men should have more right to a job as compared to women. That was among the lowest percentage on this question, comparable to the Twelve percent of the men from Britain and Spain (Remez, 2013).

In India number of female employees is far less than their counterpart in United States of America. In the year 2010 India's female labor participation rate was just 29 percent, according to the International Labor Organization. India's profile compares very unfavourably to the 68 percent female labor participation in China, and among G20 economies, only Turkey (28 percent) and Saudi Arabia (17 percent) lag behind. Women thus constitute just a quarter of India's 473 million strong workforces. Work place discrimination and harassment make their participation in workspace even more difficult.

Catalyst, a non profit research organization working to advance women in business, conducted a study of female professionals in the securities industry in their publication in 2001 titled *Women in Financial Services: The Word on the Street.* It has indicated that the top three barriers to women's advancement were lack of mentoring, commitment to personal and family responsibilities and exclusion from informal network of communication. The "Old Boys Club" as it is referred ensures that they do not form part of the decision making. Women are always under scrutiny and if they make any they are criticised much more than men. Errors committed by women leaders are invariably blown out of proportion in comparison to their male counterpart. When it comes to lower and mid-level positions in the organizational pyramid it has been found that women outperform men, but once they cross the middle level in the hierarchy, they hit the glass ceiling and future career progression opportunities start shrinking dramatically (Meyerson & Fletcher, 2000).

In the work place preventing "glass ceilings" assumes significance as it obstructs promotions or other career advancement. According to the India Spencer Stuart Board Index 2012, it has been found that only four women were in top position among the BSE 100 companies. Vasanthi Srinivasan, Associate Professor of organizational behavior and human resources management, and Rejie George Pallathitta, Aassociate Professor of corporate strategy and policy, at the Indian Institute of Management Bangalore, recently presented a study on women directors on corporate boards in India. According to them, "In most organizations, the process of identifying and grooming potential women directors is not a structured or formal one. The talent management process must work toward developing the required skills and competencies and create a pipeline of potential women directors."Better gender balance in the boardrooms can serve as a catalyst to the change in the mind set, reinforcing the values of inclusiveness and harmony at the work place.

While it is easier to deal with overt discrimination such as wage differential, problem of discrimination and harassment that are muted are more difficult to handle as far as the women employees are concerned. Often women are subjected to a hostile environment in the workplace, they are made to feel uncomfortable, unwanted and under appreciated. In fact men would go to any extent to ensure exclusion of women from the positions of power. Their line of argument is that women are not goal driven; they have different values; they don't aspire to be leaders, etc. Women are perceived to be humble. If they do not take a tough decision or stand they are seen as being weak or emotional. This is despite the fact that research indicate that women contribute to organization well being. A study by (Bass and Avolio, 1994) points out that the trend in U.S. corporations toward high-involvement work teams, consensus decision making, and empowerment may actually benefit the leadership styles that women already exhibit. According to them women exhibit transformational leadership style that has been shown to have a strong positive impact on individual, group, and organizational performance. Yet gender discrimination still exists.

How to deal with the discrimination and sexual harassment? Women tend to sweep such issues under the carpet rather than confront them. They fear that they will be subjected to further humiliations, particularly so if it is a case pertaining to sexual harassment. The first step is to openly raise the issue at the earliest. Not all discriminatory behaviour can be taken to court. Women should exercise legal options when they are available but even if that is not the case it must be dealt with using the available internal grievance system. Sexist and discriminatory behaviour in any form is unacceptable. The more you tolerate, the more difficult it will become for you to confront the situation. In corporate organization matter may be reported to HR or a higher authority. Most companies allow employees to make confidential reports and complaints, so there is no need to worry about what the repercussions may be.

Various plan proposals have addressed the issue of gender equity. India's 11th Plan document recognizes that women are not just equal citizens but also contributes as agents of socio-economic development. The draft national employment policy has a specific chapter on women workers which suggests measures to create more opportunities for gainful employment for women and increase their productivity in work. The new law to deal with sexual offences provides comprehensive measures to take up the legal recourse, if required. One would expect that glass ceiling would be easier to deal with as the number of women entering the workforce today is significantly higher than what it was two decades ago. However the ground reality is that even if they are good performers, scaling the corporate hierarchy in India Inc remains to be an arduous task for women as long as discriminatory mind-sets and practices are not rejected; till then the goal of creating an inclusive workplace shall only remain a cherished dream.

REFERENCES

[1] Bass, B.M., & Avolio, B.J. (1994). Shatter the glass ceiling: Women may make better managers. *Human resource Management*, 33(4), 549-560.

[2] Catalyst (2001) Fact Sheet .Women in Financial Services: The word on the Street, http://www.catalystwomen.org/press_room/factsheets/fact_women _in _financial _services.htm

[3] India Inc. Aims to Get More Women on its Boards, Knowledge @Wharton, http://knowledge.wharton.upenn.edu/article/can-india-inc-get-more-women-on-its-boards/

[4] Karat B. (2013), Issues of sexual assault: The Tehelka case, The Hindu Nov 25, 2013, http://m.thehindu.com/opinion/lead/issues-of-sexual-assault-the-tehelka-case/article5386951.ece/?maneref=https://www.google.co.in/

[5] Loehr, Jim and T. Schwartz (2003), *The Power of Full Engagement*. New York: Free Press.

[6] Meyerson, D.E., & Fletcher, J.K. (2000). A modest manifesto for shattering the glass ceiling. *Harvard Business Review*, 78(1), 126-136.

[7] The Spencer Stuart (2012), India Board Index, https://www.spencerstuart.com/~/media/PDF%20Files/Research%20and%20Insight%20PDFs/India-Board-Index-2012_26Jun2013.pdf

[8] Remez M. (2013) Indians Support Gender Equality But Still Give Men Edge in Workplace, Higher Education , PEW Research Center for the People & the Press January 4, 2013.

[9] Segran G. (2010), Gender discrimination in India: A reality check | December, 13, 2010, http://knowledge.insead.edu/leadership-management/women-in-business/gender-discrimination-in-india-a-reality-check-723?nopaging=1#7oVk4cQYYUl7MZo1.99

[10] Srinivasan V. and George R. (2013) , Building the Women Directorship Pipeline in India: An Exploratory Study, http://papers.ssrn.com/sol3/papers.cfm?abstract_id=2346109

Regular Papers

Promoting an Inclusive Workplace: A Study of the Tata Group

Anu Singh Lather, Shalini Garg and Sona Vikas[1]

University School of Management Studies (USMS), Guru Gobind Singh Indraprastha University, New Delhi

[1]USMS, GSIPU, New Delhi; Ansal Institute of Technology, Gurgaon

ABSTRACT

In the last few years, the focus of efforts in corporations across the world has shifted from diversity to inclusion. This sea change has happened without fanfare and almost without notice. The IT and BPO companies – both the MNC companies as well as the home-grown Indian companies – have been in the forefront of this transformation. A diverse workforce in an organisation with an inclusive culture makes the organisation more innovative, agile, and attuned to the needs of customers. Organisations that want to thrive in today's world need to have employees and managers, who are aware of, and skilled in, dealing with diversity and believe in inclusion. Tata companies have been working to integrate the spirit of affirmative action into their organisational framework and community development initiatives. This paper discusses some of the best practices at the Tata Group that has been promoting an inclusive workplace across their several offices spread across the world.

Keywords: *Inclusive Workplace, Diversity, Equality*

INTRODUCTION

In April 2006, when Prime Minister Manmohan Singh called on the Indian industry to undertake affirmative action for SC/ST communities, the Tata Group responded with the setting up of a task force to examine the issue. The task force, headed by Dr JJ Irani, Director-Tata Sons, submitted its report, committing industry to a series of time-bound commitments of voluntary initiatives under issues of Employment, Employability, Entrepreneurship and Education. Simultaneously, it was made clear in repeated interactions with the political executive and with organisations representing the SC/ST communities that industry was unequivocally opposed to reservations. The Tata Group, with a legacy of commitment to the community, established the group forum for affirmative action in November 2006. The Group Corporate Centre endorsed the Group Affirmative Action Policy in April 2007, affirming a policy of positive discrimination where, everything else being equal. Tata Companies were exhorted to employ more members of the scheduled caste communities and engage more firms owned by scheduled caste members as business associates. The Tata Affirmative Action Programme (TAAP) was initiated as a commitment by the Tata Companies to exercise a positive discrimination by employing personnel from historically disadvantaged communities and in engaging them as business partners, without sacrificing merit or quality. TAAP is a nationally acknowledged initiative that aims at taking positive steps towards inclusive growth.

At Tata Group, Workplace inclusion involves proactive behaviours that make each person feel welcome and a part of the organization. The Group accept differences and work to create a culture of unique talents and outcomes. Their Group Companies use inclusive hiring practices offer hiring and promotion policies that include a workforce with diverse sexual orientation and staff with various mental and physical abilities. They offer a working environment free from bias and discrimination. Creating an inclusive working environment is more than just giving all the employees equal opportunities. It is also about allowing people to be themselves at work, valuing the difference and letting them know that their contribution is valued. For the Tata Group, it is about ensuring that no one feels left out because of their age, gender, race, nationality, religion or belief, sexual orientation, physical or mental disabilities or social background. They offer an inclusive workplace where the human rights principles of fairness, respect, equality, dignity and autonomy are promoted and are part of the organisation's everyday goals and behaviour.

People practices followed by the Tata Group are a reflection of the Workplace Inclusion. Some of them include:

- A welcoming workplace culture where all are treated with respect and dignity and they feel valued.
- In place Policies concerning equality and human rights, working conditions, dignity at work, employee welfare and fair recruitment and procurement practices.
- The workforce is representative of the local community.
- All employees are encouraged to develop and progress.
- Members of staff at all levels are aware of the inclusive values of the Tata Group and are actively consulted and involved in policy development.
- Unnecessary hierarchies and occupational segregation are discouraged.
- Inclusive strategies are fully supported and promoted by top management.

By fully endorsing a work environment that is committed to equality and free from discrimination, the Tata Group has created a distinguished place for itself in the Indian corporate world. The Tata Group takes appropriate action to anticipate and address any potential tensions within the workplace.

ABOUT THE COMPANY

"Inclusion and fairness in the workplace . . . is not simply the right thing to do; it's the smart thing to do." – **Alexis Herman**, former U. S. Secretary of Labour

These words by Herman hold so true in the Indian context for the Tata Group of Companies. The Tata group comprises over 100 operating companies in seven key business sectors: Communications and Information Technology, Engineering, Materials, Services, Energy, Consumer Products and Chemicals. The Group has operations in more than 100 countries across six continents, and its companies export products and services to 150 countries. The total revenue of Tata companies, taken together, was $96.79 billion (around Rs. 527,047 crores) in 2012-13, with 62.7 percent of this coming from business outside India. The Tata Group has been respected in India for more than 140 years for its adherence to strong values and business ethics. Anchored in India and wedded to traditional values and strong ethics, Tata companies are in the continuous process of building multinational businesses that strive to achieve growth through excellence and innovation, while balancing the interests of shareholders, employees and civil society. Tata companies employ over 540,000 people worldwide. Workplace Inclusion is a significant feature of their work environment where all are treated with dignity and respect, where the talents and skills of all groups are values, and where customer service improves because the workforce is happier and more motivated.

WORKPLACE INCLUSION: WHAT IT MEANS FOR THE TATA GROUP

The profile of the labour force is changing rapidly. Organizations throughout the world are facing an extraordinary new challenge – the increasing cultural inclusion of the work force and the diverse globalization of business markets.

Tata Group's challenge hinges on their ability to effectively engage all of their current work force, and to retain, hire and develop the very best from all walks of life. The opportunity lies in their ability to strengthen the company by drawing upon inclusion in their workplace. Workplace inclusion at the Tata Group embraces a cooperative and supportive work environment that recognizes the value of differences. This includes race, gender, age, physical and mental abilities, sexual orientation, education, religion and cultural backgrounds. At Tata Group, their support of inclusion is a critical component of positioning their company for competitive excellence. This ethic is built upon the values of fairness, mutual respect, understanding and cooperation. All employees can contribute unique perspectives for creative ideas and solutions to sustain Tata's excellent reputation as a service provider and employer of choice. The management values workplace inclusion and views differences as assets rather than liabilities, seeing stereotypes for the restrictive viewpoints they are and getting beyond prejudice to appreciate differences. They have successfully managed workplace inclusion by actively welcoming and involving all people to accomplish organizational goals and to challenge assumptions that limit their individual and organizational opportunities. It has led to creating and managing a work environment of inclusion and acceptance beyond simply tolerating people who are different. Their focus is on fostering a work environment that encourages mutual respect and sensitivity for all employees. The company's leaders set an example of the organization's commitment to take affirmative steps to build and retain an inclusive work force. The company has embraced workplace inclusion by taking the Group's commitment to the letter and spirit of equal opportunity and affirmative action laws. While the concept of inclusion embraces a broad spectrum of significant differences in individuals, a critical sign of its presence and vitality is the full inclusion of women and minorities within their organization. The focus is on commitments and strategies that weave inclusion into the fabric or culture of the company. This is neither a short-term effort nor a program that has a beginning and an end. The Group's workplace inclusion efforts are ongoing, organizational and relevant to all employees.

INITIATIVES FOR WORKPLACE INCLUSION

The two main focus areas are related to gender inclusion and that related to minority communities. Several specific initiatives have been taken by the different Companies of the Tata Group in this regard and they are highlighted below for the disadvantaged sections of the community.

Tata Steel

Tata Steel has been striving for the cause of the scheduled castes and scheduled tribes in the spirit of affirmative action. Through affirmative action and the philosophy of inclusive growth, the company attempts to help the SCs and STs to benefit from economic opportunities, while respecting and promoting the social norms and cultural practices which are important to them. The company's efforts, directed towards the holistic development of the SC/ST communities, have included education and training, sustainable employment generation, providing entrepreneurial development opportunities and preserving the ethnic heritage of the tribes. Women empowerment is another initiative of the company. Project Tejaswini of Tata Steel has helped motivate and train women to move from menial work (from sweeping and mopping floors, cleaning office tables, serving tea and running small errands), to move out of rigid mind sets and become drivers of dumper-trucks, bulldozers, forklifts, ambulances and security trucks, elevating their financial and social status. In this process, the women acquired interpersonal skills, team building skills and positive thinking. They even went on a trekking and rock-climbing expedition with the famous mountaineer, Bachendri Pal. This was a huge initiative as it was not just about training but critical lessons for overcoming several social barriers. These women hold a record for accident-free driving and earn more than double of their earlier salaries, thus changing their lives and that of their families, significantly.

CMC

CMC commits its support to the principles and practice of equal opportunity in employment and understands that it is the duty of the organization and all its associates to ensure that diversity and inclusion are a part of their everyday business. For the Company, Diversity and Inclusion in the workplace is a good management practice and makes sound business sense. CMC is committed to respect this diversity irrespective of any individual differences, whereby creating an open, inclusive and flexible culture.

The concept of Diversity and Inclusion has been integrated with the HR and other processes within CMC. CMC Senior Management also strives to fully support and uphold the Diversity and Inclusion agenda at all times.

Trent

Trent's business relies on people power. Trained human resources, having a strong customer service orientation and steeped in the culture and values of the Tata Group, are its strength. Untrained and unskilled manpower can spell bad times on the shop floor for them, and thus they have heavily invested in the training and development of the human resources. The company has pioneered a vocational training initiative for retail. This programme, named *Saksham* (Sanskrit for capable), strives to enhance employability and provide gainful employment to the underprivileged sections of society with a special focus on SC and ST communities. Trent has established cross functional teams from corporate sustainability and the recruitment and operations departments to work together to promote the cause. These teams then disseminate the details of the initiative through formal and informal interactions with other departments in the company. Employment opportunities have been provided to these communities, whereby including them in their mainstream business.

North Delhi Power

North Delhi Power Limited (NDPL) has made the needs of the SC/ST communities a key priority, taking initiatives in the areas of education, employability, employment (workplace) and entrepreneurship. The Company seeks to provide opportunities of growth and development of the people belonging to these communities.

Tata Refractories

Tata Refractories (TRL) has committed itself to affirmative action initiatives for the benefit of SC/ST communities. With a well-articulated affirmative action policy, it has a clearly laid down code of conduct for affirmative action. The company has made great effort to introduce special facilities to encourage and motivate these people who have, so far, been unable to take advantage of economic and social development on account of various reasons. In this direction,

Tata Refractories has taken a major step by establishing the Self Employment Skill Development Institute (SESDI) in Belpahar for unemployed youth, particularly those belonging to the SC/ST communities. Unemployed youth are trained for short durations at the institute to enhance their skills and inculcate in them the spirit of entrepreneurship. This has had a significant impact on the skill enhancement of the youth belonging to the disadvantaged sections.

Titan Industries

Titan Industries through its "MEADOW" (Management of Enterprise and Development of Women) programme has created entrepreneurial opportunities for poor women from rural India. This initiative gives women an opportunity to not only earn a living but also receive business education. Women are encouraged to be part of the decision making process and play significant roles in the business matters of the company. This has helped the women achieve greater self-confidence in them and build their stature among their families and the community.

Tata Consultancy Services

Tata Consultancy Services (TCS) has been expending a lot of effort in taking forward the mandate of affirmative action. Most of these efforts like the Rural Income Generation Enhancement programme are in the area of enhancing employability. Being an Equal Opportunity and Affirmative Action Employer, the HR framework at TCS including all its functions (viz.), recruitment, retention, career management, compensation and reward & recognition programs, competency management, learning & development opportunities are designed and implemented equally without differentiation on the basis of gender, nationality, religion and other factors. For a company like Tata Consultancy Services (TCS), that has 183 offices across 42 countries, and employing 250,000 employees representing 113 different nationalities, workplace inclusion holds a significant importance. It is "the only Indian-headquartered multinational company with this kind of diversity", says Dr Ritu Anand, Vice-President and Deputy Global Head of Human Resources (HR), who, besides looking after global talent management also handles the diversity and inclusion portfolio at TCS. With changing workforce trends and an increasingly competitive market environment, developing and sustaining a healthy talent mix within the organization is an important business imperative. In this context, the areas of 'Diversity and Inclusion' have gained immense attention globally, as well as in India. To ensure greater integration among its culturally-diverse employee pool, TCS launched 'Culture Meter' in 2008 on its intranet. The company also launched 'Maitree' (friendship), a global platform for employees and their family members to join the 'caring and sharing culture' of TCS. Maitree brings TCsers and their families together in shared interests through various activities such as dance, music, photography, books, hobby clubs, nature-walks, and trekking. There are calendar events across geographies in TCS. TCS also has a Foreign

Language Initiatives (FLI) group which focuses on cultural integration and language training. Some examples are cultural workshops, English-language teaching programme for its non-English-speaking employees, and programme for expatriates to learn the local languages. TCS encourages diversity not only in terms of nationality but also on gender. It has established a platform called Diversity and Women's Network (DAWN), which sensitises employees and makes them culturally aware. The company has a successful reorientation programme for women who return to their jobs after a break.

TCS Associates have been encouraged to participate in discussion forums and theme based learning to create awareness on what Diversity & Inclusion (D&I) means at TCS and understand different perspectives on topics of interest to them.

Some such D & I initiatives include:

- Theme workshops on work-life balance, branding oneself, importance of workplace diversity, etc.
- Health and Wellness, workshops have also been organized for women specifically to create awareness and for their betterment.
- Senior associates and leaders involve themselves and conduct 'Be Inspired' sessions, which help to share success stories, inspire and lead by example for employee motivation.
- A learning module has been created specifically for managers to help them to equip themselves with the required skills to motivate and work with a diverse team.
- In order to support women in the workforce, TCS has been undertaking day-care tie-ups to provide good childcare facilities in and around office areas for their associates at discounted prices. A support group called 'workplace parents', has been formed across various centers to engage working parents through child psychology and parenting workshops.
- A stay connected program has been launched to ensure that associates on long leave continue to be updated with the latest happenings in TCS. Associates receive news and information bites in the comfort of their personal email boxes on a monthly basis that help them keep updated.
- A reorientation program has also been put together for these associates on their return from long leave. This initiative supports them back into their careers post childcare leave and sabbaticals. Associates also have opportunities to participate in industry forums and roundtables to learn and enhance their professional networks.

The above efforts are just some of the initiatives taken by a few of the companies of the Tata Group. Not only a respectable name in Corporate India, with their pro-people policies across their offices, located around the world, they have become a preferential employer globally.

ADVANTAGE INCLUSION AT TATA GROUP

Incorporating an inclusive working into the key organization values has had a threefold effect for the Tata Group: good for the business, good for the staff, and good for the community around. For the Group, the importance of an inclusive workplace includes the advantages of competitiveness and increased productivity. Also as an employer, it is their legal obligation to comply with the statutes related to equality and to stamp out discrimination from the workplace. This means developing policies and practices that guarantee equal treatment for all. And such actions on equality and human rights issues by the Group have a significant impact upon their brand reputation. They are able to attract new talent, retain productive and committed staff, create wider customer appeal and access to untapped markets and create culture change that spreads to communities. It requires a consistent effort of the management and the seniors in the Tata Group to put together an effective process to create Inclusion at the workplace. A diverse workforce in Tata Group with an inclusive culture has made the organisation more innovative, agile, and attuned to the needs of customers. Indeed organisations like the Tata Group that want to thrive in today's world will need to have employees and managers, who are aware of, and skilled in, dealing with diversity and believe in inclusion. Workplace inclusion goes beyond employing individuals with diverse backgrounds to creating an environment where every employee is valued. Organizational structures, values, policies, and day-to-day practices all influence the degree to which employees with disabilities feel truly valued by and included in their workplaces.

The Tata Group has realized that effective inclusive workplace practices and policies relate directly to key metrics important to overall organizational success. As employers, the Tatas have moved beyond simply recruiting a defined number or percentage of candidates from diverse backgrounds toward creating workplaces that value a broad range of perspectives. A diverse group of employees in their various companies has led to an increased employee engagement, job satisfaction, commitment to the company and improved Organizational citizenship behaviours. It has led to a reduced employee turnover intention.

Diversity is no longer simply a buzzword but a reality. The workforce and the general population are becoming more diverse in terms of new entrants. Companies are asking for guidance about how to engage in leadership that is inclusive to all employees. Organizational leaders who include diversity and inclusiveness as part of their company strategy have put themselves in a good position to prepare for the future of their company. As diverse and inclusive workplaces, the Tata Group has a distinct strategic advantage over less diverse competitors as they get the opportunity to capitalize on the diverse knowledge-base of workers when relating to different groups, including customers, partners and staff. It has led to increased innovation and creativity, helped in reducing skills shortages, improved customer services, increased opportunities for external interactions and communications, reputational benefits related to valuation of social responsibility and increased organizational stability. The various surveys on employee satisfaction and feedback from their employees have indicated this to the HR department.

CONCLUSION

Tata Group is one of those organisations that have realised the business imperative in making workplace inclusion a core value, and are quickly assimilating best practices that provide them the competitive advantage needed in a dynamic work environment. They are amongst the companies for whom providing employees the opportunity to balance work and personal life is no longer a "nice to do" but a fundamental pre-requisite to attract and retain the best. They have also seen measureable benefits for their Group organization through consistent inclusion in the workplace. An inclusive climate and inclusive leadership has contributed to employees' perceptions of being included in their work groups, which increase job performance, job satisfaction, employee retention and employee creativity.

REFERENCES

[1] https://www.avma.org/News/JAVMANews/Pages/111001c.aspx

[2] http://www.equalityhumanrights.com/uploaded_files/publications/an_employer_s_guide_to_creating_an_inclusive_workplace.pdf

[3] http://www.forbes.com/sites/karenhigginbottom/2013/11/26/organizations-lacking-inclusive-leaders/

[4] http://www.tata.com/aboutus/sub_index/Leadership-with-trust

[5] http://www.equality.ie/Files/Building%20an%20Inclusive%20Workplace.pdf

[6] http://interweave.cc/downloads/Diversity-handbook.pdf

[7] http://www.equalityhumanrights.com/uploaded_files/publications/an_employer_s_guide_to_creating_an_inclusive_workplace.pdf

[8] www.tata.com

[9] http://www.indousstf.org/pdf/Tata-Consultancy-Services.pdf

[10] http://www.tata.com/careers/articlesinside/xkCI0qGuLcE=/TLYVr3YPkMU=

Constitutional Imperatives of the Inclusive and Accessible Workplace in India

Anuj Vaksha

University School of Law and Legal Studies, Guru Gobind Singh Indraprastha University, New Delhi

ABSTRACT

The paper titled "Constitutional Imperatives of the Inclusive and Accessible Work place in India" reflects on the constitutional provisions of the Indian Constitution and argues that there are a number of provisions in it which seek to promote inclusive and accessible workplace in India. The paper argues that the Constitution outlines the process of the making of the nation and seeks the provide participation of all citizenry in this onerous exercise. However, the paper identifies the problems of the nation because of which these constitutional imperatives have not been realized even after more than six decades of the adoption of the Constitution.

Keywords: *Constitution, Preamble, Poverty, Illiteracy, Untouchability, Social, Political, Economic, Patriarchal, Caste, Communal, Inclusive, Participative, Legal System, Non-Exploitative Economic Order, Corruption, Mis-Governace*

INTRODUCTION

Inclusive and accessible workplace is the buzzword now. The corporate employers, the public sector undertakings, the multinational organizations, the government institutions etc. are now realizing the merit of perfectly inclusive and accessible workplace. The psycho, social and economic merits of such perfect inclusive and accessible workplace is a subject of enormous interests and shall remain so for years to come. Through this paper I seek to explore the constitutional perspectives and imperatives of such inclusive and accessible workplace based on the provisions of the Constitution of India.

CONSTITUTIONAL CONCEPT OF INCLUSIVE AND ACCESSIBLE WORKPLACE

The Constitution of India does not have any specific provision outlining the concept of inclusive and accessible workplace. This is not to say the Constitution of India in anyway negates the idea of inclusive and accessible workplace. On the contrary, the Constitution of India is one legal framework which has enabled and shall further enable the making of all legal edifice for making of every working platforms in the country, be it economic, social, cultural, political, a thoroughly inclusive and accessible workplace. To this end one is to only read the preamble to the Constitution, which begins by the words, "We the people of India, having solemnly resolved to constitute India into a …"

It is fascinating to imagine the scholastics of the framers of the Constitution, who in late forties of the previous century could understand the unqualified involvement of all Indians in making of the nation called India. A newly independent modern nation in 1947, which inherited with its independence a legacy of wide spread poverty and illiteracy, deeply entrenched caste and communal divisions, pervasive patriarchal family orientations, it must have been an utopian vision to think of a nation where every single citizen shall be secured what may be called constitutionally guaranteed content of citizenship benefits in the form of justice, social, economic, and political; liberty of thought, expression, belief, faith and worship; equality of status and of opportunity.

Thinking in terms of realization of the vision of the constitution makers, it must be reckoned as an enormously difficult task to secure to all its citizens the constitutionally guaranteed content of citizenship benefits, more so with the kind of society which it inherited at the time of adoption of the Constitution. Thanks to the scholastics of the Constitution makers, while outlining what is called hereinabove, the enormously difficult task, they envisaged the participation of all citizens in making of the nation where in to all its citizens the constitutionally guaranteed content of citizenship benefits can be secured. Thus in its opening sentence the Preamble to the Constitution declares, "WE, THE PEOPLE OF INDIA, having solemnly resolved to constitute India into a sovereign socialist secular democratic republic and to secure to all its citizens…", what has been called here in above the constitutionally guaranteed content of citizenship benefits. Thus as far as the constitution of India is concerned, on the one side it promises to all its citizens a guaranteed content of citizenship benefits and on the other side makes each one of them an avowed active participant in the realization of this promise. Thus, from the constitutional perspective it is argued that the concept of inclusive and accessible workplace is holistically ingrained and outlined with respect to the process of the nation building. Nation building, by any paradigm and perspective is more complex and onerous exercise than any other business, social, political or corporate enterprise which one may think of. If the constitution of India could envisage an inclusive and accessible participation of every Indian in the nation building exercise, it is further argued that it mandates inclusive and accessible workplace for every process within the domain of the Indian nationhood. The preamble to the Constitution further strengthens the imperatives of the inclusive and accessible workplace by seeking to promote among the fellow citizens and the co-workers of the nation building process the spirit of fraternity.

The preamble to the Constitution outlined significantly lofty ideals for the nation, however the problem which the nation inherited from the history was that significant section of its population was ordained in the then existing poverty, illiteracy, untouchability, caste and communal divisions, exploitative socio-economic structures and thus they were either disabled, disqualified or disdained from relishing or realizing the lofty ideals enshrined in the Preamble to the Constitution. The challenge of the nascent nation was to bring them in the mainstream of the nationhood. To this end the Constitution provided for a number of special measures within the constitutional framework. Mention may be made of some of the constitutional provisions for what has generally been called empowerment of the weaker sections of the society. Article 15 of the Constitution prohibits discrimination on grounds of religion, race, caste, sex or place of birth; however it allows the State for making any special provision for women and children,[1] for the advancement of any socially and educationally backward classes of citizens or for the Scheduled Castes and the Scheduled Tribes.[2] Similarly Article 16 of the Constitution provides for equality of opportunity in matters of public employment; however it allows the State for making any provision for the reservation of posts in favour of any backward class of citizens.[3] In exercise of its powers under Articles 15 and 16 of the Constitution the State has undertaken a number of measures which have the affect of empowering the traditionally disempowered section of citizens and thus facilitating their wholesome participation in the socio-economic and political processes of the society and also enabling them to reap the benefits of the nationhood in living their lives. Every citizen of the country has been guaranteed the same fundamental rights enshrined under Part III of the Constitution and thus in matters of scope of such fundamental rights all citizens have same rights except for the special provisions which are in the nature of affirmative action for empowerment of one or other disadvantaged class of citizens.

The provisions of Part III of the Constitution are in the nature of mandatory clauses and thus are enforceable by the Supreme Court and the High Courts of the States by the appropriate constitutional remedies.

There are a number of provisions in Part IV of the Constitution which have the affect of supplementing and complementing the objectives of Part III of the Constitution. Unlike Part III of the Constitution, the provisions of Part IV of the Constitution are not enforceable in any Court, but the principles therein laid are nevertheless fundamental in the governance of the country. Article 37 of the Constitution mandates the State to apply those principles in the making laws and thus in the governance of the Country. Some of these principles which have the affect of promoting inclusiveness and accessibility at work place are the principle of welfare of the people,[4] the principle of non-exploitative economic order of the society,[5] the provision of legal system that promotes justice,[6] the provision for rights to work, to education and to public assistance,[7] the provision for just and humane conditions of work and maternity relief,[8] the provision for living wage etc., for workers,[9] the provision for participation of workers in management of industries,[10] provision for early childhood care and education to children,[11] the provision for promotion of educational and economic interests of scheduled castes and scheduled tribes, ands other weaker sections,[12] the provision for raising the level of nutrition and the standard of living and to improve public health.[13] All these provisions, *inter alia*, have the cumulative effect of enhancing the capability, competence, entitlement and eligibility of the individuals for a wholesome participation in the socio-economic affairs of the society.

The Supreme Court in a number of cases has captured the spirit of the Constitutional provisions and has reinforced them through their judicial intervention, expansion, innovation and application.[14] A particular mention of the famous *Vishakha* case may be made where the Supreme Court invoked Article 14 of the Constitution to prohibit sexual harassment of women at work place and went ahead to frame mandatory guidelines for ensuring safe work place for the women of the society.[15] In one of the judgments it notes;

"Providing adequate means of livelihood for all the citizens and distribution of the material resources of the community for common welfare, enable the poor, the Dalits and tribes, to fulfill the basic needs to bring about a fundamental change in the structure of the Indian society which was divided by erecting impregnable walls of separation between the people on grounds of cast, sub-caste, creed, religion, race, language and sex. Equality of opportunity and status thereby would become the bed-rocks for social integration. Economic empowerment thereby is the foundation to make equality of status, dignity of person and equal opportunity a truism. The core of the commitment of the Constitution to the social revolution through rule of law lies in effectuation of the fundamental rights and directive principles as supplementary and complimentary to each other. The Preamble, fundamental rights and directive principles – the trinity are the conscience of the Constitution. Political democracy has to be stable. Socio-economic democracy must take strong roots and should become a way of life. The State, therefore, is enjoined to provide adequate means of livelihood to the poor, weaker sections of the society the Dalits and tribes and to distribute material resources of the community to them for common welfare, etc."

The State and various authorities constituted under the State have taken a number of measures for realization of these constitutional provisions. These measures have often been called as 'unprecedented in their scope and radical in content[16]. These unprecedented and radical measures have had significant impact in bringing about critical changes in making of an egalitarian Indian society, yet the full realization of the constitutional promises for a number of citizens of the country remains a distant dream. Even by the year 2010 no less than 32.7%[17] of the people of India were living under situations of extreme poverty, which meant even in the most ideal situation, just because of their poverty they are deprived of wholesome participation in the socio-economic affairs of the society. The extent of exclusiveness and inaccessibility for the persons reeling under extreme poverty becomes more accentuated in degree and nature, when the state of poverty is combined with other socio-economic evils like corruption, mis-governance, illiteracy, inaccessibility to judicial remedies, extraneous political considerations, often an insensitive administrative machinery, unjust gender, caste and communal relations, etc. The affects of these socio-economic evils gets further accentuated by the situational hazards which individuals often encounter in one's life. Given all these considerations, if 32.7% of the people are in the state of extreme poverty, one can guess from the experiences around that more than 50% of the population would be in the state of deprivation of an inclusive and accessible workplace. It is frightening to imagine that more than 50% of the Indian population would be in the state of denial of a decent, dignified, inclusive and accessible workplace, but that is what the crude reality of the India is even after more than six decades of the adoption and working of a Constitution which promises to every citizen justice, social, economic, and political; liberty of thought, expression, belief, faith and worship; equality of status and of opportunity. Often these words in the preamble to the Constitution and the guaranteed constitutional promises sound unrealistic, illusive and possibly even deceptive. However these are pessimistic outbursts which occur in the state of extreme frustrations at the state of affairs going on around the country. The truth remains that Constitution of India is the cornerstone of all socio-economic changes taking place in the country since its independence in 1947. A nation which inherited with its independence massive poverty, masse illiteracy, vicious caste and communal divisions, heart wrenching exploitative socio-economic affairs, a traditional society marooned in superstitious belief and rituals, it was an unbelievable journey of unprecedented socio-economic and political changes. Almost every institution of the one of the most ancient civilization of the world, which India was, was to be reformed and restructured. In last sixty plus years India has been persistently moving towards reformation and restructuring of its social, political and economic institutions and the process. It is significant to note that all these changes transcending now almost the third generation of Indians have been taking around the Constitution of India for realization of the goals enshrined in the Constitution of India. As we think the tedious yet sanctimonious task of making of the nation where every Indian finds justice, social, economic, and political; liberty of thought, expression, belief, faith and worship; equality of status and of opportunity, one is reminded of and finds some solace in the poetic words of Robert Frost

> The woods are lovely, dark and deep,
> But I have promises to keep,
> And miles to go before I sleep,
> And miles to go before I sleep.

REFERENCES

[1] Article 15(3).
[2] Article 15(4).
[3] Article 16(4).
[4] Article 38.
[5] Article 39.
[6] Article 39-A.
[7] Article 41.
[8] Article 42.

[9] Article 43.
[10] Article 43-A.
[11] Article 45.
[12] Article 46.
[13] Article 47.
[14] See generally.
[15] Vishakha v. State of Rajasthan, AIR 1997 SC 3011.
[16] Equalizing Access Zoya Hasan & Martha C. Nussbaum, Oxford University Press (2012), p. 5.
[17] ILO 2012.

Gendered by Age and not by Knowledge at Professional Working Places: A Case Study for Professional Environment

Ramani Swarna

Delhi Technical Campus, Knowledge Park-III, Greater Noida

ABSTRACT

A good and healthy professional environment is essential for any employee. In case there is any kind of discrepancy present in such a working place, then there would arise many complications for the respective employee as well as others present in the immediate surroundings of the respective place. In the present paper, an attempt would be made to give a real life case study. Furthermore a complete analysis would be studied with logical arguments. This would enable us to understand whether we need A Good Professional Environment Based on Knowledge Sharing or not. Apart from this, there would be a philosophical discussion to arrive at a concrete.Certain questions are raised and pondered upon to know the nature of the problem present in the professional environment. The focus is either on the age factor or on the skills acquired through good education,knowledge acquired, grooming and other set of experiences of the person. In other words, what should be more important for us-Is it the Age of the Individual Which Matters to US or is it the Knowledge, Education And Experience? At the end of the paper, it would be shown that in any given professional environment,the important factors are Knowledge, Education and the Qualification for which one person is hired and given the opportunity to work in the Organization or Company or any kind of Institution. This is observed in the popular Corporates or the Multinationals or the educational Institutions.

Keywords: *Professional, Environment, Age, Knowledge, Experience, Communication, Hiring, Senior, Organizations, Ethics, Correct, Wrong*

PROFESSIONAL WORK: A CASE STUDY FOR PROFESSIONAL ENVIRONMENT–AGE OR KNOWLEDGE AND QUALIFICATION

The case study is the following one:

A. A Senior person joined the company with recommendation from the side of the immediate relative associated with the Senior Management level and a professionally naïve person with a Post graduate Degree

B. A young talented employee who had registered for higher studies after the completion of the Post-Graduation Degree, highly professional person and a good research scholar

A member of the senior management :

One fine day, A approaches a colleague and narrates the differences between two concepts of a theory. However, the individual is confused and gives wrong information. On the other hand, B-a young person-raises the objection and corrects A's knowledge. Consequently, A is hurt and is egoistic and does not accept the mistake and raises the voice that B is wrong and should apologize immediately or face the grave results of losing the job. What is thereason behind this: A is much more senior in age and the knowledge was given by other higher designated officials This takes place in front of C. Surprisingly, C does not take any action or intervenes or ponders to know more about the situation before taking any action. The result was very simple: B had to apologize in front of other employees.

The dilemma in front of us is of the following form:

1. If A has a very strong hold in the company, then B has no other choice other than apologizing to A; and if B is a very professional person, then B is ethically right to correct A irrespective of the age or experience.
2. Either it is the case that A is a very strong position in the company or it is the case that B is a professional person.
3. Therefore, it is the case that B had to apologize A or it is the case that B is ethically right to correct the wrong knowledge gained by A.

How should we resolve the two horns of the dilemma?This is the main motive behind this research paper.

Given this case in front of us, a question arises immediately: IS THIS CORRECT? An argument is given in the following way:

(a) If it is the case that only senior and aged people are always correct, then their knowledge is right one without any errors.
(b) However, it is not the case that the knowledge is always free from errors.
(c) Therefore, it is not the case that only seniors and aged individuals are correct.

Given this argument, there are few questions to be answered immediately for the professional work and the environment wherein one is working and spending maximum of time. These are the following:

1. What factors are necessary in any professional environment?
2. How should the hiring take place to make the environment highly professional?
3. Is AGE an important factor?
4. Should we focus on skills, knowledge and education of an individual before hiring for an appropriate position or designation?
5. Is it wrong to share the knowledge irrespective of the age?

Each of these above mentioned points would be discussed in short manner and an argument would be deduced and associated with the case study in order to resolve our dilemma present in the professional environment.

FACTORS NECESSARY IN ANY GIVEN PROFESSIONAL ENVIRONMENT

What is the definition of a professional environment? In simple words, it is a place wherein following factors play a very important role:

(a) Communication in both UPWARD and DOWNWARD.

(b) Healthy association between different employees.

(c) Focus on the work for which one is hired and employed.

(d) Boundary less Environment wherein one employee is free to talk and discuss the work related issues and looks for somekind of grooming. This should take place both ways. The main reason being that sometimes senior individuals are wrong and do not possess the knowledge pertaining to the contemporary times. Thus, it becomes necessary to gain new knowledge from young scholars and learners. In the same way, it is necessary for the young researchers to learn and lend their ears to the senior persons so that they might learn something new. In this manner, knowledge is gained for both the parties.

(e) No fear of anyone irrespective of the fact that one is related to the senior management or not and what matters most is the WORK and the OUTPUT.

(f) Sharing of knowledge amongst the employees irrespective of the age or field(in other words, if I am good in something, then I must be able to deliver it to others).

(g) Be a Whistle Blower and this would alert others of something wrong that is occurring in the given environment

(h) Open to the feedback and ready to learn from others irrespective of the age or creed or sex or experience or religion or relations

(i) Be an INNOVATION LEADER who is ready to accept the knowledge and technological management wherein learning and changing are always present. The individual must be ready to ACCEPT THOSE CHANGES WITHOUT ANY KIND OF INFERIOR COMPLEXITIES.

(j) Respect for all individuals irrespective of the age or sex or creed or religion

Now given these factors, let's move towards the case study. A should be ready to accept the knowledge from the younger employee of the organization. There is nothing wrong in accepting the fact that our knowledge is limited one. We are not the PERFECT AND ALL PERVASIVE God who knows everything. I think we should be COMPASSIONATE Like Buddha towards our fellow beings and learn from them. It might be possible that they are joining the industry just after the completion of their studies. In other words, their knowledge is not outdated. Rather it is other way round.

Mill's utilitarianism really works with wonders in this case-"MAXIMUM HAPPINESS FOR MAXIMUM NUMBER OF INDIVIDUALS". If C was right in informing the correct knowledge and correcting the other person, then it is not only C's happiness. In fact it is the HAPPINESS FOR ALL. One should look at the Kantian ethics in this scenario. Kant made it very clear in his CRITIQUE OF PURE REASON, true knowledge is always right and one should acknowledge it immediately without any kind of biasness.

Thus, the above mentioned factors do play very important role in any kind of professional place and must be adhered without any partiality and should not be depending on factors like AGE or EXPERIENCE. In fact the important ingredients of the contemporary working places are SKILLS, KNOWLEDGE AND READY TO CHANGE TO BE TRUE LEADERS.

HOW SHOULD THE HIRING TAKE PLACE?

With respect to the CASE STUDY, the hiring process must be focused on the following skill set:

1. Soft Skills.
2. Educational background.
3. Specific traits like good at communication ,open for learning, readiness for changes, flexible and respect for other fellow beings.
4. No relatives of any kind must be hired within the SAME organization as this might bring in grave issues and problems. In case such individuals are being hired, then enough care should be taken that they are being handled with care so that they are not causing any difficulty to other employees who are hired after going through rigorous interview rounds of the company.
5. Activities which might exhibit the so called prospective employee to be a LEADER and a LEARNER rather than a BOSS-ER and PROBLEM CREATOR.
6. Test the knowledge of the person.
7. Observe the behavior of the individual in different situations.

These are some of the new ways in which hiring should take place in any organization. This would surely help us to create a healthy and professional environment without any kind of partiality and biasness,

IS AGE AN IMPORTANT FACTOR?

Rather than discussing in length, it would be better to comprehend it in the form of an argument:

1. If age is the main factor for considering the employment, then young scholars and learners should not be given any chance to work in any of the professional working places.
2. However, it is not the case that any of the professional working areas are not recruiting young and dynamic learners or scholars. This is necessary for any kind of organization

as the new generation is quick in learning and adaptable to new environment. They do not carry any kind of ego with them. They are not easily hurt and are flexible to changes. They are energetic and trainable candidates. In other words, they do not have any mental blocks. If something wrong is taking place in front of them, then they are sensitive enough to blow the whistle and alert others like a child. This factor is missing in individuals who are in the age group above 40 years.A survey was conducted and a following was the result for this:

Table 1

S. No.	*Age Group*	*Ego Hurt*	*Adaptability*	*Flexibility*	*Superior Complex*	*Open to Changes*	*New Learnings*	*Energy Levels*	*Attitude*
1	18-20	15	75	82	12	85	92	95	48
2	20-24	18	83	85	14	95	86	92	28
3	25-30	20	75	86	15	82	87	82	34
4	30-35	24	74	65	21	76	82	86	52
5	35-40	15	75	65	22	72	65	54	67
6	40-45	55	35	31	65	12	12	42	83
7	45-50	52	25	25	75	14	12	35	85
8	50-55	65	22	12	78	12	10	28	82
9	55-60	63	15	10	87	10	8	18	90

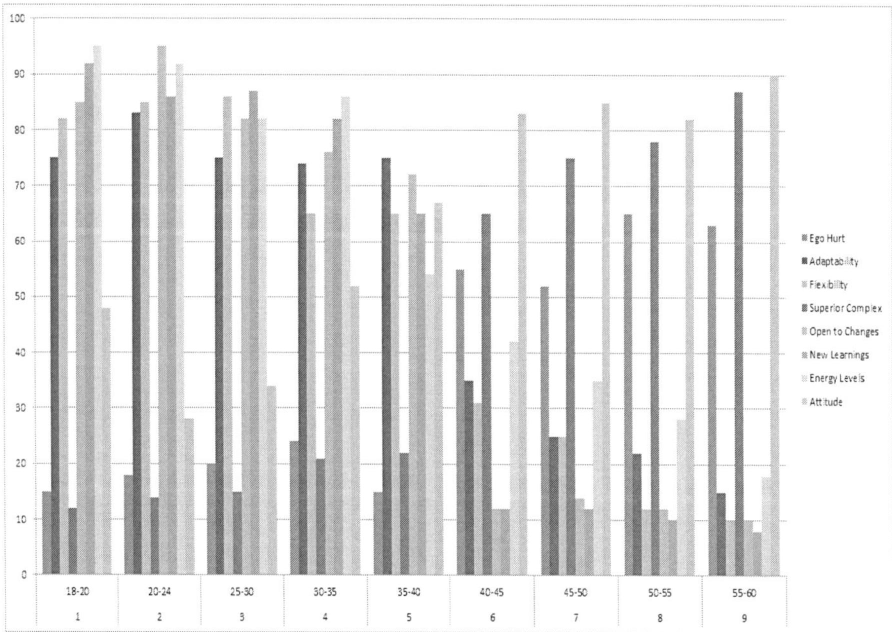

Fig. 1

3. Therefore, age is not the main factor for employment.

   Any individual above the age of 18 years can be employed in a professional organization and must be given equal rights as an employee.

SHOULD WE FOCUS ON SKILLS, KNOWLEDGE AND EDUCATION BEFORE HIRING?

The answer to this question is simply YES. There is no doubt that one should not look out for the presence of good skills in an individual. The knowledge and education also plays very important role and hiring team would never bargain on these two important factors also. All three are essential and necessary points as to why an individual is selected and offered the job in the respective company.

What is mandatory is the fact that the respective individual exhibits and shows the caliber to be selected by the hiring team. Once it is observed that the person possesses these characteristic features, there should not be any doubt of his or her selection. After the selection, let the individual show the reality of his or her abilities. One area wherein abilities might be showcased is from the knowledge domain.Such a person would be sensitive and would certainly highlight the following features-

(a) Identify the wrong inputs of the knowledge
(b) Raise the voice against the wrong information
(c) Open the eyes of others who do not possess such knowledge
(d) Correct the wrong piece of information
(e) Share the knowledge as much as possible
(f) Introduce new knowledge domains to everybody in the form of trainings or class room sessions or through presentations
(g) Always be a learner
(h) Be ready to learn whenever and whatever place it might be
(i) There is no age criteria for the right and correct knowledge giver

IS IT WRONG TO SHARE THE KNOWLEDGE IRRESPECTIVE OF THE AGE?

A simple argument is enough to answer this question and it might be shown in the following manner:

1. If it is the case that age is the important factor for sharing knowledge in this world, then there should be cases wherein knowledge is always shared by elders only.
2. However, this is not case and certainly not correct. The knowledge might be shared irrespective of what age we belong to-maybe we are young or senior in age or in experience. This is the reason why new gateways are always open for new learners.

Consequently, there are so many new inventions and discoveries made in the world every day. Not only this, there is growth and research in each and every department due to young and dynamic young scholars and readers.

3. Therefore, it is not the case that age is the important factor for sharing knowledge. If a young person corrects my knowledge, then I should not feel bad or hurt. In fact I should encourage and motivate myself that my wrong knowledge had been identified and corrected. That's the true learning in real essence.

Given this conclusion, do we get the resolution for our dilemma raised at the beginning?

CONCLUSION

First of all, let us analyze the steps one by one for the quick resolution:

(a) A is senior in age and introduced to the job with high recommendation at the work place.

(b) A is a professionally naïve person, i.e. not a highly professional person. However, the individual had been always working in organizations due to recommendations only.

(c) A is seriously hurt due to the fact that the respective person is senior in age as compared to B.

(d) A's ego had been touched in the negative manner that a young scholar or employee is correcting A's knowledge gained through the learning process.

(e) B is young in age and sensitive towards the environment.

(f) B is sensitive enough to BLOW THE WHISTLE as soon as wrong knowledge was being shared by A.

(g) It is the nature and sensitivity of B to share the correct knowledge with A and this is professionally and ethically correct also.

(h) Given this situation, A should have immediately taken the opportunity TO BE A REAL LEARNER and appreciated B.

(i) However, the situation was the other way round. A demanded B to apologize or face the immediate consequences.

(j) B apologized to A.

(k) However, A did not amend and accepted the fault.

From these steps, it is very clear that our work places are NOT ONLY GENDERED BY SEX, RATHER WE ARE IN THE GRIP OF BEING GENDERED BY AGE.This need to be corrected and one should welcome and share the knowledge irrespective of sex, creed, religion, caste, states and NOT DEFINITELY BY THE AGE.

Therefore, the resolution for the dilemma is very simple. B should have apologized to A. In fact A should be mentored or groomed in a very professional manner that A is wrong and correct knowledge should be shared.

REFERENCES

[1] Chalapathi Rao, I.V., Communication and Leadership, Hyderabad: Book Links Corporation, (1999).

[2] Davar, R.S., The Management Process, Bombay, Progressive Corporation (P) Ltd., (1984).

[3] DonH, Slocum, J.W. and Woodman, R.W., Organizational Behavior, Thomson Learning, Australia

[4] Keith D, Human Behavior at Work, New Delhi: Tata McGraw-Hill.

[5] Kumar, N Communication and Management , New Delhi: Gyan Publishing House (1997).

[6] McGraith, S.J.: Basic Managerial Skills for All, New Delhi, Prentice-Hall of India, (2003).

[7] Myers and Myers: Management Communication, New York: McGraw-Hill.

[8] Reddy, M.N. and Sinha B.P., Organizational Communication – A Structure and Functional Analysis, New Delhi: Mittal Publications (1991).

[9] Robbins, S.P. and Sanghi, S. Organizational Behaviour; Pearson Education, (2009).

[10] Singh, Kavita, Organizational Behavior: Text and Cases, Pearson Education (2010).

[11] Luthans, Fred, Organizational Behavior, 11th Edition, McGraw-Hill Education (2008).

[12] Mirza, S., Organizational Behavior, 1st Edition, McGraw-Hill Education (2003).

[13] Mcshane, Steven, Von, Glinow and Sharma, Radha, Organisational Behaviour, 4th Edition, McGrawHill Education (2008).

[14] Kinicki, Angelo and Kreitner, Robert, Organisational Behaviour, 2nd Edition, McGraw-Hill Education, (2005).

[15] Durai, Praveen, Human Resource Management, Pearson Education (2010).

[16] Monappa, A. and Saiyadain, M., Personnel Management, McGraw-Hill Education, (2001).

[17] Dessler, Gary, Human Resource Management, Pearson Education, (2004).

[18] Jyothi, P. and Venkatesh, D.N, Human Resource Management, Oxford Higher Education, (2006).

[19] Aswathappa, K., Human Resource Management, McGraw-Hill Education (2010).

[20] DeCenzo, D. A. and Robbins, S.P., Fundamentals of Human Resource Management, 9th edition John Wiley, (2007).

An Inclusive Workplace: A Great Place to Work

Shruti Sargam

Computer Sciences Corporation India Pvt Ltd, DLF IT Park, Sector-62, Noida

ABSTRACT

The aim of this article is to list the benefits of creating an inclusive workplace and to describe the obstacles encountered in the process. Organizations need to expand their notion of diversity to include not only the organization itself, but also the larger systems that constitute its environment. The concept of "the inclusive workplace", introduced here, refers to a work organization that is not only accepting and using the diversity of its own work force, but also is active in the community, participates in state and national programs to include working poor people, and collaborates across cultural and national boundaries with a focus on global mutual interests. A case study of an IT company has been incorporated to list the various factors that make a workplace inclusive.

Keywords: *Inclusive Workplace, Diverse Workforce, Great Place to Work*

INTRODUCTION

While the backbone of today's global economy is an increasingly diverse workforce, many individuals still perceive themselves as outsiders, according to a new book by University of Southern California Professor Michàlle Mor Barak (Barak, 2005).

Though with the increased competition to hire the best talent available in the market, employers have realized the importance of building their brand reputation and create an environment that is underlined by dignity, respect, equality, fair treatment at workplace. Many organizations pay lip service to a culture of acceptance, but few have adopted measures for a truly inclusive workplace. Many companies struggle and do not realize the full potential of a diverse and inclusive workforce. These organizations might still be focused on numbers and lack a complete understanding of the business imperative (Garland, 1991).

While diversity in organizations is increasingly respected as a fundamental characteristic, mere acceptance has not made a difference to the work culture. Inclusion enhances an organization's ability to achieve better business results by engaging people from diverse backgrounds and perspectives through participatory decision-making. The organizations that ultimately will thrive are those prepared to divest themselves of their prejudicial attitudes and effectively unleash the potential embedded in a heterogeneous workforce.

THE INCLUSIVE WORKPLACE—A PRACTICE-BASED MODEL

Table 1

	System Level	*Benefits*	*Benefits*	*Obstacles*
		Individuals	*Organization*	
Inclusion and diversity within work organizations	Individuals, groups	Promotions and benefits Job satisfaction Well being	Lower Turnover and absenteeism Attract potential employees Access to diverse client populations	Discrimination Prejudice Access to power
Inclusion and corporate-community relations	Organizations, communities	Job training employment More services in the community	Improve corporate image Advantage in corporate recruitment and in labor disputes	Economic pressures to demonstrate profitability Limited company vision (shortsighted and internally focused)
Inclusion and welfare to-work programs	State, federal government	Employment Improved Job prospects	Expand potential Employee pool Loyal workforce Improve customer relations	Misunderstanding the bigger picture Stereotyping welfare recipients
Inclusion and economic globalization	International	International Job Opportunities	Expand geographic markets Increase economic activities	Cultural and national barriers in international communications Poor preparation of expatriates

Barak, 2000

Inclusion and Diversity within Work Organizations

Benefits

Inclusion policies within an organization would facilitate equal employment opportunities to women and ethnic minorities. Such policies open the doors to job advancement and promotions that have clear monetary benefits to individual employees and their families. They also open channels of communication and provide real decision-making power. Real participation in the decision-making process has been linked to job satisfaction, which in turn can potentially affect worker retention and effectiveness on the job (McNeely, Sapp, & Daly, 1998; Whiddon & Martin, 1989). The benefits for the organization include:

1. **Attracting and Retaining Talent:** Diversity and inclusion attracts the best employees and leaders from the widest possible talent pool in a competitive labour market. Candidates care about workplace diversity and judge an organisation's commitment to diversity by their perceptions of inclusion in the workforce. A diverse and inclusive organization increases employee intent to stay by as much as 24% (Corporate Leadership Council, 2010).
2. **Performance:** An effective diversity approach supports equal opportunity and mitigates legal risk and costly outcomes where antidiscrimination regulation is not complied with. Diversity strategies improve employee engagement, motivation and productivity; reduce absenteeism and turnover and improve employee health and well being; increases commitment to colleagues and drives team collaboration and effectiveness by as much as 21% (Corporate Leadership Council, 2010); contributes to employee flexibility and adaptability.
3. **Innovation:** Diversity fosters creativity and innovation. Employees from diverse backgrounds bring new and different perspectives, experiences and styles to problem solving and decision making, thereby increasing capability and return on investment Attract new talent working teams that are diverse in their make-up are able to come up with a wider range of solutions to business problems. Inclusive workplaces that openly communicate their values and strategies on equality, human rights and inclusion are capitalizing on this as they are able to attract a wider pool of applicants and talent.

Obstacles

The main obstacles have to do with managers' and employees' attitudes and behavior. Specifically, prejudice (biased views) and discrimination (biased behaviors), are at the core of the barriers for implementing inclusive policies at the workplace. In today's "politically correct" environment, people may be embarrassed to show their ignorance about other cultures, may not want to invest time and energy in learning them, or feel threatened by other people who may take their jobs. Women, older adults, and ethnic and racial minority groups lack of support in career planning. They also don't get the required time and exposure for job advancement. An unsupportive working environment is an obstacle in creation of an inclusive workplace.

Inclusion and Corporate-Community Relations

Benefits

Corporate houses are capable of providing essential resources to groups and communities given their economic power. A wide range of activities fall under the title of corporate social responsibility, such as supporting educational or cultural institutions in the community, providing mentorship to youths, or tutoring children in local schools, running old age homes and NGOs. Corporate social responsibility actions now focus on positive benefits such as advantages in recruitment and increased employee loyalty. Social responsiveness generates goodwill from employees and customers alike that may result in fewer labor problems and a more favorable customer view of the company's products. Studies indicate that reputations have potentially favorable consequences because they enable companies to improve their standing by charging premium prices (Klein & Leffler, 1981; Milgram & Robert, 1986) and by enhancing their access to capital markets (Beatty & Ritter, 1986).

Obstacles

The main obstacle for initiating and maintaining activities that benefit the company's social environment are economic pressures to show profits in the short run. When companies are under pressure to demonstrate profitability on a quarterly basis, it is often difficult for managers to make a decision to allocate the money necessary for long-term commitments to social causes. Firms often perceive the relationship between social responsibility and financial performance as a trade-off. They view the costs incurred from socially responsible actions as an economic disadvantage compared with other, less responsible activities (Aupperle, Carroll, & Hatfield, 1985; Ullmann, 1985). A secondary, but important, obstacle is finding the right leaders to be champions of such programs, people who can initiate and maintain these activities.

Inclusion and Welfare-to-Work Programs

Benefit

The economic benefits include improved wages for this segment of the population that increases the pool of consumers with discretionary income. Also, better treatment of low-wage employees who are often frontline workers improves the company's customer relationships. In addition, value-based organizational practices are often attractive to customers. Companies gain a more loyal work force (given that it is treated well) that is committed to the organization and has lower turnover rates as a result (Kossek et al., 1997). With the expanding economy and the current and anticipated labor shortages, employers may need to expand their employee pools by tapping into the potential resource of former welfare recipients. A strong corporate commitment to hiring and retaining former welfare recipients that includes help with employment barriers can facilitate the difficult transition and increase the chances of long-term employment. In addition, opening up advancement opportunities for this population may increase their chances of obtaining higher-paying jobs with better benefits that will release them from the vicious cycle of low paying jobs that do not leave much income above the job-related expenses such as child care and transportation.

Obstacles

The main obstacle here is a limited corporate vision. Companies often focus only on the immediate needs and objectives of the company rather than considering the bigger picture that includes moral and ethical values as well as labor-force trends and the larger organizational environment. The other obstacles are stereotypes held by management and workers against welfare recipients and against people of color. The latter is based on a common misconception that the majority of welfare recipients are people of color when, in fact, the majority are white (Gottschalk, Mclanahan, & Sandfur, 1994).

Inclusion and Economic Globalization

Benefits

Companies today can reap the benefits of an increasingly global market place employing workers from different nationalities in, or outside, their native countries. This expansion creates new jobs, including international job opportunities, for these companies' employees. Multinational companies such as IBM, General Electric, British Petroleum, Siemans, and Eastman Kodak do business with more than 50 countries. Of the 1,000 largest industrial companies in the United States, 700 expect their growth abroad to exceed their domestic growth in the next five years. With foreign production currency accounting for more than 25 percent of their domestic production, U.S. multinationals have a great stake in the international scene. These global ventures and international collaborations allow companies to expand their geographical markets and to increase their economic activities.

Obstacles

Expatriates are the primary contact between the home organization and their international partners. An *expatriate* is a professional/manager/employee moved from country to, and for employment in, another country. There are two obstacles related to applying the principles of the inclusive workplace with respect to the deployment of expatriates.

The first is discrimination or inappropriate consideration of age, gender, race, or other personal characteristics with respect to the expatriate's selection (Adler, 1987), and the second is lack of preparation or under preparation for the values, norms, and overall cultural differences in the foreign assignment (Giagalone & Beard, 1994). Failed foreign assignments cause direct as well as indirect costs, such as losses in business opportunities, which are estimated in billions of dollars annually (Copeland & Griggs, 1985).

CASE STUDY

BrickRed Technologies, a software development company located in Noida has been ranked one of the "Best Places to Work" during 2011. "A great place to work is one in which you trust the people you work for, have pride in what you do, and enjoy the people you work with" — Robert Levering, *Co-Founder, Great Place to Work.*

Employees believe they work for great organizations when they consistently:

- **TRUST** the people they work for;
- Have **PRIDE** in what they do; and
- **ENJOY** the people they work with.

The Great Place to Work started operations in India in 2003 and it established itself as an independent entity in India on 21st May 2007.

In collaboration with Business world, Great Place to Work in India published lists of Best Workplaces in India in 2003, 2004, 2005 and 2007. In 2008, however, it published the Best Workplaces in India list in collaboration with *The Economic Times*, the largest-circulation business daily in India and the second largest globally. Over 500 organizations registered for the 2011 Study making it one of the largest studies in workplace culture in the world.

How are the Best Places Determined?

Trust Index Assessment & Employee Survey

Great Place to Work Institute's Trust Index Assessment and employee survey is the starting point for organizations invested in building a better workplace. Great Place to Work analysts precisely measures the underlying level of trust within the organization, while making targeted recommendations on how to improve your workplace.

Questions in Employee Survey

All the below questions have two options – **Agree or Disagree**.

1. This is a friendly place to work.
2. I am given the resources and equipment to do my job.
3. This is a physically safe place to work.

4. Everyone has an opportunity to get special recognition.
5. People here are willing to put in extra effort to get the job done.
6. You can count on people to cooperate.
7. Management makes its expectations clear.
8. I can ask management any reasonable question and get a straight answer.
9. I am offered training or development to further myself professionally.
10. Management shows appreciation for good work and extra effort.
11. People here are paid fairly for the work they do.
12. My work has special meaning: this is not 'just a job'.
13. When people change jobs or work units, they are made to feel right at home.
14. Management is approachable, easy to talk with.
15. Management recognizes honest mistakes as part of doing business.
16. Management genuinely seeks and responds to suggestions and ideas.
17. When I look at what we accomplish, I feel a sense of pride.
18. I feel I receive a fair share of the profits made by this organization.
19. Management keeps me informed about important issues and changes.
20. Management has a clear view of where the organization is going and how to get there.
21. Management trusts people to do a good job without watching over their shoulders.
22. Management involves people in decisions that affect their jobs or work environment.
23. Managers avoid playing favorites.
24. I feel good about the ways we contribute to the society.
25. Management does a good job of assigning and coordinating people.
26. People here are given a lot of responsibility.
27. This is a psychologically and emotionally healthy place to work.
28. People here are treated fairly regardless of their age.
29. Promotions go to those who best deserve them.
30. People look forward to coming to work here.
31. I can be myself around here.
32. Management delivers on its promises.
33. People here are treated fairly regardless of their race or caste.
34. People care about each other here.
35. Management's actions match its words.
36. Our facilities contribute to a good working environment.
37. People here are treated fairly regardless of their sex.

38. I'm proud to tell others I work here.
39. There is a "family" or "team" feeling here.
40. People celebrate special events around here
41. I believe management would lay people off only as a last resort.
42. People avoid politicking and backstabbing as ways to get things done.
43. People are encouraged to balance their work life and their personal life.
44. Management is competent at running the business.
45. If I am unfairly treated, I believe I'll be given a fair hearing if I appeal.
46. We have special and unique benefits here.
47. We're all in this together.
48. Management is honest and ethical in its business practices.
49. Management shows a sincere interest in me as a person, not just an employee.
50. I want to work here for a long time.
51. I am treated as a full member here regardless of my position.
52. I am able to take time off from work when I think it's necessary.
53. I feel I make a difference here.
54. When you join the organization, you are made to feel welcome.
55. This is a fun place to work.
56. Management hires people who fit in well here.
57. Management does a good job of developing managers for leadership positions.
58. Management does a good job of attracting talent for key positions
59. People here are treated fairly regardless of their religion.
60. There are opportunities here for my career growth
61. Performance of employees here is fairly evaluated.
62. Taking everything into account, I would say this is a great place to work.

Free Text Questions

63. Is there anything unique or unusual about this organization that makes it a great place to work? Please give specific examples.
64. What would make this organization a better place to work? Please give specific examples.

Demographic Details

Which Option best describes your role?

Your age bracket?

How long have you been with the company?

What's your gender?

What region do you work in?

What's your work status?

While the survey findings show how one can maximize effort to become a great place to work, workplace is measured on other parameters like the Culture of workplace through The Culture Audit instrument that includes The Trust Audit and *360 degree Management Trust Appraisal and* Internal Customer Perception Index.

- The detailed report gives deep insight into people processes
- Best practices of some of the best workplaces in all the 15 people practice areas as per the Great Place to Work® Framework
- Interactive sessions with Senior Managers on the findings of the analysis where the consultants help the organization prioritize some of the people practices for short term as well as long term action. (www.Greatplacetowork.com/India)

After being measured by the various indices and metrics it was found that people at BrickRed feel engaged and relate to the company culture. They feel free to work in an environment which is friendly, helping, and flexible as well as helps them to maintain a good work life balance. BrickRed is highly devoted to the wellbeing of its employees and it can be determined through its Employee Engagement initiatives like The Employee Recognition Program, Review and Increment Guidelines, Training and Certification Policy Referral Bonus Scheme, Joining Anniversary Recognition Program, Wedding Gift Policy, Home Drop Facility for women during late hours, Flexible Timings, Relocation Policy, Casual Dress Code, Interest Free Loans, Fun Fridays, etc.

The management not only is doing its best in engaging the employees but also values and respects the perspectives and contributions of individuals and groups of employees versus the exclusionary workplace that promotes employees conforming to organizational norms.

CONCLUSION

There is still a long distance to be travelled by organizations to create an inclusive workplace. While the private sector specially the IT industry has realized the importance of valuing the employee resources, government holdings are far behind when it comes to taking initiative to create an inclusive workplace. Incorporating inclusive working into the key values of an organization in a way that is practical for the organization can have a threefold effect: good for the business, good for the staff, and good for the community around it. Equality and human rights training for all employees, along with culture-changing initiatives such as mentoring, work placements and information-sharing events, all help to promote the benefits of inclusive working and reduce any tension between different groups. Culture change cannot happen overnight, but the ideas set out in this guide will help you to begin the change and the resulting benefits.

BIBLIOGRAPHY

[1] Adler, N.J., (1987). Pacific basin managers: A Gaijin, not a woman? *Human Resource Management,* 26(2), 169-191.

[2] Aupperle, K., Carroll, A., & Hatfield, J. (1985). An empirical examination of the relationship between corporate social responsibility and profitability. *Academy of Management Journal,* 28,446-463.

[3] Beatty, R.P., & Ritter, J.R. (1986). Investment banking, reputation, and underpricing of initial public offerings. *Journal of Financial Economics,* 15, 213-232.

[4] Brick Red Employee Handbook.

[5] Copeland, L., & Griggs, L. (1985). *Going International.* New York: Random House.

[6] Giagalone, R. A., & Beard, J. W. (1994). Impression management, diversity, and international management. *American Behavioral Scientist,* 37,621-63.

[7] Gottschalk, P., Mclanahan, S., & Sandfur, G. D. (1994). The dynamics and intergenerational transmission of poverty and welfare participation. In S.H. Danzinger, G.D. Sandfur, & D.H. Weinberg (Eds.), *Confronting Poverty: Prescriptions for Change,* pp. 85-108. Cambridge, MA: Harvard University Press.

[8] Klein, B., 8 Leffler, K. (1981). The role of market forces in assuring contractual performance. *Journal of Political Economy,* 89, 615-641.

[9] Kossek, E.E., Huber-Yoder, M., Castellino, D., 8c Lerner, J. (1997). The working poor: Locked out of careers and the organizational mainstream? *Academy of Management Executive,* 11(1), 76-92.

[10] McNeely, R.L., Sapp, M., & Daly, A. (1998). Ethnicity, gender, earnings, occupational rank, and job satisfaction in the public social services: What do workers say? In A. Daly (Ed.), *Workplace Diversity: Issues and Perspectives,* pp. 144-165. Washington, DC: NASW Press.

[11] Michael. Mor Barak (2000). The Inclusive Workplace: An Ecosystems Approach to Diversity Management: Social Work, Volume 45, Number 4.

[12] Milgram, P., & Robert, J. (1986). Price and advertising signals of product quality. *Journal of Political Economy,* 94, 796-821.

[13] Mor Barak, Michalle (2005) Managing *Diversity: Towards Globally Inclusive Workplace.* Thousand Oaks: Sage.

[14] Social Networks and Health (Garland, 1991).

[15] U Umann, A. (1985). Data in search of a theory: A critical examination of the relationships among social performance, social disclosure, and economic performance. *Academy of Management Review,* 10, 540-577. www.Greatplacetowork.com/India

[16] Whiddon, B., & Martin, P.Y. (1989). Organizational democracy and work quality in a state welfare agency. *Social Science Quarterly,* 70, 667-686.

Inclusion in Consulting Firms

Rupa Mittal

KPMG India

ABSTRACT

This paper explores the prevalent practices for inclusion in the services industry with special reference to consulting firms. It mentions some of the policies being followed in the industry to make the work place an egalitarian one with people exhibiting mutual respect for each other.

There are various facets of inclusion which through relevant HR policies can make day to day work at the organization more balanced and conducive for efficiency. Be it the work life balance, transparency in promotion and bonuses, facilities that the administration provides, the approachability of senior members in the organization or retention of the talent in the firm; the aspects are countless. Yet a common thread of mutual employee respect and work satisfaction runs through them all.

Hence, this paper is a modest attempt to throw some light on such policies which cover the aforementioned aspects in the consulting domain where the companies are competing with each other in order to make their workplaces the most favorable.

Keywords: *Consulting Firms, Inclusion, Employee, Employee Satisfaction, Working Conditions*

BACKGROUND

According to a survey in India, before joining a prospective employer the major parameters on which the aspirants rate a firm are: career growth, learning and development, job profile, job security and opportunities to go abroad.

However, from the employer's perspective; another survey tells us that some of the major challenges faced in order to retain its employees are to keep the work place interesting, to give them freedom to speak their minds, to provide facilities based on individual needs and to encourage work life balance.

Hence, we can clearly see a disconnect between pre joining expectations of an employee and post joining priorities. Most of the employers within an industry can provide the former; but the latter is more about Esteem and Self actualization which as Maslow's hierarchy of needs clearly portrays becomes more important once the basic needs are in place. This is where inclusion comes into picture.

In the services industry, if we focus mainly on the consulting firms we find that to implement policies for inclusion is a different ball game altogether. Most of the employees are stationed at the client site for long periods of time. If the projects are very long the employees tend to lose touch with the work culture of the firm and get more accustomed to the working conditions of the client. Interaction between colleagues also becomes a challenge as they don't meet for months and hence, the bond that one feels with the firm and his co-employees tends to weaken.

Also to be mentioned are the stressful deadlines to meet the clients demands, late working hours and a lot of travel requirements, be it domestic or international.

Hence, in such kind of working conditions, to foster employee satisfaction and a feeling of oneness among its employees is a herculean task. Not to mention the frequent poaching of employees by competition as talent/human resource is the most important asset in this industry. If we were to draw an analogy with the manufacturing industry both the raw material and the final product are the employees in the consulting domain.

Therefore, inclusion is of paramount importance for consulting firms.

POLICIES EMPLOYED AT CONSULTING FIRMS

We can now talk about the various measures that consulting firms have taken to build loyalty and employee satisfaction among its employees.

If we see **from a point of view of work life balance**, firms have come up with innovative ideas in terms of leave structures, office timings and travel. A few companies have started with a concept of Block Leaves from 25th December to 1st January which means that all employees from all divisions would be taking compulsory annual off at this time of the year. Keeping in mind the client's needs, a partner's approval is must for the employees who have to work on those days. Not only does it help the employees plan their vacation better with their families and friends; it also sends a message about how much their firm cares for their well being.

Another interesting concept is "leave sharing". If an employee has exhausted all leaves and needs more in case of an emergency; medical or otherwise, other fellow employees who have unused leaves can share them with the concerned person. It is not hard to fathom that this kind of culture helps build camaraderie among its employees. It also reinforces the belief of the employee in the organization's genuine concern for the person facing hard times; as it means that the person would still be getting paid for those leaves and the firm is putting the interests of the employee above its own.

Although now very common among organizations across industries, flexible timings to work and work from home policies help employees balance their personal and professional lives better.

As mentioned earlier, consulting firms face a challenge as most of the times their employees are stationed at the client's site. Hence, they are granted a "flyback" to their base office at regular intervals depending on the time period of the project. This helps them interact with their colleagues and managers better and build a bond with the firm from which they had been away for a long time. Also, more often than not the base location coincides with the home town of the employee which gives them a chance to spend time with their families too. The employees are also given the options of flying back to their native cities rather than reporting at the base office.

In terms of **creating a bond among its employees**, the firm organizes various events and outings for giving a chance to interact with each other. Apart from local outings within the city that are held 2-3 times a year; an "offsite" is organized every year where people from the entire division go to an outstation location and spend time with each other. Many fun group activities are organized which help people get to know their colleagues better; even the ones that they have never worked with and build a relationship which goes beyond a merely professional one. At various festive occasions, such as Diwali and Christmas, games and competitions among divisions are organized to foster a feeling of unity within the department.

All these make the **senior management more approachable** too, as in all these activities, events and outings everyone, starting from the partner to an analyst is involved. The teams are also formed in such a way that people across designations interact with each other.

Providing facilities such as company cabs, car pool options etc. to employees helps increase their efficiency at work, reduce absenteeism and increase bonding between fellow employees.

Given the late working hours at times, women employees are provided assistance for security such as:

- A security escort guard in each cab or radio cab (if the employee is at the client site), post dusk.
- Help lines to assist in case of a cab breakdown or any other such emergency
- Escort guards in the parking bay if the employee wishes to use her own vehicle

Fairness is another aspect that matters a lot to the employees. Ambiguity in ratings, bonuses and promotions are some of the key issues that a number of organizations face. Transparency in the system is extremely important as the employees need to understand the reasons due to which an individual gets a promotion/bonus etc. Firms have come up with innovative ideas such as quick feedback mechanisms through which one can get a feedback before the entire assignment is over. There are provisions to get feedback from those managers with whom you have worked on non-chargeable assignments. Meeting up with the manager on regular intervals is highly encouraged and tangible goals are set by the manager and employee in the beginning of any assignment to remove any ambiguity.

And finally the most important point is **valuing the talent within the firm**. Most consulting firms have a number of divisions such as management consulting, risk consulting and transaction advisory to name a few. After a while, an employee may want to explore other divisions to maintain interest and excitement of doing something new at the workplace. This is something which is encouraged in most firms in order to retain the talent in house.

The organizations believe that rather than people applying outside the firm to explore new opportunities, the opportunities should be created within in order to retain the services of the employee who understands the firm well and has build a reputation for it in front of the client. Companies offer inter department transfers after a certain years of experience and the partners are encouraged to relieve their resources.

Thus, we see that despite the various challenges faced by consulting firms; they have come up with innovative ways to bring about inclusion in the firms. In India especially, these policies hold a lot of importance as according to Business Standard; India has high attrition rate of 14 % which is higher than the global rate. The firms have understood that it's not just the paycheck that motivates the employee. A number of other factors such as fairness, mutual respect and individual dignity are cornerstones of employee satisfaction and hence, the relevance of inclusion is increasing by the day.

BIBLIOGRAPHY

[1] Best Companies to Work for in INDIA by Nishad P.I.

[2] Websites of Consulting firms.

[3] Website of Princeton University on the topic of inclusion.

[4] Blog HR Vigilance.

[5] 'Indian cos attrition rate at 14%, higher than global average' published in Business Standard.

The Image of Persons with Disabilities as Portrayed in a Daily Newspaper: A Short Term Content Analysis Study

Shalini Garg, Sanchita and Puneet Kumar Gupta[1]

University School of Management Studies, Guru Gobind Singh Indraprastha University, New Delhi

[1] *AYJ National Institute for the Hearing Handicapped (AYJNIHH), Mumbai*

ABSTRACT

The newspaper dailies have the ability to link persons with disability to the world. Still, no research has been found specifically on persons with disabilities and their portrayal in the newspaper daily in India. Many studies have focused on the more general topic of disabilities in the news (Mick 1996; Power 2006; Haller, Dorries, and Rahn 2006). Person with disabilities are also part of the society. The newspaper dailies depict the persons with disabilities, as reflection of the society's perspective about them. Content analysis of media is a traditional mass communication research method used to assess a wide range of media content trends (Poothullil J.M. Martin 2008). This research paper advocates for increased newspaper analysis within the disability studies field. Using a short term media research study about Hindustan Times (HT) Newspaper daily and its news coverage of disability issues, this paper explores the shifting nature of recent disability coverage in Mumbai newspapers for a period of 3 months in 2012. Content analysis based research found that the newspaper under study reported sensational and gender biased news related to disability issues.

Keywords: *Disability, News, Media, Study, Gender, Issues, Society, Image*

INTRODUCTION

Persons with Disabilities have their image in society. It may be positive or negative. Media plays a significant role in creating the right image of persons with disability in society. Today world population is 7,113,968,427 billion (GeoHive 2013) and hence estimated population of person with disabilities is 711 million, if we consider that 10% of world population are persons with disabilities as estimated by World Bank (2004), Sanchez (2010) and Cumberbatch (1992). If the current population (on 29th April 2013) of India is 1,271,876,934 billion, then the population of person with disability is estimated to be more than 100 million. However,

India is signatory to the UNCRPD since 2007 as it ratified the same on 1st Oct.2007. Adhering to the UNCRPD guidelines, it is mandatory in a country like India, to create awareness in the society about disability (article-8 of UNCRPD). Hence it is imperative that both government and non-government sectors in India adhere to these guidelines. In his exploration of the principles for media representations of disabled people in society Colin Barnes (1992) states that 'the overall view of disabled people is decidedly negative and a threat to the well- being of the non-disabled community'. The reason for this is that the person with disabilities lives in such condition that, media which have the ability to link persons with disability in society to the world, do not portray them as persons and discover their abilities. As a group, they are often grossly underrepresented in the media. The underrepresentation then entails that the mass society who watch/view and listen to media may end up not knowing much about them. This paper seeks reaction which is necessary to convey a sentiment and priority of togetherness in the fight for equal distribution of human rights, using a short term media research study about a newspaper daily and its news coverage of disability issues, this paper explores the shifting nature of recent disability coverage in Mumbai newspapers for a period of 3 months in 2012. Content analysis based research found that the newspaper under study reported sensational and gender biased news related to disability issues.

CONTENT ANALYSIS

Content analysis is a research tool used to determine the presence of certain words or concepts within texts or sets of texts. In his research on Canadian disability studies, Janowitz (1968) explains that the content of the mass media can provide two contrasting indicators of social culture: 'The contents of the mass media are a reflection of the social organization and value system of the society or group interest involved. In their research studies on content analysis of print media (Denis McQuail 1968, Poothullil, J.M. Martin (2008) explains that the purpose of the cultural indicator analysis is often to test propositions about effects from media on society over time, but it is also a method for the study of social change in its own right and for the comparison of different national societies and cultures'.

DISABILITY IN INDIA

Disability is the permanent or temporary restriction on the use of sight, sound, color or motor skills. According to Census 2001, (Orissa review 2010) there are over 21 million people in India, suffering from one or the other kind of disability. This is equivalent to 2.1% of the population. Across the country, the highest number of disabled has been reported from the state of Uttar Pradesh (3.6 million). Significant numbers of disabled have also been reported from the state like Bihar (1.9 million), West Bengal (1.8 million), Tamil Nadu and Maharashtra (1.6 million each). Tamil Nadu is the only state, which has a higher number of disabled females than males. Among the states, Arunachal Pradesh has the highest proportion of disabled males (66.6%) and lowest proportion of female disabled.

Table 1: Number of Disabled Population and Type of Disability

	Population	*Percentage (%)*
Total population	1,028,610,328	100.0
Total disabled population	21,906,769	2.1
Disability rate (per lakh population)	2,130	–
Type of Disability		
(a) In seeing	10,634,881	1.0
(b) In speech	1,640,868	0.2
(c) In hearing	1,261,722	0.1
(d) In movement	6,105,477	0.6
(e) Mental	2,263,821	0.2

Source: Census of India 2001.

THEORIES ON IMAGES

By nature the visual medium demands receiver attention. HT newspaper daily depicts news with text and images. The news photograph connects the reader to a story in a way that text alone cannot. Graber (1996) said "combining pictures with words makes the message more memorable" (p. 87). The overall content of pictures differs in the emotion, immediacy, and environment captured. These elements of a picture can produce dramatic information, which are not necessarily conveyed or included through textual information alone. Graber attributes this to the fact that the human brain absorbs larger amounts of information when messages are visual (1996). Medium theory also explains this phenomenon. Chesebro (1984) argues each individual's mind is conditioned to view and digest media modalities in different ways. He asserts that "specific media are linked to particular modes of understanding". In print media image on disability does depict its impact and understanding on the minds of persons in the society. With respect to photographic images, the aspect of human sensation is an important one.

An operational assumption of media is that "attention is best gained by appealing to sensation and human interest" (Myerowitz, 1985, p. 13). This assumption directly relates to arousal and the evidence that humans like to "feel." An image can capture human interest within a momentary glance and evoke sensation soon after. While words alone have the same ability, it takes more effort on the part of the receiver. It is a less instantaneous and perhaps less vivid, effect. Myerowitz (1985) argues that all media focus on dramatic or exciting events and spectacles to gain attention. Yet it is possible photographic images may win more attention than the printed word simply due to ease of use. Once that attention is gained, do the images create a stronger arousal or emotional response?

HINDUSTAN TIMES (HT) DAILY

HT (HT), Mumbai edition, was launched on July 14, 2005. The Mumbai edition has its own character, reflecting the vibrancy and diversity of the great metropolis. The core values of HT, integrity, fairness and maturity are respected. HT is the first smart-age newspaper in India to evolve into a new international size. Sleeker and smarter, it ensures enhanced ease of reading and convenient handling. The publication has completely redesigned its format with an all-new masthead, sporting a contemporary international look. On an average the number of pages of the daily is 26 on a particular day. The content analysis study focused on the total area of the daily, including the supplements. According to Indian Readership Survey (IRS Q2-2011), HT daily has consolidated its number 2 position in terms of circulation in Mumbai, i.e., 7.2 lakhs readers.

NEED OF THE STUDY

The media is a powerful means of disseminating information to the mass Barnes (1992) and Klepper (1996) state that 'the history of the portrayal of disabled people is the history of oppressive and negative representation'. In many countries, people with disabilities and organizations that advocate for their mainstreaming, lament that media coverage of their issues are scanty and not impacting positive attitudes concerning them to the wider society. Media images and stories influence thinking and establish social norms. People with disabilities have endured misrepresentation, defamation, and lack of representation in the media news and entertainment. This lack of awareness is a problem in the sense that the wider society may not have a positive attitude towards PWDs and this may slow down the process of mainstreaming and their being included in the normal daily activities. Catlet (1993) asserts that policy issues that a country has put in place to address the plight of people with disabilities affects the attitudes that the wider society may have towards them. Sanchez (2010) puts it rightly that the media – television, radio, newspapers, magazines, the Internet, social media and other forms – play an important role in influencing public opinion and attitudes. The choice of words, images and messages can determine perceptions, attitudes and behaviors. Hence there is a need for content analysis of a daily to understand the perspective of the society in Mumbai. In fact according to Jay Cope et al. (2011) Visual images demand a viewer's attention. Photos have the ability to convey drama and emotion and realism in a way that text alone cannot.

This study is an attempt to depict the illicit support from the print media and journalism in its efforts to bring not only rights bearing legislation to those who are in need, but to create a powerful image of a population. In the toolkit of OHCHR, according to UNDP (2010) Media and the positive portrayal of persons with disabilities will make the necessity for fair human rights treatment apparent to citizens, advocacy organizations and legislative bodies.

OBJECTIVE OF THE STUDY

This paper seeks to depict the reaction which is necessary to convey a sentiment and priority of togetherness in the fight for equal distribution of human rights. It uses a short term media research study of content analysis, about a Newspaper daily and its news coverage of disability issues. This paper also explores the shifting nature of recent disability coverage in Mumbai newspapers for a period of 3 months in 2012. This content analysis based research study aims to find sensational and gender biased news related to disability issues.

RESEARCH QUESTIONS

1. What is the image of persons with disabilities in the Newspaper daily?
2. How many news Items on disability issues depicts involvement of Government and Non-Government agencies?
3. Which disability has been featured more frequently in the Newspaper daily?
4. Is there gender bias in the news on disability issues in the Newspaper daily?
5. Is there any gender bias in success stories on PWDs are featured in the Newspaper daily?

HYPOTHESIS

1. The image of persons with disabilities depicted in the Newspaper daily is positive
2. The newspaper daily depicts involvement of Government and Non-Government agencies in disability related news
3. Mental illness is featured more frequently in the Newspaper daily
4. There is gender bias in the news on disability issues in the Newspaper daily
5. There is no gender bias in success stories on PWDs are featured in the Newspaper daily

METHODOLOGY

The methodology of the research study consisted of the content analysis of newspaper daily selected for the study for a period of 3 months. The exact period of the research study was from 1st October 2012 to 31st December 2012. A sample size collected, consisting of 50 news articles/advertisements pertaining to disability issues. A research tool was developed for content analysis of the daily (Appendix-1) and the same was used for the purpose of the study. The focus of research study was to analyze the coverage of disability related news with respect to the image portrayal of person with disability. The coverage was measured in terms of the type of news area of coverage, gender, color used, and depiction of news with graphical representation, sources of news and various stages of life. The data gathered with the help of the research tool was analyzed using the computer software Statistical Package for the Social Sciences (SPSS) Version-19.

LIMITATIONS

1. The period of the research study was for 3 months from 1st October 2012 to 31st December 2013.
2. Only Mumbai edition of HT, English newspaper daily was considered into the research study.

3. A sample size collected consisted of 50 news articles / advertisement pertaining to disability issues.
4. The study of the disability related issues was restricted to only 6 types of disabilities as mentioned in the PWD Act 1995. The disability related to leprosy was not considered, during the research.

RESULTS AND DISCUSSIONS

In order to find the significance of the coverage of disability related news in the HT Mumbai, daily, a research was done using a research tool (Annexure – 1) created for the purpose of the study. This research tool consisted of various parameters to analyze image, gender, news related with govt. & non govt. agencies and depiction of news with graphical representation, sources of disability related news.

Disability News and Images as Depicted in the HT Daily

In order to find out the projection of image of persons with disability related news in HT Mumbai daily, analysis of the data collected using the research tool was done. The analysis was done based on the parameters defined for the projection of news, number of news stories, number of images and type of stories. The results of the study in terms disability, with reference to projection of image of persons with disabilities are depicted in the Chart 1 and Table 1.

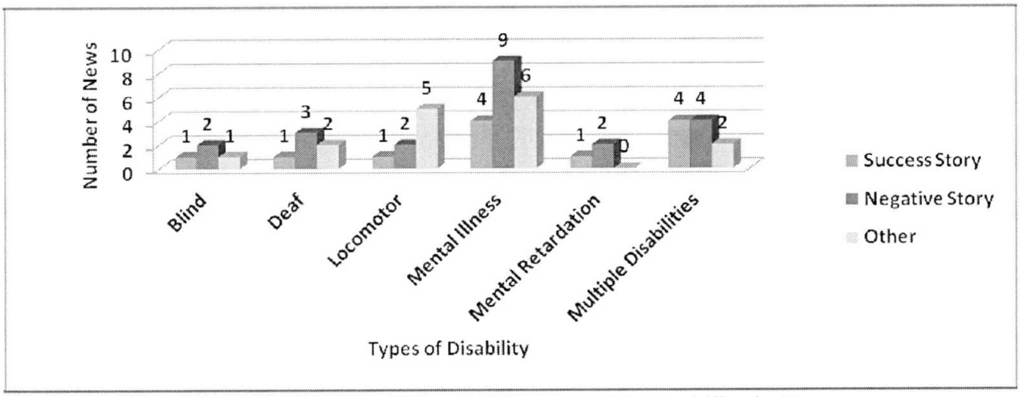

Chart 1: Depicting Image of Persons with Disability in News

In the Table 1 given above, it is found that there was negative image projection in the disability related news. In fact the negative projection of the news with reference to various disabilities was also significantly different as the p-value is 0.74. It was also found that, out of 50 news articles studied during the research 22 (44%) news articles had a negative projection of news with reference to various disabilities.

Table 1: Image of Persons with Disability in News

Type of Disability	*Type of News*		
	Success Story	*Negative Story*	*Other*
Blind	1	2	1
Deaf	1	3	2
Locomotors	1	2	5
Mental Illness	4	9	6
Mental Retardation	1	2	0
Multiple Disabilities	4	4	2
TOTAL	12	22	16

p value = 0 .74

Frequency of Disability Images in HT Daily

In order to find out the frequency of image of persons in disability related news of HT Mumbai daily, analysis of the data collected using the research tool was done. The analysis was done based on the parameters defined for the projection of news, number of news stories, and types of stories. The results of the study in terms disability with reference to projection of frequency of image of persons with disability are depicted in the Chart and Table 2.

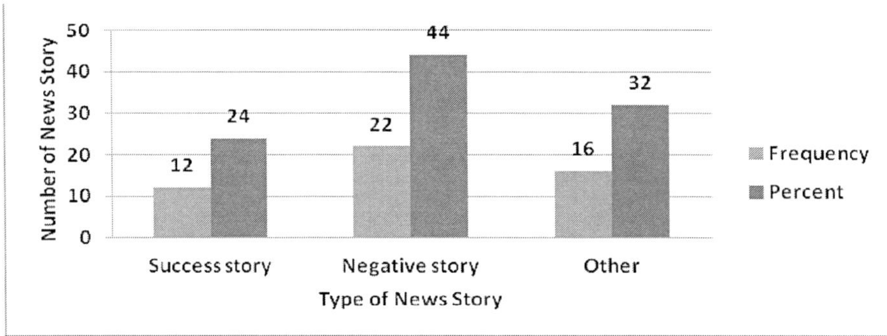

Chart 2: Frequency of Disability Images in HT Daily

Table 2: Frequency of Disability Images in HT Daily

Types of News Story	*Frequency*	*Percent*
Success story	12	24
Negative story	22	44
Other	16	32
Total	50	100

In the Table 2 it was found that there was a negative projection of disability related news. It was also found that out of 50 news articles, 22 news articles had a negative projection of news with reference to various disabilities.

Gender Biased Image of Disability

In order to find out the projection of gender biased image of person with disability related news in HT Mumbai daily, analysis of the data collected using the research tool was done. The analysis was done based on parameters defined for the projection of news, number of news stories, and type of stories were success story, negative story, other depicting gender biased. The results of the study in terms disability with reference to projection of gender biased image of person with disability are depicted in the Table 3.

Table 3: Gender-wise Classification of Disability Related News

Gender	*Success Story*	*Negative Story*	*Other*
Male	2	7	2
Female	0	5	0
Male & Female	4	4	3
Other	6	6	11
Total	12	22	16

p-value = 0.05

In the Table 3 above it was found that there was a negative projection of female gender disability related news. In fact the projection of the news with reference to various disabilities was significantly different as the p-value is 0.05. It was also found that out of 50 news articles, 5 news articles had a negative projection of female gender news with reference to various disabilities and no positive projection. It is also strengthen a small 2004 survey in Orissa, India, found that virtually all of the women and girls with disabilities were beaten at home, 25 per cent of women with intellectual disabilities had been raped and 6 per cent of women with disabilities had been forcibly sterilized. The Women Watch of the United Nations Internet Gateway, on Gender Equality and Empowerment of Women (UN-2012) states that girls and women of all ages with any form of disability are generally among the more vulnerable and marginalized of society.

Gender-wise Classification of Disability Related News

In order to find out the projection of gender wise classification of disability related news in HT Mumbai daily, analysis of the data collected using the research tool was done. The analysis was done based on parameters defined for the projection of disability news and gender. The results of the study in terms disability with reference to projection of gender of person with disability are depicted in the Table 4.

Table 4: Gender-wise Classification of Disability Related News

Types of Disability	*Male*	*Female*	*Male & Female*	*Other*	*Total*
Blind	2	1	0	1	4
Deaf	0	0	0	6	6
Locomotor	2	1	2	3	8
Mental Illness	4	3	5	7	19
Mental Retardation	2	0	1	0	3
Multiple Disabilities	1	0	3	6	10
Total	11	5	11	23	50

p-value = 0 .21

In the Table 4 above it was found that there was less than half of news of female compare to male with reference to disability related news. In fact the projection of the news with reference to various disabilities was not significantly different as the p-value is 0.21. It was also found that out of 50 news articles, 11 news articles had news of male with compare to 5 news article of female with reference to various disabilities.

Visual Representation of Disability Related News

In order to find out the visual representation of disability related news in HT Mumbai daily, analysis of the data collected using the research tool was done. The analysis was done based on parameters defined for the projection of disability news and visual representation. The results of the study in terms disability with reference to visual representation are depicted in the Table 5.

In the Table 5 above it was found that there was 6 visual image representation of locomotor disability out of 10 visual image representations where as 21 visual image representations is not related with the news and 19 new articles did not carry any visual. In fact the visual image

Table 5: Visual Representation of Disability Related News

Types of Disability	*Visual Representation Disability Wise*				
	Blind	*Locomotor*	*Multiple Disabilities*	*Not Related with Disabilities*	*No Image*
Blind	2	0	0	0	2
Deaf	0	0	1	5	0
Locomotor	0	2	0	3	3
Mental Illness	0	1	0	10	8
Mental Retardation	0	0	0	2	1
Multiple Disabilities	0	3	1	1	5
Total	2	6	2	21	19

p- value = 0.001

representation of the news with reference to various disabilities was significantly different as the p-value is 0.001. It was also found that out of 50 news articles, 2 news articles had visual image representations of blind as well as same number of news articles of multiple disabilities had visual image representation.

Classification of Disability Related News with Reference to Govt. and Non-Govt.

In order to find out the classification of disability related news with reference to govt. & non-govt. in HT Mumbai daily, analysis of the data collected using the research tool was done. The analysis was done based on parameters defined for the classification of disability news and govt. & non-govt. The results of the study in terms disability with reference to govt. & non govt. are depicted in the Table 6.

Table 6: Classification of Disability Related News with Reference to Govt. & Non-Govt.

Types of Disability	*News Reference to Govt.*	*News Reference to Non-Govt*	*Neither Govt. & Non-Govt.*	*Both – Govt. & Non-Govt.*	*Total*
Blind	2	1	1	0	4
Deaf	3	0	1	2	6
Locomotor	3	1	4	0	8
Mental Illness	5	3	11	0	19
Mental Retardation	1	0	2	0	3
Multiple Disabilities	6	1	2	1	10
Total	20	6	21	3	50

p-value = .26

In the Table 6 above it was found that there was equal distribution of disability related news with reference to govt. & non govt. of disability related news. In fact the classification of the news with reference to various disabilities was not significantly different as the p-value is 0.26. It was also found that out of 50 news articles, 21 news articles had reference of govt. and 20 had non govt. of news with reference to various disabilities.

CONCLUSION

Persons with disabilities have endured misrepresentation, defamation, and lack of representation in the print media news. It is evident from this research study that gender bias and negative image is dominant in the print media reports. Among the 50 news articles analyzed for its content during the research study, 22 (44%) news articles had a negative projection of news (Table 1) on persons with disabilities. In Table 3, it may be noted that the number of news items with negative image of female gender related disability news is higher. The newspaper daily under study has thus depicted the opinion of the public with reference to woman with disability. In fact Sanchez (2010) puts it rightly that the print media play an important role in influencing public opinion and attitudes. The choice of words, images and messages can determine perceptions, attitudes and behaviors. In Table 5 it may be noted that there were visual image representation of locomotor disability visual image representations. Whereas 21(42%) visual image representations are not related with the news and 19 (38%) disability related new articles did not carry any visual. It was also found that on 2 news articles related to disability had visual image representations of Blind. It is observed that even on 'World Day of the Disabled' i.e., 3rd December, there were no news reports on persons with disabilities or on disability issues in the daily. This shows that print media is influenced by society's negative attitude towards persons with disability.

REFERENCES

[1] Barnes, C. (1992). Disabling Imagery and the Media: An Exploration of the Principles for Media Representations of Disabled People.

[2] Catlett, S.M. (June, 1993). Newspaper images and messages: People with disabilities. Paper presented at the Annual *Meeting of the American association on Mental Retardation*, Washington, D.C.

[3] Chesebro, J.W. (1984). The media reality: Epistemological functions of media in cultural systems. *Critical Studies in Mass Communication*, 1, 111-130.

[4] Denis McQuail, (1989). *Mass Communication Theory* (London: Sage, 1989): 178.

[5] Graber, D. (1996). Say it with pictures. *The Annals of the American Academy*, 546, 85-96.

[6] Geohive (2013). Global Statistics/Population Statistics, Accessed on 29th April 2013, available at:www.geohive.com/earth/population_now.aspx

[7] Halifax: The British Council of Organisations of Disabled People and Ryburn Publishing Limited disability community identity.

[8] Haller, Beth, Bruce Dorries, and Jessica Rahn (2006). Media labeling versus the US disability community identity: A study of shifting cultural language. *Disability and Society* 21, No. 1: 61-75.

[9] Hurst. R. (1995). Overcoming obstacles to the integration of disabled people. Copenhagen: Disability awareness in Action.

[10] Jay Cope, et al. (2011) Image Impact in Print Media: A Study of How Pictures Influence News Consumers University of Oklahoma, Impact of News Images, Taylor and Francis, Brisbane, Australia.

[11] Meyrowitz, J. (1985). No Sense of Place: The impact of electronic media on social behavior. New York: Oxford University Press.

[12] Klepper, Robert (1996). The Cinema of Isolation: A History of Physical Disability in the Movies. www.silentmajority.com/FeatureBook/book19.htm.

[13] Mick, Kristin Anne (1996). Framing disability: A content analysis of disability-related newspaper coverage from 1986-1994. MS diss., San Jose State Univ.

[14] Morris Janowitz, "Harold Lasswell's contribution to content analysis." *Winter 1968-69, Public Opinion Quarterly* (1968): 648.

[15] Penas, E. (2007, September, 1). Media and Disability. Interview Report, 1: Fundacion ONCE.

[16] Poothullil. J.M. Martin (2008). Content Analysis of "Disability Communication", The Daily Newspaper DNA (Daily News Analysis) A Short-term Study Report, Language in India, Vol. 8 11 November. Available at : www.languageinindia.com/.../disabilitycommunication.pdf

[17] Sanchez, J (Ed). (2010). Media Guidelines for Portrayal of Disability.

[18] UN Enable - Factsheet on Persons with *Disabilities* www.un.org/disabilitics/dcfault.asp?id – 18

APPENDIX 1

Disability-related News/Story Content Analysis Form

(Fill out one form per story. Below you will find descriptions of each question and how to answer them.)

Story ID

Newspaper Date (6 digit) – Story # (2 digit)

November 11, 2013 newspaper story 4 would be: 111101-13

If analyzing more than one newspaper title, on the same day, add another code at the front indicating paper. For example 2-111101-13

Jump

A story is said to have "jumped" when it is continued on another page – usually with a tag such as "see Tree Page 8" at the end. Jumping applies only to the text of the story itself and doesn't apply to a promotional bit (like a skybox) that may appear independently of the story.

Types of Disability

Various types of disabilities have been depicted in the news/advertisement carried by the dailies. The types of disabilities classified by the Person with Disabilities Act, 1995 are:

1. Blind
2. Deaf
3. Mental Retardation
4. Mental Illness
5. Orthopedic/Locomotor
6. Multiple Disability

Projection of News

1. Success Story
2. Negative Story
3. Other

Treatment of News

It is related to determine the general focus of the story.

Following question been considered to portray the image of person with disability:

1. Is a story portraying person with disability with his achievement?
2. Is the story significantly focusing on person rather than his /her disability?
3. Does the story seem to be tailored for person with disability to represent them in pity or for empathy?

By answering these questions, the image of person with disability should become clear.

Gender

The identification of news article was with reference to gender. The news representing male it will get a code for male category similarly for female, both male and female and other.

Parameters for Terminologies used to Address Disability Issues

1. Acceptable – Eg. Person with Disability,
2. Derogatory – Eg. Dumb, Mute
3. Politically Correct – Eg. Differently challenged
4. Medical – Eg. Impairment

Visual Image Representation Disability wise:

All the news carrying visual representation of disability had been categorized under

- Blind
- Locomotor
- Multiple Disabilities
- Not with related Disabilities
- No image

Disability Related News with Reference to Govt. & Non-Govt.

News articles mentioning about government policies and welfare and their involvement had been identify to study the portrayal of disability in the light of success story.

A category had been formed: News reference to govt., non govt., both govt. & non govt., neither govt. or non govt.

Perception of the Employed Sexual Minorities (LGBT) on their Inclusion in the Workplace in Bangalore

Justin J. Philip and Bino Thomas[1]

Department of Social Work, Christ University, Bangalore
[1]Christ University, Bangalore

ABSTRACT

As reported in various studies, homosexual orientation is common in almost every culture and every society. In India the number of Lesbian, Gay, Bisexual and Transgender (LGBT) are approximately 42-84 million. An understanding of the issues faced by LGBT to the workplace starts with the recognition that a diverse and inclusive business environment is directly linked to enhanced business performance. Peoples' Union for Civil Liberties, Karnataka (PUCL-K) reports that discrimination against sexuality minorities is embedded at workplaces. LGBT people have experienced a long and pervasive history of employment discrimination which still continues to be present in India even though initiatives are taken by the companies such as Google, IBM, and Goldman Sachs to protect their rights and treat them equal. Study on sexual minorities is important as diversity and inclusion at workplace is more than racial and gender diversity. In this context, this study was conducted to find out the perception of employed sexual minorities on their inclusion in workplace with 50 participants (N=50) from Bangalore who are working in organised industries using Snowball sampling method. The results also suggest importance of Employee Resource Groups (ERG's) at workplace and LGBT friendly policies are essential to join any industry.

Keywords: *LGBT, Workplace, Inclusion, Sexual Orientation, Sexual Minority, Discrimination, Employee Resource Groups*

INTRODUCTION

Historically, lesbian, gay, bisexual and transgender (LGBT) people have been heavily stigmatised and therefore subject to harassment and discrimination. However, in recent times, most western countries have made considerable moves to afford legal rights on a basis of sexual orientation and/or gender identity. Sexual identity and orientation and are the issues that are not openly discussed in Indian society or at the workplace. For many parts of Indian society and work culture LGBT identity is perceived as a foreign evil – with the common held belief that

LGBT individuals did not exist in Indian history and culture but came from Western influence (Business, 2012). Google, Microsoft, IBM, Goldman Sachs, JP Morgan, Cisco, Citibank, etc. and some Indian firms such as Wipro, TCS, Infosys and Mind tree have sexual orientation on their anti-harassment policy (Business, 2012). Still Gender identity is not covered by many of them. Having sexual orientation/gender identity on the company's anti-harassment policy means that they are protected against overt/covert discrimination/abuse/harassment for being LGBT. They have the right to report their colleagues/managers to the relevant HR authorities if they feel they are being targeted because of their sexual orientation/gender identity. The policy is also supposed to protect them against any backlash for making such a complaint.

Google, Infosys, and Goldman Sachs have taken tangible initiatives for their LGBT employees in India. IBM in 1984 had included sexual orientation in its *Manager's Handbook* and later covered LGBTs in their Equal Opportunity Policy.

A well-motivated and productive set of employees are essential for business success. Individuals who do not fit with organisational culture will tend to feel marginalised and may be dissatisfied with their work and their organisation (Miller & Katz, 2002). It's important to examine the impact how this can emerge in workplaces particularly in relation to sexual and gender diversity. According to a study in Queensland results suggest GLBTI workers are disclosing their sexuality more and are experiencing more discrimination in the workplace, despite anti-discrimination policies (Barrett, Lewis, & Dwyer, 2011).

LGBT inclusion can be attained by creating a place which provides Safety, Acceptance and Equality, ensuring safety from harassment, bullying and violence, acceptance in fostering understanding, building relationship, and equality to ensure respect.

Discriminatory workplace treatment more specifically found that employees who were covered by a non-discrimination policy were less likely to have experienced discrimination than those who were not covered (Human Rights Campaign, 2009). Studies show that Factors such as LGBT-supportive policies leads to less discrimination (Button, 2001), openness at workplace leads to positive business relationship, greater commitment and positive workplace behaviour and attitudes (Badgett, 2001; Tejeda, 2006; Rostosky & Riggle, 2002).

In India approximately 42-84 million are Lesbian, Bisexual, Gay and Transgender (LGBT). An understanding of the issues faced by LGBT to the workplace starts with the recognition that a diverse and inclusive business environment is directly linked to enhanced business performance. Peoples' Union for Civil Liberties, Karnataka (PUCL-K) has reported discrimination against sexuality minorities is embedded at workplaces.

This paper outlines the results of a quantitative study examining Perception of the employed sexual minorities on their inclusion in workplace in Bangalore.

The objectives of the paper are:

1. To study the Socio demographic data of the employed sexual minorities.
2. To assess about Sexuality status (at family and workplace).

3. To understand employment/work related information.
4. To assess the usefulness of Employee Resource Group (ERG) at workplace.
5. To study about the perception of employed sexual minorities on their inclusion in workplace.

LITERATURE

A study by **Badgett, Durso, Kastanis, & Mallory (2013)** found that there are no studies which says that there is a positive relationship with policies and outcomes. Having policies reduced discrimination and less discrimination leads to better psycological health and higher job satisfaction. Also companies which have policies are profitable and get more customers in market.

In the quantitative study by **Barrett, Lewis, & Dwyer (2011)** on effects of disclosure of sexual orientation at work for 152 LGBT employees in Queensland, found 36% of their respondents had experienced sexual orientation discrimination at one workplace and 34% at two workplaces based on their sexual identity. High discrimination is still occurring (54%) despite 74% of workplaces having policies addressing discrimination.

According to the study by **Sears, B., & Mallory, C. (2011)** a variety of methodologies has consistently documented high levels of discrimination against lesbians, gay men, bisexuals and transgender (LGBT) people at work. 78% respondents of the largest survey of transgender people to date reported experiencing at least one form of harassment or mistreatment at work because of their gender identity; more specifically, 47% have discriminated against in hiring, promotion, or job retention. Discrimination and harassment in the workplace can have a negative impact on the wages and mental and physical health of LGBT people.

A study carried out by **Robinson and Berman (2010)** found that 1100 GLBTI had been harassed or abused within the last two years on the basis of their sexual orientation. Five most prominent forms of abuse experienced were: verbal abuse, spitting and offensive gestures, physical violence, written threats and abuse and physical attack or assault (without a weapon).

Drydakis, N. (2009) examines the possible discrimination faced by gay men compared to heterosexuals when applying for jobs in the Greek private sector. This was observed by employer hiring decisions. Survey was conducted from December 2006 to September 2007 in Athens, Greece. In total applicants were sent to 1714 job openings. Hence, net discrimination against the gay applicant was found to be in 448 cases, or 64.3%. Moreover there were differences and was found that gay applicants faced a 34.8% lower chance of being invited for an interview. Despite the introduction of antidiscrimination legislation 3 years ago, the current results showed a strong negative effect of gay orientation on hiring chances.

Irwin (1999) in a study on the workplace experiences of 900 gay men, lesbians and transgendered employees found that harassment and prejudicial treatment on the basis of sexual orientation and gender identity was widespread with 59% of her respondents experiencing heterosexism in their workplace. Forty one percent of the participants considered they had been dismissed from their most recent job because of their homosexuality.

A survey conducted by **Industrial Relations Counselors, Inc. (IRC) in 2011,** of 64 employers and interviewed ERG program managers in 10 organizations study found that many companies are experiencing a resurgence of enthusiasm for ERGs. The majority of participating organizations are parent companies doing business in multiple regions of the world. Silva & Warren (2009) explains the need of the coming out and reasons why being in closet and also explains the need of building inclusive place for LGBT.

A study done by **Peoples' Union for Civil Liberties, Karnataka (PUCL-K)** in 2012 found out that discrimination against sexuality minorities is still present at workplaces which needs to be removed for an inclusive and diversified business culture.

METHOD

Data collection was done through self-made questionnaire comprising all the required domains for the study. More importantly reaching the LGBT was difficult, therefore this study used an online survey to access LGBT individuals and allowed respondents the capability to complete the survey at a time convenient to them. To connect with potential respondents, snowball sampling was used. Once respondents finishes the survey they are encouraged to recruit other potential respondents the new sample members are then asked to further recruit other potential respondents from within the target population. The total respondents were 50 (N=50). The inclusion criterion for the respondents was that they need to be employed in organised sectors in Bangalore. On completion of the survey, data was analysed using SPSS.

RESULTS

Demographic Details

Of the 50 respondents, the age range of respondents varied from 18 to 38 years of age with the mean age of the respondents between 25 and 31. Most of the respondents are working in BPO sector (44%). 70% of them are single, followed by 22% married. It was found that 42% and 52% are graduate and post-graduate and above respectively. The participants were 30% gay, 26% lesbian, 22% bisexual and 22% transgender.

Sexuality Status

74% of the respondents have disclosed their sexuality status with family and friends out of which 58% are not accepted by family and 79% are accepted by friends. Only 20% respondents feel supported after disclosing to family, on the other hand 60% feel that they are supported by the friends. The results show that 66% of LGBT have disclosed, 3% are partially out at work place to their managers and co-workers and rest are still in closet. 60% of those who are out reported as not accepting at workplace, 17% feel that they are partially accepted and only 23% are accepted. The major reasons which made them to be in closet were such as fear of rejection, criticism, to be judged, non-acceptance in society and reasons which made them to disclose at workplace are the presence of ERG, confidence on the employer, support from other LGBT.

Work/Employment Related Information

76% of respondents know other LGBT present in their organisation and 42% agrees that initiative is taken by the company. 16% have faced discrimination during recruitment. 48.5% of who are out have trust and 52% are loyal with their employer. 44% are not in comfort interacting with the managers/supervisors including both who are out and in closet. It was found that the entrepreneurial ambitions and contribution towards success of the organisation are higher in those who have disclosed than in closet. 81% of respondents who are out feel that it is important to disclose at work and 29% of closet respondents.

LGBT Employees Resource Groups (ERG)

68% of respondents are aware about the LGBT ERGs. Among those who have ERG at workplace 82% have membership and 70.6% agrees that it has helped them and workplace. Companies where LGBT ERG is not present, all the respondents who do not have ERGs at workplace want to have and participate. 96% support the presence of LGBT ERGs/LGBT friendly policies at workplace as factors which determine joining a new company or continuing at the same place.

Inclusion at Workplace

For respondents who have disclosed, 45.45% feel that their contributions are not recognized by the organisation. 69.7% feels that they are included in taking managerial decisions and posts. The most astonishing results were, 51.5% have faced discrimination because of their sexual orientation/identity and faced harassments/bullying/taunts/verbal abuse at workplace from managers/supervisors and co-workers. 63.6% have heard homophobic comments/jokes/anti-gay rhetoric at workplace.

80% out of closet respondents feels that being in closet has made them grow professionally. 82.4% says that being in closet reduces productivity.

92% respondents out of all feel that discrimination faced at workplace reduces work productivity directly and indirectly. 40% of Respondents categorize their workplace environment as not LGBT friendly, 46% neutral and 14% LGBT friendly.

CONCLUSION

This study was relevant in order to understand the perception of the inclusion of LGBT in workplace and their growth as an employee which is directly linked with the job satisfaction. Study has highlighted that still LGBT employees face discrimination even after having policies at place. Human Resource practitioners must incorporate the need for removing the issues faced by them. It was found that even after the presence of ERG at workplace they decided to remain in closet which they felt important to grow professionally. Discrimination and harassment which is faced in workplace can create negative impact on the wages and the mental health of LGBT people also. The result clearly shows a great need of a workplace of treating all the employees equally and with respect and dignity. This is essential in Human Resource Development (HRD) which makes a workplace happier for higher growth and satisfaction as well creates a diversified and inclusive workplace for all the employees' especially sexual minorities (LGBT) who are facing it from a long time. There is a great need of further research in this field in India and higher awareness of their issues to everyone.

REFERENCES

[1] Badgett, M. (2001). *Money, Myths, and Change: The Economic Lives of Lesbians and Gay Men.* Chicago: University of Chicago Press.

[2] Barrett, N., Lewis, J., & Dwyer, A. (2011). Effects of disclosure of sexual odentity at work for gay, lesbian,bisexual, transgender and intersex (GLBTI) employees in Queensland. *The 25th Annual Australian and New Zealand Academy of Management Conference.* Wellington: Australian and New Zealand Academy of Management (ANZAM).

[3] Business, C. (2012). *Creating Inclusive Workplaces for LGBT Employees in India, Resource Guide.* India: http://www.communitybusiness.org/.

[4] Button, S. (2001). Organizational efforts to affirm sexual diversity: A cross-level examination. *Journal of Applied Psychology*, 17-28.

[5] Campaign, H.R. (2009). *Degrees of Equality: A national Study Examining Workplace Climate for LGBT Employees.* Retrieved from Human Rights Campaign: http://www.hrc.org/files/assets/resources/DegreesOfEquality_2009.pdf.

[6] Dhar, U. (2012). *OUT @ WORK: A Guide for LGBT Indians at the Workplace.* Community Business.

[7] Drydakis, N. (2009). Sexual orientation discrimination in the labour market. *Labour Economics*, 364-372.

[8] Irwin, J. (1999). The pink ceiling is too low: Workplace experiences of lesbians, gay men and transgender people. *The University of Sydney, Australian Centre for Lesbian and Gay research.*

[9] Mercer (2011). ERGs Come of Age: The Evolution of Employee Resource Groups. New York: *Mercer LLC, Industrial Relations Counselors, Inc. (IRC)*Miller, F., & Katz, J. (2002). The

inclusion breakthrough: unleashing the real power of diversity. *Berrett-Koehler Publishers Inc.*

[10] People's Union For Civil Liberties-Karnataka. (2001). *Human Rights Violations against Sexual Minorities in India.* Bangalore: PUCL-K.

[11] Robinson, S., & Berman, A. (2010). Speaking out: Stopping homophobic and transphobic abuse in Queensland. Brisbane: *Australian Academic Press*

[12] Rostosky, S., & Riggle, E. (2002). Out at work: The relations of actor and partner workplace policy and internalized homophobia to disclosure status. *Journal of Counseling Psychology, 49*, 411-419.

[13] Sears, B., & Mallory, C. (2011, July). Documented Evidence of Employment Discrimination & Its Effects on LGBT People. Retrieved from the Williams Institute, California.

[14] Silva, C., & Warren, A. (2009). Building LGBT-Inclusive workplace. *Catalyst*, 1-34.

[15] Tejeda, M. (2006). Nondiscrimination policies and sexual identity disclosure: Do they make a difference in employee outcomes? *Employee Responsibilities and Rights Journal, 18*, 45-59.

[16] Badgett, M.L., Durso, L.E., Kastanis, A., & Mallory, C. (2013). The Business Impact of LGBT- Supprotive Workplace Policies. *Other Recent Work, The Williams Institute, UCLA School of Law*, 1-38. Retrieved from http://williamsinstitute.law.ucla.edu/wp-content/uploads/Business-Impact-of-LGBT-Policies-May-2013.pdf

Work-Life Balance in Socio-Professional Life: Need, Necessity and Utopia

Rajesh S. Pyngavil

Gitarattan International Business School, Rohini, Delhi

ABSTRACT

Work-life balance has now become a sensitive issue. Successfully addressing this issue can lead to a healthy synergy in the working environment of an organisation and individual. Work-life balance (WLB) refers in maintaining a balance between professional and personal life. It is not only merely confined to balance profession and family, but balancing mental status quo and thereby balancing the emotional intelligence of an individual. It has crucial impact not only on individuals but also on organizations as well. Organizations are formed through the people and by the people; satisfied employees help building a better work culture and enhance productivity. When both the company and the employee understand their responsibility and try to make the work-life coin stand vertical, employee show dedication and willingness to perform the job with emotional commitment not with rational commitment. This paper primarily deals with various facets of work-life balance. The paper also proposes a suggestive framework in which work-life balance can be achieved by balancing work satisfaction and social satisfaction which leads to personal satisfaction, and hence results in organizational benefits (productivity and efficiency) and individual benefits (happiness and health).

Keywords: *Work, Work Life Balance, Emotions, Physical Health, Mental Health*

INTRODUCTION

In this competitive world, firms are under pressure of long-term existence for which they need societal acceptance of the firm so that more people invest in their organization and more people to apply for employment. 'Life' means existence of an individual. To exist satisfactorily people give birth to 'needs'. To fulfill needs people 'work'. Hence, work is a phenomenon to lead the life. This ideology dissevered the life into two, personal life and professional life. Life and work are two faces of a coin. While tossing a coin you could select one side of the two, but while choosing your way of living this technique is not helpful. Ideal living situation is attained when the coin stands vertical, balancing Life and Work. Earlier, when there were simple needs the work needed to be performed was also simple. People were available with ample time to prefer their personal lives as well. With the evolution of civilization, new needs evolved, new desires came into existence, new procedure got discovered & modern industries were formed. And the complexity increased in work and in life. Such complications generated a concept, a demand of time, a necessity to be achieved-Balance-making the coin stand vertical.

Family and work influence each other in a significant manner and hence conflicts arise. An individual has responsibilities on both sides and to lead a happy life one need to fulfill both. Initially, it was the work-family concern that further broadens up and became the work-life concern. The story of this shift finds its way back from an era where work and family were entirely separate arenas of life; we call that era the Machine age. It was the time when traditional definition of working was all about men going out working and women staying at home. With the demand of time to change, the society entered an era which we address as the Industrial age. Men and women both started working outside the domain of four walls and another need of housekeepers originated backing up further opportunities of employment. The present age is the Networked age, when the time barrier and space have been nullified due to the technological and network enhancements. Work span is of 24 hours a day and system spares no time for family or relations and hence, life is dramatically and drastically got restrained again in 4 walls. Wants have increased and time has shrunk; relation, which was the integral part of life and living, has become a burden. So, we need an approach that can enable us to balance ourselves between desires and relations.

NEED OF AN EFFECTIVE WORK-LIFE BALANCE

Work – Family literature has moved beyond family to incorporate the whole of personal life an individual has. To increase their financial balance, individuals often disturb their personal lives, and it leads to many problems. Sometimes it becomes difficult to focus even on the job they are performing. Hence, the companies require some strategies to tackle various work-life related problems of employees who lead to the concept of Work-Life Balance. Work-life balance is about creating and maintaining supportive and healthy work environments, which enables employees to have balance between work and personal responsibilities and thus strengthen employee loyalty and productivity. Work-life conflicts are the initiators of finding the approach of Work-life balance. Biggest of those factors is the time. As the hours spent at work are increasing the personal time has shrunk to the minimum. Most people working for longer hours are reportedly having work-life issues. Job security, job satisfaction, overload, work-role conflicts, and ambiguity, are few more causes with the severest is the usage of technology. Technological advancements and connectivity have been a revolution in working sector but have steeled the privacy of people. Communication technology narrowed the edges

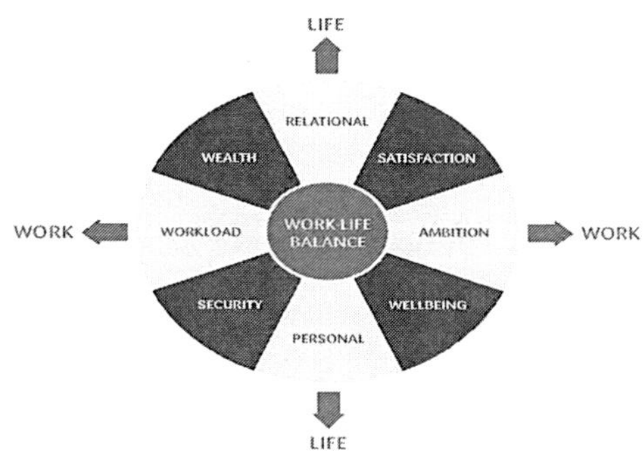

between home and office. Maintaining that distance of home and office needs balancing of work and life.

To reach that level and enjoy the benefits for long-term, company should initiate a change that favors individual lives along with work. This cannot be achieved all of a sudden, thus require a permanent change in culture of the organizations that supports such programs.

Table 1: Transition of Work through Ages

	The Machine Age	*The Industrial Age*	*The networked Age*
Work-Life Issues	Work and Family were two independent domains	Work started spilling into family time and was often carried over home	Workdays span 24 hours with brief time intervals for non-work activities
Home Issues	Traditional roles with men working and women taking care of household chores	Dual Career couples with both men and women working but women still tending to household chores	Dual career couples with both men and women working as well as attending to home issues
Support	None	Availability of help like baby sisters, crèches, old-age homes, and maids	Hands-free executive support firms that provide services as diverse as managing the laundry and kids' homework

Source: Agarwala, T. (2007), *Strategic Human Resource Management*, New Delhi: Oxford University Press, p. 711)

VARIOUS THEORIES USED BY FIRMS TOWARDS WORK-LIFE BALANCE

Institutional Theory: Institutional theory refers to the deeper aspects of Social structure. It considers the processes by which structures, including schema, rules, norms, and routines, become established as authoritative guidelines for social behavior. It inquires into how these elements are created, diffused, adopted, and adapted over space and time. Firms adopt work-life policy in order to gain lawful acceptance within the society and environment. It is a reactive theory which assumes that firms react to pressures.

Resource Dependence Theory: Resource dependence theory is based upon the notion that environment is the source of resources that are scarce in nature; especially the qualified workforce and organizations are dependent on these finite resources for survival. A lack of control over these resources thus acts to create uncertainty for firms operating in that environment. Organizations tend to develop ways to exploit these resources, which are also being sought by other firms, in order to ensure their own survival.

Managerial Interpretation Theory: Work Life initiatives can be adopted only when the key management persons interpret the work life policies as an important strategy for a firm to sustain itself in the environment. It is the manager who needs to understand the mindset of employees and also their ego states so that they effectively work towards the organizational goals. It depends on the management to adopt any work-life policy or not, as they understand their firm's situation in a better way.

Organizational Adoption Theory: Growing organizational resources are being devoted in many contexts to 'work–life initiatives' that aim to adapt employment settings to the workforce's changing work–life needs, and to respond to government regulations for fostering employee's integration and protecting working families. According to this theory, firms adopt work-life initiatives in an attempt to align themselves with the dynamic business environment.

APPROACHES TOWARDS WORK-LIFE INTEGRATION

There is a give and take relationship between an employee and the organization he is working with. It is not just the firm's responsibility to take care of the employee's needs, but also the employee's responsibility to give his best at the job he is performing along with looking after his personal life. So, there are two approaches, viz., Organization Approach and Employee Approach.

Organization Approach: While selecting approaches towards work-life integration, organizations need to look the extent up to which an organization should interfere in the employees' personal lives. The approach an organization chooses must be complementary with organization goals, mission, values and the need of the workforce.

Jobs have become more complex and employees have been put under pressure to produce quality results in shorter time frames and with fewer resources that have resulted in a redefinition of 'normal working hours'. Furthermore, the very nature of the employment contract has necessitated that organizations effectively manage their employee's well- being, stress and job satisfaction.

Organizational Approaches include:

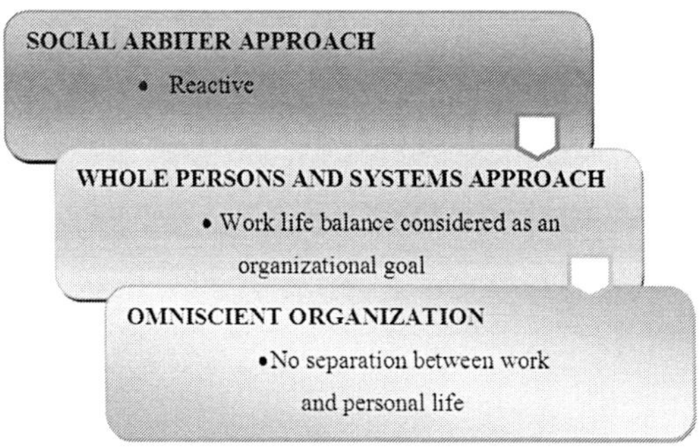

Source: Developed by Authors

- **Social Arbiter Approach:** The firms following Social-Arbiter approach emphasize that employer should get involved only if the employees request help or the managers feel that the employee's personal life problems are hindering his performance. There is a strong separation between work and family. Hence, this approach is reactive that is, if the employee does not perform well, then only employers help them to balance their work and life. The organization does not get involved in the non-work lives of their employees until there is a performance problem. Examples of this approach include providing concierge services, on-site crèche, ATM services, etc.
- **Whole Persons and System Approach:** The Firms opting for this approach consider work-life balance to be an organizational goal. According to this approach, the organizations should view employees as internal customers and demonstrates more sensitivity to their needs. This perspective reflects the human relations approach to management and promotes 'whole systems' and 'whole persons' approach to employment. Organizations feel that by implementing various work-life programmes, organizations will have employees who will be more loyal and committed. Various organizations are based upon the belief that an environment of belonging and trust goes a long way in retaining employees and maximizing their full potential. Various organizations that follow this approach include American Express, Reliance, Tata steel, NIIT, etc.
- **Omniscient Approach:** According to this approach, the organization attempts to make the workplace as a home to employees. There is virtually no separation between work and personal life. In today's network age, most of the time of employees is spent in offices as the business needs have changed and with globalization it becomes difficult to manage office and work hours together, so recognizing this, companies like Infosys provides dormitories and gymnasium for employees. With flexible workplace, the boundaries between the work and personal domains. It has become a disagreeable necessity to separate these two domains of the employer. In this approach, it becomes difficult to measure the performance appraisal because this approach provides the flexibility to employees to work from home.
- **Employees Approaches:** Work life integration is not the sole responsibility of the firm. It is the employee who has to work throughout his career and along with it has to manage his personal life. The work should not spill over the personal life because both are important for survival, but most of the employees are not able to distinguish between the two and eventually let their work life spoil the personal life. Employees need to self-reflect on their own value for managing the integration of work and personal life.

Employees tend to cope with family issues by psychologically minimizing their attention that families actually need. Employees start relying on paid help for various off-work demands. Employees develop a mentality that present is the time to earn, and these earning will give them a rich and rewarding family life in the future. Organizations with a long-term strategic view of work-life balance provide employees with training to help them focus on both the professional and personal life. In reality, work-life balance can only be achieved when both Organizational and Employee approaches complement each other.

ORGANISATIONS, WORK AND EMPLOYEE LIFE: A RELATION IN NEED OF DISCOVERY

Firms need human resources to achieve their objectives. Work-life policies provide employees and potential employees with the incentives. Hence, such firms attract a larger applicant pool and are able to secure necessary human resources. While there's no one size fits all, making employees happy, increasing job satisfaction and building a culture where people can thrive is the foundation for a strong employment brand and a key to becoming an employer of choice – especially in a market like India where staff turnover is always an issue.

Trak.in, a leading HR research and consultancy organisation recently covered a survey which pointed out that Indian employee and Indian companies scored better on the work-life balance ratio in 2012 than in 2010. The implementation of the concept of work-life balance essentially stems from Western management theories. While the same may not have been entirely present in traditional Indian businesses and corporate, increased focus on work-life balance in India is being seen. Companies like Infosys, Wipro, Yahoo India, Google India, Dell India, Microsoft India, Accenture and HCL Technologies amongst many others have already begun taking steps in this direction.

Employees know that salary is not the only thing required to make a living. People have personal commitments, want to enjoy their lives, raise family, take care of their parents and so on. Companies apart over the past year is employee speaking favorably about flexible schedules, work from home options, and demanding managers who understand life outside of work.

1. **Google India Pvt. Ltd.:** With employee strength of 1503, Google, apart from being the first choice of the young talent in India; it has been recently voted as the finest company to work with by the popular Forbes magazine survey. It has been voted as the best place to work by not only one, but by several surveys. The most popular reason is Google's sensitivity towards its employees. It values the talent of employees in today's knowledge economy and does the best possible it can do to maintain the work-life balance of its talented workforce. Google is known for promoting flexible schedules and personal and professional balance, where employees learn how to manage their time, be multitasking and collaborative. This is not all, there are several other perks offered by Google to ease the stress of its hard-working employees.
2. **Accenture:** Accenture, another big company to work with, offers tremendous scope for the development of its employees as well as relates to their day to day problems. Superiors realize the importance of striking a balance between people's personal and professional life, adding to the satisfaction level of its employees. Accenture offers a flexible approach—giving options for how, and where, its employees do

their work. They offer programs and tools to help individuals and teams understand how encouraging flexibility and a balance between work and personal life enhance and not impede productivity. It engenders diversity, and offers various programs like **Life-Works Employee Assistance Program, Backup Dependent Care, Eldercare resource program, Nursing mother's program, etc.**

3. **Tata Consultancy Services**: Tata Consultancy Services, popularly known as TCS, has been a hot favourite of fresh graduates from various disciples. TCS not only is a fun place to work at, but also offers healthy career development options to its employees. Apart from this, the working hours are designed in a way that they facilitate a balance between the personal and professional commitment of its employees. People at TCS are very aware of the crucial ways that would make its workers work in a stress-free manner, which would ultimately improve their productivity as well as would add to the level of satisfaction of its employees. As a part of TCS' work-life balance programs, 'Maitree' actively promotes a series of scheduled fun and cultural events and activities, and also keenly promotes community development projects.
4. **Infosys:** Infosys is a brand name, and many dream to be a part of the Infosys team. This company is not only rapidly developing its business but also has shifted its focus from working employees to happily working employees. It is a known fact that work-life balance has been a newly introduced concept at Infosys. Infosys has around 90,000 employees worldwide and 15,000 of those employees who have children across 72 countries are expected to benefit from it. This network is designed to provide parenting counseling, demystify work-life balance policies and give employees a platform to ask questions and discuss their views with others about their experiences as working parents. The portal also provides useful information about schools, day-care facilities and doctors – to those who relocate.
5. **IBM:** IBM is well known organization that focuses on the work-life balance of its employees. At IBM, flexible work options are available to assist employees in balancing their responsibilities to work, family, education, and other personal needs. IBM gives the flexibility to manage work hours, so the employees can meet the needs of their personal life. Employees, in consultation with their manager may agree on a special working hour schedule provided the same does not hinder the departments working. Flexibility in work is a significant feature that helped IBM to retain its position in the best places to work at. No doubt one would enjoy working according to his or her convenience at the workplace.

It is evident from the examples stated above, that companies today not only recognize the importance of work-life balance but also are leaving no stone unturned to make its talented and hard-working work force maintain a cordial balance between personal and professional needs. Apart from this, the developments of new and fast technologies have made it possible for the working people to carry on their lives and responsibilities outside the boundaries of their office, according to their own comfort.

BALANCING THE LIFE: PROBLEMS STILL PERSISTING

With the evolution of Tertiary sector or rather the services' sector the need of work—life balance grew, as these services include hefty working hours, which lead to problems related to health and disturbance in personal lives. Though some measures were taken by the organizations initially, but they were not as effective as required.

Certain problems that still persist include:

- Employees doing a lot of overtime: With increased work pressure and increased hunger for power leads employees to work as more and more.
- Employees taking a lot of time off to deal with personal problems which lead to an imbalance with work in this competitive era.
- High levels of employee stress: with growing business, the stress grows proportionately.
- High rates of absenteeism lead to problems in work.
- High levels of staff turnover.

Relation of Work and Life: The Existing Framework

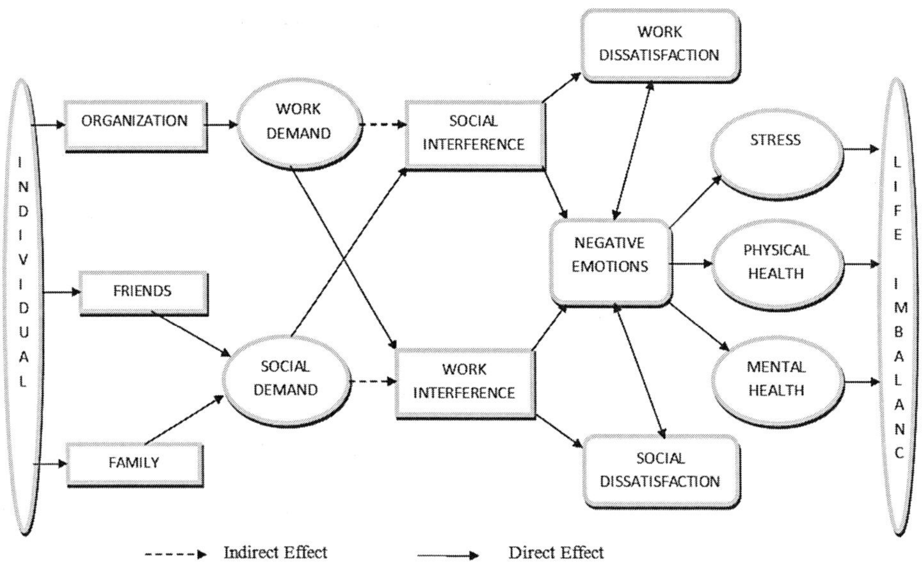

Source: Developed by Authors.

An organization and a society both are composed of individuals. People have responsibilities towards both the society and the organization, and the individuals of network age feels disassembled as the working hours are extended to 24*7. The enhanced modes of communication had diminished the personal time of people and thus, people develop negative feelings regarding his working scenario. The responsibilities and expectations of both sides demand complete attention from the individual. Responsibilities towards organization generate work demands, the commitments to the position one have in the organization; responsibilities towards family & friends generate social demands, the right of the people you are living with. Both, when taken into consideration affect each other in a significant manner and without the proper care and balance they cause interference into one another's arena. Such interference again induce a demand that needs a collaboration from the work and the society so that to help the individual manage both effectively. In condition when people do not get that supportive collaboration from his work and society he starts developing negative emotions. This negativity retards the capacity of the person to cope-up with the demands and reduces his competency. People not competent enough will start developing work sickness, that results in work dissatisfaction. People overburdened by work or incompetent enough are not left with quality time to satisfy their social needs and leads to problems like work dissatisfaction, life dissatisfaction, stress, health issues, etc. These issues can never create balance between work and society, hence, cause Imbalanced Life. It is thus the responsibility of both the individual and the society & organization he represents to help him create balance between personal and professional lives.

Relation of Work and Life: The Proposed Framework

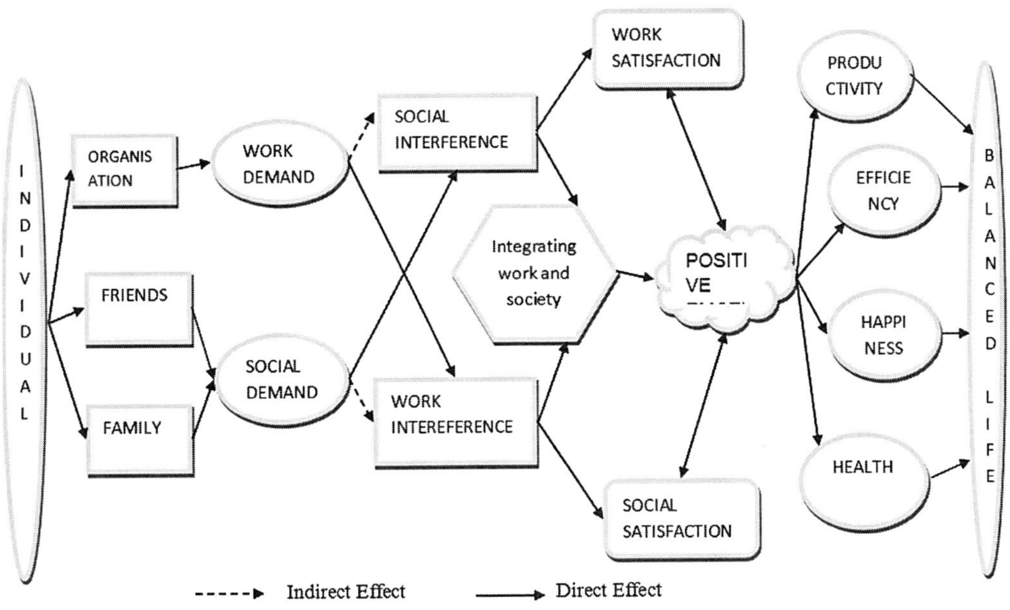

Source: Developed by Authors

As discussed above, an individual is linked with his organization, friend circle and his family. He has responsibilities that he needs to fulfil to satiate these arenas and for his personal satisfaction. An organization demands work, and family and friends demand social get-together. When the two are not interconnected it creates interference in both personal and professional life. If there are initiatives from both the organization and the society towards the other domain of one's life, an individual can be self-satisfied by performing his duties effectively and efficiently towards both society and the organization. If initiatives are taken from both the sides, that is, organization and society for everyone and the individual responds to them willingly, it will create positive essence everywhere and will lead to happiness, Productivity, self-satisfaction, efficiency, good health, etc. An organization and a society both are comprised of individuals and hence if they work together for each other, then only the balance between personal and professional life can be attained.

Here, the 'integration of work and society' defines various attempts that can be made from both organization and society like family tours, office parties, stress-bursting exercises, equitable treatment for all individuals within the organization and on part of the society. If individual's views are considered to make social decisions, he feels himself as an important part of society, and this gives him positivity and freshness to take good decisions. It is the individual who has to respond to these positive initiatives in a positive way to achieve that balanced state.

CONCLUSION

Work-life balance is crucial not only for individuals but have an indirect yet deep impact on organizations as well. Organizations are formed through the people and by the people; satisfied employees help building a better work culture and enhance productivity. When both the company and the employee understand their responsibility and try to make the work-life coin stand vertical, employee show dedication and willingness to perform the commitments.

Work life balance is a big question of great concern with the changes of personal life style and organisational life style. This got triggered with advent of technology and automation that facilitated changes in personal and professional life of individuals. Every organisation is vigour to exploit time, availability and potential of employees to the fullest. This paper addresses the issues related to work life balance. The focus was on gaining an insight into the problems which are addressed due to ineffective work life balance and bio medical affects. Moreover, the paper also tried to concentrate on organisational policies and practices to ensure proper and conducive work life balance which results healthy organisations and employees which ultimately can transform into unbalanced life of an individual into a balanced life with results in individual happiness and organisational commitment.

REFERENCES

[1] Agarwala, T., (2007), *Strategic Human Resource Management*, New Delhi: Oxford University Press.

[2] Cascio, W.F., (2005), *Managing Human Resource: Productivity, Quality of Work Life, and Profits,* New Delhi: McGraw-Hill (6th Ed).

[3] Joshi, M (2010), Work Life Balance: A Major Need of the Hour, *Effulgence,* Vol. 8, No 2, pp 65-70.

[4] Pyngavil, S Rajesh and Singla, A., (2009), Effect of Quality of Work Life on Work Life Balance: An Empirical Analysis, *J K Journal of Management and Technology,* Vol. 1, No 2, pp 189-199.

[5] Varkkey, V and Dessler, D., (2009), *Human Resource Management.* New Delhi: Pearson Education, (11th Ed).

[6] http://www.bia.ca/articles/AReportontheImportanceofWork-LifeBalance.htm (last accessed on 2, December 2013)

[7] http://www.evancarmichael.com/Human-Resources/840/Resource-Dependence-Theory-In-Management.html (last accessed on 2, December 2013)

[8] http://icos.groups.si.umich.edu/Institutional%20Theory%20Oxford04.pdf (last accessed on 2, December 2013)

[9] http://theglobaljournals.com/gra/file.php?val=ODk (last accessed on 2, December 2013)

[10] http://convergeinternational.com.au/docs/WorkLifeBalanceWhitePaper-Smallfilesize.pdf (last accessed on 2, December 2013)

[11] http://www.forbes.com/pictures/efkk45jihk/top-25-companies-for-work-life-balance-2/ (last accessed on 2, December 2013)

[12] http://www.businessinsider.in/The-25-Best-Companies-For-Work-Life-Balance/articleshow/21170024.cms (last accessed on 2, December 2013)

[13] http://trak.in/tags/business/2012/06/11/top-5-tips-work-life-balance-in-india/ (last accessed on 2, December 2013)

[14] http://careers.accenture.com/us-en/your-future/rewards-benefits/Pages/work-life-balance.aspx (last accessed on 2, December 2013)

[15] http://www.careers.tcs.com/CareersDesign/Jsps/WorkingatTCS.jsp (last accessed on 2, December 2013)

[16] http://bprao.wordpress.com/2008/07/31/a-work-life-balance-intiative-by-infosys/ (last accessed on 2, December 2013)

[17] http://www-07.ibm.com/in/careers/lifeatibm.html (last accessed on 2, December 2013)

The Problems of Discrimination Faced by Women at their Workplaces: Experiences and Lessons

Bhavya Nain

Advocate, Supreme Court; and Former Law Clerk-cum-Research Assistant, Supreme Court

ABSTRACT

The Hon'ble Supreme Court of India in G. Sekar V/s. Geetha [AIR 2009 SC 2649] has held that Gender Equality is recognized by the world community in general in the human rights regime; and also under the Indian Constitution. But, in reality, Gender Equality does not exist, as also noted in Medha Kotwal Lele v. Union of India [(2013) 1 SCC 297]. This is particularly true in respect to work place environments. Prevalence of concepts such as Glass Ceiling, Sticky Floor (effect), Sex-Role Orientation, Gender Stereotyping, Sexual Harassment, Workplace Incivility, Queen Bee Syndrome, etc., are a conclusive indicator to this effect. Gender Inequality exists in many forms, such as, women's under-representation at the corporate hierarchy, gendered wage gap, occupational segregation, discriminative corporate policies, lack of attention to the specific needs women have, sexual discrimination, and exclusion of women from informal networks. The gender disparity at work place is an extension of the patriarchal system (Dr. P. Dey, 2013). Gendered relations extend to the work places as well (B. Aggarwal, 1997).

We must look for solutions. Solutions must exist beyond law because laws will never be fully effective as long as there is no societal will. Gender sensitization and gender equity training beyond the facade of empty company policies, etc., is required. It is a known fact that women provide more value altruism, team-building, conscientious work than men. These advantages of having women workers in the team must be emphasized and must be made to be understood to the employers (Budhwar, P.S., Saini, D.S. & Bhatnagar, 2005).

Keywords: *Women, Work, Gender, Organisation, Discrimination, Society, Biases, Harassment*

"Women can do anything, even besides home-making, but the men must not prevent them from doing so by putting the hurdles of gender biases, prejudices and glass ceilings, etc."

INTRODUCTION

It is a trite fact that the women have been a subjugated section of the society in India. It is also a known fact that the women have earlier been deprived of their real place in the society. This has happened despite the fact that the ancient Indian texts have advocated honour and dignity for the women. This phenomenon has perpetrated even in the modern work place scenario in India. The working women, in India, face a lot of gender biases and problems. These gender biases hinder the professional growth of the working women. The working women always have to work on a tightrope in order to balance the duties at home and the duties at the work place. But, it is most unfortunate that inspite of this the work of the women is not appreciated and not given their due. The reason behind this is the apparent regressive psychology of a significant section of the Indian males. All this has caused the women to continue to feel that they are the weaker section of the society. Apparently, many a times, they are made to feel as if they are the weaker sex at the home; and beyond.

THE LEGAL POSITION

This deplorable phenomenon has also been elucidated by the Hon'ble Supreme Court of India. The Hon'ble Supreme Court in the case of C.M. Mududaliar v. Idol of Sri S.S. Thirukoil [(1996) 8 SCC 525] has held, "Women have always been discriminated against and have suffered and are suffering discrimination in silence. Self-sacrifice and self-denial are their nobility and fortitude and yet they have been subjected to all inequities, indignities, inequality and discrimination." In 2013, in Medha Kotwal Lele v. Union of India [(2013) 1 SCC 297], the Supreme Court noted that even now many women still struggle to have their most basic rights protected at workplaces in India.

This dismal position of women exists despite the fact that the Hon'ble Supreme Court has time and again tried to come to the rescue of the women facing gender discrimination. In Valsamma Paul (Mrs) v. Cochin University [(1996) 3 SCC 545], the Hon'ble Supreme Court has held: "Human rights are derived from the dignity and worth inherent in the human person. Human rights and fundamental freedoms have been reiterated in the Universal Declaration of Human Rights. Democracy, development and respect for human rights and fundamental freedoms are interdependent and have mutual reinforcement. The full development of personality and fundamental freedoms and equal participation by women in political, social, economic and cultural life are concomitants for national development, social and family stability and growth – cultural, social and economic. All forms of discrimination on grounds of gender are violative of fundamental freedoms and human rights."

THE EXPERIENCES ABROAD

Traditionally, it has been maintained by the society that a woman's place is at home (Jacob, 1999; Moore, 1995; Dr. Maheshwari, 2012). Pratto et al. (1997) have shown that hierarchy roles are gendered ;and men are over-represented in hierarchy enhancing roles (defined as serving the interests of the elite) and women are over-represented in hierarchy attenuating roles (serving the interest of the downtrodden). Hierarchy-enhancing jobs generally benefit those who hold them in terms of compensation, social status, and power. Over a period of time, power begets power. Thus, the differentiation among role holders widens. Such deep-rooted perpetuating processes cumulatively increase the gender gap in organization (N. Vohra, 2009). Thus, it is apparent that even outside India, the woman has not been her due place neither in the society nor at the work place. The position did, however, improve a bit in recent times but not to the satisfaction of most of the people. However, there is one difference in the Indian and the Western culture, which is the prevalence of a revered traditional patriarchal system in India since time immemorial. This means that the problem of gender inequity is apparently more in India because of the tradition of senior most male member being the all-powerful person in the family.

THE PATRIARCHY IN INDIA

In India, the concept of Karta and the Hindu Undivided Family always gave the men an upper hand over the women. The concept of Karta was that the senior most male member of the family was the main decision maker of any Hindu family. His decision was of utmost importance and the same could generally be rebutted by only other male members of the Hindu family. The role in the decision making of the women members was kept at the minimal. The role of the women was apparently confined to household/ domestic chores. This system has prevailed for a very long time in India. It cannot be said that the said system is per-se ineffective or per-se bad. However, wanton use of this system has indeed apparently contributed somewhat to the weaker status of the Indian women. The biased use of the said system by some section of Indian men has further led to the subjugation of the Indian women. In the male-dominated society, women suffered to extreme levels of exploitation. Some factors – like death of bread winner, sudden fall in family income or inadequate family income – forced women to seek employment in informal sector (small trader, artisan or field labourer on a family farm) but yet, that did not result in women empowerment (Dr. K. Sundar & Ashok Kumar, 2012). A woman, in India, has always been seen as only a home-maker, or as a wife, or as a mother. The women psychology has been adversely affected by this.

It is most unfortunate that the Indian patriarchal system, as practiced by some, has also extended to the work place (Dr. P. Dey, 2013). As per many, the gender inequality and unequal power relations at the work place are primarily due to the misuse of the patriarchal system in India at home and beyond. It is a known fact that the gender relations within the household are unambiguously depicted in the labour market and workplaces (B. Aggarwal, 1997). In other words, unfortunately, gender inequality and gender biased ideology has perpetrated beyond the home-space and has entered even in the public-space. The women psychology has been adversely affected by this because it may affect the job satisfaction of the career women.

THE GENDER BIASES OPERATING AGAINST THE WOMEN AT THE WORKPLACE

The male psychology, of a considerable section of the society, suffers from many gender biases. It is a trite fact that there is existence of gender insensitivity and gender biases in India. The ordinary working woman has to deal with a lot of biases, and problems, at workplace, these are:

(a) She is more often than not taken less seriously; and is even considered lesser than the male counterparts.

(b) She is considered not fit for challenging and outdoor roles.

(c) Her leadership capabilities are underrated and often ignored and often not cultivated properly.

(d) She faces gender based discrimination at every step of the ladder.

(e) She is often underpaid, in comparison to her male counterparts.

(f) Her family responsibilities are considered as hurdles in her official work.

(g) Her career goals are considered less important compared to her male counterparts (Ambarish, 2013).

(h) Her any kind of platonic association with male counterparts is seen as a sexist move by her to further in her career.

(i) She is often considered unfit for higher management because of her gender only.

(j) She is often considered as an object to be pursued by her male counterparts for their time pass.

(k) She is considered a weaker performer in comparison to her male counterparts.

(l) She is considered less decisive; and less equipped to make decisions than her male counterparts.

This is also the paradox of the Indian work place scenario. On one hand, though in fact the female workers work hard at the work place and try to contribute their best but, on the other hand, the gender biases and gender assumptions are always to the contrary and to their detriment. All this leads to mental dissatisfaction and mental discord in the minds of the career women and the female workers.

SOME OTHER APPARENT PROBLEMS AT THE WORKPLACES

The Problem of the Glass Ceiling(s)

It has been the experience that there is always an invisible ceiling that stops the progress and career progression of the working women. This glass ceiling is created by the male chauvinist thinking and the policies of the employers and the management. This glass ceiling can be seen in the form of invisible obstacles in the path of the career women. The psychology of the working women is adversely affected by it because the barriers to progress affect the thinking and the motivation of the working women. The glass ceiling creates a negative work environment for the career women. Many a times, it happens that the working women tacitly accept their subjugation or the working women end up having up job stress. It is a known fact that job stress on the women has psycho-social effect on the women which causes adverse physical and mental health problems on the women. As per R. Kaur, et al. (2013), these reduce her energy, lead to difficulty in dealing with others and in completing the required tasks and duties of job. She has a feeling of low control, helplessness and powerlessness. As per Foot & Venne (1990), there is positive co-relation between blocked career and job related stress.

The Problem of the Sex Role Orientation

It has been the experience that the work organisations tacitly approve and promote that the working women accept submissive and non-leadership roles. This is because work organisations tacitly approve and promote the traditionally thought sex roles performed by men and women. This means that the work organisations also tacitly admit the fact that a man is the main leader and the woman is the follower. This leads to mental regressive conditioning of the working women as they also start thinking in the same regressive manner. Such passive conditioning of the career women is not acceptable because it only leads to a passive and regressive society.

The Problem of the Gender Stereotyping(s)

In this cliché, some work organisations generally accept that certain kinds of work are male type of work; and the rest are female kinds of work. Assuming this to be correct, the work organisations delegate the work while keeping this job classification in mind. Khandelwal, in his study on Gender Stereotypes at Work: Implications for Organizations (2002) notes that stereotypes and perceptions of Indian women in the workplace appear to have a significant negative impact on the position of women managers. The study suggests that male Indian managers are viewed, stereotypically, as working in the areas of sales, marketing and production; being good leaders, decision makers and bosses; and handling challenging assignments. On the other hand, Indian women are viewed as working in HR and administrative positions at low to junior levels, and in fields such as fashion and beauty (S. Sharma and Manju Sharma, 2012). This kind of job classification system though being regressive is indeed promoted by certain work organisations. This leads to mental regressive conditioning of the working women as they also start thinking in the same regressive manner. There is also a possibility that this may lead to conflict between job role talent and job role expected and job role delivered. It is a known fact that there is positive co-relation between job role conflicts and job related stress.

The Problem of the Sexual Harassment

The career woman is often seen as an object by the male co-workers. Many a times, the career woman is pursued by the male co-workers as a sexual object. Work place harassment occurs in many forms ranging from taunts/ comments to actual physical transgressions. The underlying common result of any kind of sexual harassment is that the working woman involved is greatly dissatisfied with the job and the job satisfaction is greatly diminished. As per C.S. Swarnlatha et al. (2013), all forms of workplace harassment are detrimental to employee's well-being; and indeed one of the most consistent findings from literature is that harassment represents a potent interpersonal stressor and as such it produces strain outcomes as well as poor psychological and physical health like anxiety, depression, neck strain, dissatisfaction.

The Problem of the Queen Bee Syndrome

Sometimes, women managers do not promote women employees. The main reason behind this irony is that because the women managers would not want the potential women employees to break the glass ceiling and advance in the organisational hierarchy. This is a big irony because men do promote men but women might not promote women even though they are from the same gender. Queen Bee Syndrome has great effect on the job satisfaction. The psychology of the existing women managers must be improved and developed. The women managers need to be trained in the object of gender inclusive growth of the work organisations.

The Problem of the Workplace Incivility

The ignorance of the male co-workers to the travails of the working women leads to anomalous results. Many a times, it happens that the working women are not given the due respect and care they deserve from their male co-workers. This is because many of the male co-workers have the same psychology and mental conditioning that the women occupy a subjugated position both at home and beyond. This regressive psychology must be replaced by gender sensitisation. This will need both time and effort by the work organisations and the employers. Otherwise, retention of female employees might become a problem for the work organisations where work place incivility is an issue. Work place incivility may lead to job alienation. Thus, work place incivility is an issue which needs immediate redressal by adopting policies on gender sensitisation.

The Problem of the Sticky Floor Effect

It happens many a times that even if a career woman reaches at a managerial position or a leadership position she is not adequately compensated. The main reason behind this is that because there is lack of alternative job offers available to such career woman in comparison to men. This happens generally because traditionally women are not seen as corporate leaders or entrepreneurs. This anomaly causes job dissatisfaction amongst women managers and women leaders because they are not compensated adequately. Their motivation to work for their organisation is reduced considerably. It is a known fact that there is positive co-relation between unfavourable work environment and job stress. This is detrimental both for the advancement of the career woman and for the growth of her work organisation.

SOME STARTLING STATISTICS REGARDING THE WOMEN

The women are not given their due place in the work organisations. This may reduce their motivation and stimulus for work and their jobs. According to a survey done by Economic times, there are only 16 women on the board of directors of the 30 Sensex companies, or only 4.8% of the 335 people who hold directorship positions. According to Poonam Barua, founder chairperson of the Forum for women in Leadership, India's 500 million strong female populations does not find representation in even 10% of the managerial posts across companies (Dr. Kulkarni; and Dr. Rushi Bakhare, 2013). The gender disparity and inequality is also reflected, at lower positions, from the fact that the women's wage rate in India is only 75% of the men's wage rate and the female share of the non-agricultural wage employment is only 17%. Even otherwise, in India, Gender Inequality is also reflected in India's low rank on the 2013 UNDP Gender Inequality Index, which is 132 out of 187 countries (with even countries like Pakistan doing better than India).

RECOMMENDATIONS

It is not that no attempts have been made by the corporate sector to ameliorate this gender disparity and unequal power equation. Many companies, in fact, have employed measures such as crèches, flexi-time, refresher programs, orientation on company policies only scratch the surface of the real problems. However, there is need and requirement for increased awareness for the contribution of women and the need to nurture their talent at the workplace (Dr. Anil Sarin & Sonal Pathak, 2011). There is need for gender sensitisation. There is need for gender equity training. This must be done by the work organisations. This should not be seen as a redundant cost. This should be seen as an opportunity for job retention of female employees because there will be more job satisfaction and less job stress. It is the known fact that employees who are less strained and have more job satisfaction are likely to perform better. Women employees must be seen as an asset. It is a known fact that women provide more value altruism, team-building, conscientious work than men. These advantages of having women workers in the team must be emphasized and must be made to be understood to the employees (Budhwar, P.S., Saini, D.S. & Bhatnagar, 2005). Gender sensitisation can be done by the use of talks on women equality, organising seminars on women equality, etc., by the work organisations for the exclusive benefit of their employees in order to make them understand the utility and the reasons behind the same.

Further, the work organisations must treat women employees at par with men employees. There should be deliberate effort to break and/or dissolve the glass ceiling and sticky floor. This can be done by having special women cell within the work organisation where women employees can complain and where their work related grievances can be heard. The work organisations must emphasize their policy of inclusive growth. Moreover, certain facilities for making the lives of women employees easier must be provided by the work organisations such as providing pick up facility, ATM machines, work from home options, etc. All this should be seen as an investment towards an inclusive growth mechanism. Women managers must be trained to act as mentors for other women employees (Kaila, 2007). The work organisations must develop a work culture where equal voice should be lent to the female employees. All these measures must be adopted so that the female employees and workers can be provided appropriate level of job satisfaction and so that there should be less job alienation and less job dissatisfaction and more job/ work efficiency and more employee retention.

As far as the law is concerned, even, the Indian Government has recently passed the Sexual Harassment of Women at Workplace (Prevention, Prohibition and Redressal) Act, 2013. But, this alone cannot eliminate gender power inequality because *laws will never be fully effective as long as there is no societal will to promote gender equity*. Moreover, on the legal front also the fight is far from over. This is so because gender equity is even beyond the issue of sexual harassment. For e.g., there is no Equal Opportunity Employment Act in India and there is no law that requires that all companies must provide life balancing/support mechanisms for women employees.

Thus, to conclude, there is need for gender sensitization and gender equity training. This may be a long process towards equal rights from women at the workplace, but there are no shortcuts to gender equality. Removal of gender biases and prejudices will take time. But, we must act now. We must act now because we should prevent any more women from being a victim of workplace discrimination. It is our solemn duty as a society. The laws will also automatically change with changes in mind-sets of the people.

REFERENCES

[1] Agarwal, Bina (1997). Bargaining' and Gender Relations: Within and Beyond the Household, *Feminist Economics*, 3(1), 1-51.

[2] Ambarish (2013), *Gender Bias at Workplace – A Fact or a Myth?*, Retrieved from http://www.citehr.com/27810-gender-bias-workplace-fact-myth. html.

[3] Budhwar, P.S., Saini, D.S., & Bhatnagar, J. (2005), Women in Management in the New Economic Environment: The Case of India, *Asia Pacific Business Review*, 11(2), 179-193.

[4] C.M. Mududaliar v. Idol of Sri S.S. Thirukoil [(1996) 8 SCC 525].

[5] Dey, Dr. P.(2013), Sexual Harassment At Workplace – An Empirical Study to Understand Through the Lenses of Working Women of Guwahati, Assam, India, *IOSR Journal of Humanities and Social Science,* 8(6), 77-82.

[6] Eugene, J.W. (1999), The Impact of Work Resources on Job Stress Among Correctional Treatment Staff. *Journal of Addictions and Offender Counseling*, 20(1), 26-34.

[7] Foot, D.K. & R. Venne (1990), Population, Pyramids and Promotional Prospects, *Canadian Public Policy*, 14 (4), 387-398.

[8] G. Sekar V/s. Geetha [AIR 2009 SC 2649].

[9] Jacob, J.A. (1999), *Handbook of Gender & Work*, Thousand Oaks, CA: Sage.

[10] Kaila (2007), Women Managers in Indian Organization, *Journal of the Indian Academy of Applied Psychology*, 33(1), 93-102.

[11] Kaur et al. (2010), *Psycho-Social Problems of Women Teachers Working in Schools and Colleges of Punjab*, Retrieved from http://www.aiaer.net/ejournal/ vol22110/2.Kaur%20.... pdf.

[12] Khandelwal, P. (2002), Gender Stereotypes at work: Implications for Organizations. *Indian Journal of Training and Development,* Vol. XXXII(2), 72-83.

[13] Dr. K. Sundar & Ashok Kumar (2012), Problems Faced by Women Executives Working in Public Sector Banks in Puducherry, *International Journal of Marketing, Financial Services & Management Research*,1 (7),180-193.

[14] Dr. Kulkarni and Dr. Ruhi Bakhare (2011), Women Leadership in Indian Corporate: Analyzing Social Perceptions, *Zenith International Journal of Multidisciplinary Research*, 1(4), 113-128.

[15] Maheshwari, Kalpana Dr. (2012), *The Glass Ceiling impact on Indian Women Employees*, Retrieved from http://domsiitr.minddevicetech.com /allpaper/The%20Glass%20Ceiling%20 impact%20on%20Indian%20Women%20Employees_Kalpana%20Maheshwari_HRM003.pdf.

[16] Medha Kotwal Lele v. Union of India [(2013) 1 SCC 297].

[17] Moore, D. (1995), "Role Conflict: Not Only for Women? A Comparative Analysis of 5 Nations", *IJCS* XXXVI, Vol. 1, No. 2.

[18] Pratto et al. (1997), The Gender Gap in Occupations Role Attainment: A Social Dominance Approach, *Journal of Personality and Social Psychology*, 72(1), 37-53.

[19] Sharma, S. and Sharma, Manju (2012), Gender Equality in the Workplace: The Perceptive Reality, *Social Sciences Directory,* 1(1), 19-33.

[20] Swarnalatha, C.S. et al (2012), Workplace Harassment and Job Satisfaction: An Empirical Study Among Employees of Automotive Industries in India, *Journal of Management Research and Development,* 2(1), 27-34.

[21] Pathak, Sonal and Sarin, Dr. Anil (2011), Management of Stress Among Women Employees in BPO Industry in India: A Contemporary Issue, *IJMBS,* 1(3), 65-70.

[22] Vohra, N. (2009), Gendered Behaviour of Men and Women in the Workplace: Time to Move On. In colloquium "Gender and Workplace Experience". *Vikalpa: The Journal for Decision Makers*, 34(4), 79-118.

[23] Valsamma Paul (Mrs) v. Cochin University [(1996) 3 SCC 545].

Predictive HR: Paving the Way for an Inclusive and Accessible Workplace

Rekha Mishra and Shalini Garg

University School of Management Studies, Guru Gobind Singh Indraprastha University, New Delhi

ABSTRACT

One of the biggest mandates for modern HR has been to create an inclusive and accessible work place. So HR minds are fraught with questions like how to measure the needs of different employee populations? How will the organization recognize, which HRM policies, practices, plans and processes are working properly to achieve its inclusive agenda etc.? This situation is becoming increasing complex due to multiple sources and multitude of data required for such kind of decision making. Can HR analytics and in particular predictive analytics assist in resolving some of these issues faced by modern day HR? In this review paper we have tried to understand, what is HR analytics all about, how does predictive analytics help HR. We have looked at some cases of companies that benefited by Predictive HR analytics solutions by being able to pinpoint areas in need to improvements or factors that needed attention to achieve the goals for creating an inclusive and accessible work place. It is hoped that this review paper will enlighten HR manager and others who are involved in making decision concerning modern day workforce and would pave the way for more structured and global mind-set that welcomes diversity in all its form and yet manages to achieve structure and consonance.

Keywords: *Inclusive, Accessible, Analytics, HR, Predictive Analytics*

INTRODUCTION

Use of HR analytics in HRM has a very long history. In western part of the globe we find that the credit for introducing analytics in management is often contributed to Frederick Winslow Taylor's work on task-management system using time study and selection of workers [1]. In Indian context also we see the reference of use of HR analytics in HRM in the work of Chanakya's Arthasastra [2].

In Modern times, around 1980s, with the use of Human Resources Management Systems (HRMS) we saw the beginning of use of reporting and basic metric capabilities. The 1990s marked the process driven focus and the use of balanced scorecard position goals and measure progress and outcomes. By the advent of 2000s, companies that were already making heavy use of analytics in other areas of the business introduced more robust Business Intelligence (BI) capabilities to HR data [3].

In todays hyper connected world the biggest mandate for HR has been is to create an inclusive and accessible work place. Decision making around people is crucial for any business and this situation is becoming increasing complex due to multiple sources and multitude of data required for such kind of decision making. Can HR analytics and in particular predictive analytics assist in resolving some of these issues faced by modern day HR? An accurate assessment in some of the HR areas like recruitment, employee retention, development and succession planning is of immense value to HR. So can predictive analytics base decision making ensure success for HR? This is a highly debatable topic and proponents of analytics would argument for the motion and those who people that decision around people cannot be concluded based on the conclusion drawn from analytics would argue against the motion [4].

WHAT IS HR ANALYTICS?

HR analytics is being considered useful for comprehending and assessment of usefulness of HR activities and for making an impact on the business strategy and performance. It assists in understanding the way HR practices and policies propel organizational performance and is thus of huge assistance for HR functions for value addition to their organization [5]. The influence results due to effect it has on the decisions and behaviours of those in the organization [6].

HR analytics is an application of statistical techniques for example, factor analysis, regression and correlation and the synthesis of multiple sources of data to create meaningful insights for example, employee retention in office X is driven by factors Y and Z [7]

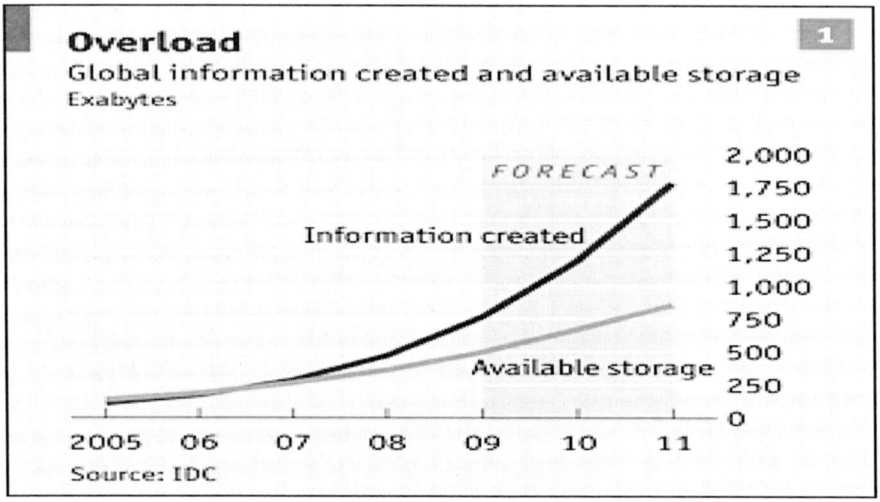

Fig. 1: Global Data Today

Source: IDC

The need and demand for predictive analytics is set to increase. There are many reasons for this situation but three main changes that have led to the hike in demand for predictive analytics in today work environment are as follows [7]:

- Huge growth in computing power and its affordability by masses: As the hardware and software technology is evolving, advancing and becoming increasing cost effective we find that computing power of very high standards is within the reach of masses.
- Huge digitalized HR data accessible via the cloud for processing: Now varied and huge amount of data can be easily accessed via power of cloud computing and analysed to get results in real time.
- Global talent war: As the world become hyper connected, organisations, especially those with global presence are facing a hue dearth of talent that could be utilised immediately. This has led to company's talent strategy into jeopardy and risking the long term integrity of talent streams internally

As per IDC, the importance of analytics as such can be assessed from the fact that much more operational data is being created and captured because of the increasing use of technology. This data come from various Enterprise software like ERP, CRM, and SCM. Much more unstructured data is being captured and stored especially via social media data from website like Facebook and Twitter. Much more unstructured data being captured from sources like Web transactions and Smart objects [8].

APPLICATIONS OF HR ANALYTICS

Harris, Craig and Light (2010) sited five different categories of human capital analytical applications. First are those applications that identify and manage critical talent, e.g. high performers, high potentials, pivotal workers. Second are those that manage critical workforce segments accordingly, e.g. underperforming units are identified and helped to improve. Third are those that predict employee preferences and behaviours and tailor HR practices to attract and retain talent. Fourth are those that forecast business requirements and staffing requirements, e.g. workforce skills needed in different business scenarios and fifth are those that adapt rapidly and scale recruiting supply channels and targets in order to make use of best talent sources available to meet changing business conditions, objectives, and competitive threats [9]. Following are some of the HR domain activities that make use of analytics.

(a) **Turnover modelling**. This is used to predict future turnover in business in specific functions, business units, geographies and countries by looking at factors such as commute time, time since last role change, and performance over time. This means one can scale hiring efforts accordingly, reducing empty desk time and panic hiring, which can lead to lower cost, higher quality hiring.

(b) **Recruitment advertising measurement**. This is used for modelling response for advertising jobs. One can use experience gained from previous campaigns to avoid contacting candidates or using channels that don't yield a response and focus on those channels that do work.

(c) **Targeted retention**. This is used to find out which employees or groups of employees are at high risk of churn in the future and focus retention activities on those who are more in need and reduce it in other areas where it is not needed as much.

(d) **Risk Management**: This is done to develop a profile of candidates with a higher risk of leaving prematurely or performing below standard.

(e) **Talent Forecasting**. This is done to be able to predict which new hires, based on their profile, and are likely to be high fliers and then moving them in to high potential programs.

A survey done by Economic Intelligence Unit in the year 2012, on performance of HR showed that majority of the CEOs agreed that HR does a good job of managing internal affairs like evaluating employee performance and leading day to day HR functions but they did a poor job when it comes to activities like developing key talent, global outsourcing and succession planning.

One main reason for this situation was identified was severe lack of required data and insight in order to make decision on those issues. It is thus imperative for HR to incorporate smart use of predictive analytics in its day to day affairs to remain viable, competitive and sustainable.

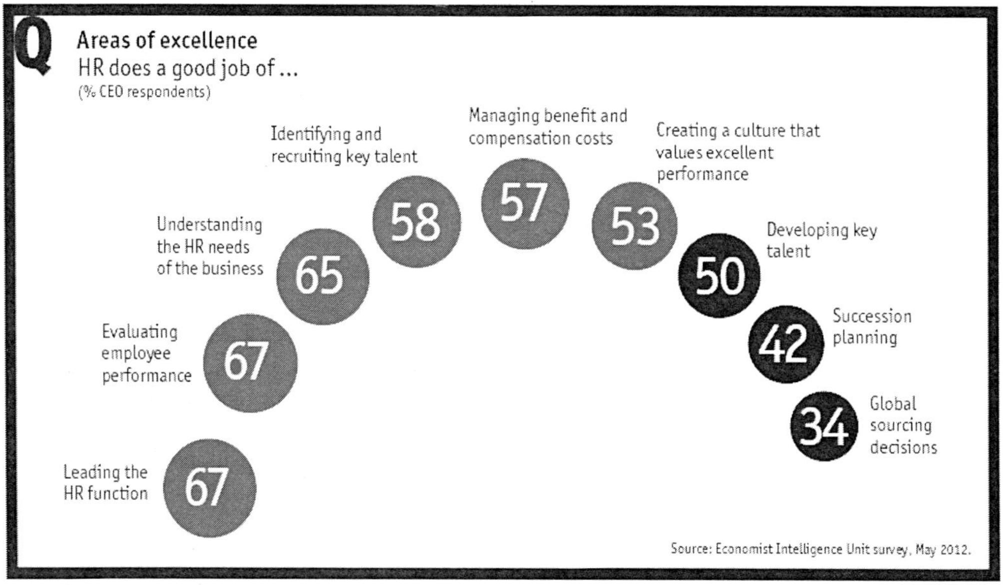

Fig. 2: Study: Rethinking Human Resources in a Changing World, 2012

Source: Economist Intelligence Unit.

ANALYTICS FOR AN INCLUSIVE AND ACCESSIBLE WORKPLACE

Some of the questions that fraught HR mind on daily basis in order to create inclusive and accessible work are as follows [10].

1. How to measure the needs of different employee populations in mind (e.g. nursing rooms for mothers, handicap access for the disabled, workplace ergonomics for older workers)? So that they are able to design a workplace that is inclusive and accessible.
2. How to find out who are employees who share a certain interest or characteristic (e.g. working parent network, women's network, and network of employees of the same nationality) so that a an employee resource group can be created to facilitate the career development of individuals by providing an avenue to share personal experience and obtain advice?
3. How will the organization recognize, which HRM policies, practices, plans and processes are working properly to drive improvements in business and/or mission outcomes?

In order to ensure that HRM delivery system has operational efficiency and robustness, strategic enablement and high quality/cost effective/rapid time-to-market HRM service delivery. It needs Predictive analytics solutions to assist HR in pinpointing areas, modelling techniques to solve workplace issues and factor out processes that need improvement or modification in order to achieve the inclusive and accessible workplace mandate.

Analytic solutions provide proactive, event-based, and scheduled alerts, delivered directly by email, cell phones and other mobile devices, or to personalized dashboards. With this information, HR can quickly correct the deviation, examining alternatives solutions to problem faced and thus as a result, profit margins can be preserved. Alert are of immense importance. Following are some cases of the companies that have already achieved success at workplace using Predictive HR solutions [10].

Harrah's entertainment: Uses insights derived from data to do job fit and job matching with employee and have thus modelled an approach that estimates the optimal number of staff member's requirement at service side and especially at front desk. As of today the company uses analytics for accountability for the things that are of utmost importance to staff, since happier and healthier employees create better-satisfied guests [10]. This approach has also helped in getting to know their employees on an individual basis to determine each person's strengths, interests, priorities, challenges and commitment to the business.[11]

Sprint has spotted the factors that best foretell which employees will leave after a relatively short time which helps control employee attrition [10]. Thus adapting a flexible policy towards work arrangement as per the need of the employee rather than having single policy for all. And also linking employee goals and ambitions to the goals and future plans of the business and thus making sure that employees are more engaged and feel part of the company, both now and in the future [11].

To protect its investments, soccer team AC Milan created its own biomedical research unit which draws on some 60,000 data points for each player. These units help the team gauge player's health and fitness and make contract decisions. [10]. Thus providing both positive and constructive feedback to employees on their work as soon as possible and also praising publicly, but if correcting or reprimanding in private[11].

Public relations firm Ketchum analysed its intra company network in London to understand how the information flowed in the organisation. [10]. Thus are able to acknowledge and accommodate employees with diverse backgrounds and priorities and ensure they use language that is respectful and welcoming of all ages, gender, ethnicity, personal priorities and experiences. All internal and external communications such as newsletters, memos, job ads and websites should follow this guideline [11].

The current global and diversified workforce and work environment have raised concern regarding issues that has sent HR domain requiring thinking out of the box to face the current reality. Need for creating an inclusive and accessible work place has been globally recognised by most organisations to remain sustainable [11].

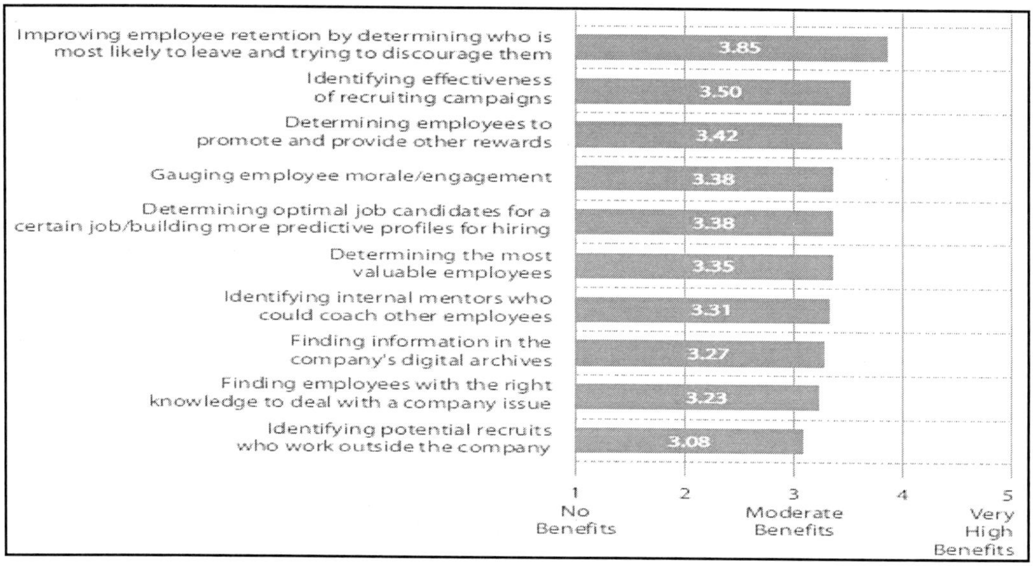

Fig. 3: Degree of Potential Benefits Big Data and Analytics Could Generate – Mean Summary – Human Resources

Source: (www.tcs.com)

Ernst & Young is a global professional services firm has 141,000 employees across 140 countries. The Singapore office has over 2,000 employees, with approximately one-third of the workforce made up of international employees spanning across different age groups. Ernst & Young believes that embedding an inclusive culture in the organisation will enable its employees to achieve their potential and make a difference, and better enable the organisation to deliver high quality services to its clients, create competitive advantage and drive market leadership [11].

HR of many of many several organisations like Ernst & Young are using Inclusiveness Pulse Check, a tool that assesses employees' perception of the organisation's state of workplace inclusiveness and harmony and is completed on a periodic basis. Using predictive analytics on the data obtained from pulse check was combined with existing employee surveys which are conducted in organisation via employee focus groups. HR was thus able to gather feedback on employees' perception of the organisation's inclusiveness [11].

Analytics provide legitimate and reliable foundations for human capital decisions. Human capital metrics potentially can and often should influence the development and implementation of business strategies. Organizational capabilities and core competencies are both highly talent dependent and involves development of organizational social capital and individual skills and knowledge for which the role of HR is critical. Mayo (2008) mentioned that very few organizations have a fully integrated approach to Human Capital Measurement (HCM) [12].

The main focus of HR in general is on collecting and reporting data about activities instead of outcomes, while the analyses are mostly very simplistic e.g., limited analyses of drivers of outcomes. As a result, there is a need for HR to develop itself from descriptive metrics to predictive analytics.

Hence if HR wants better performance from their top employees who are perhaps their greatest asset and their largest expense then they have done well to favour analytics over their gut instincts.

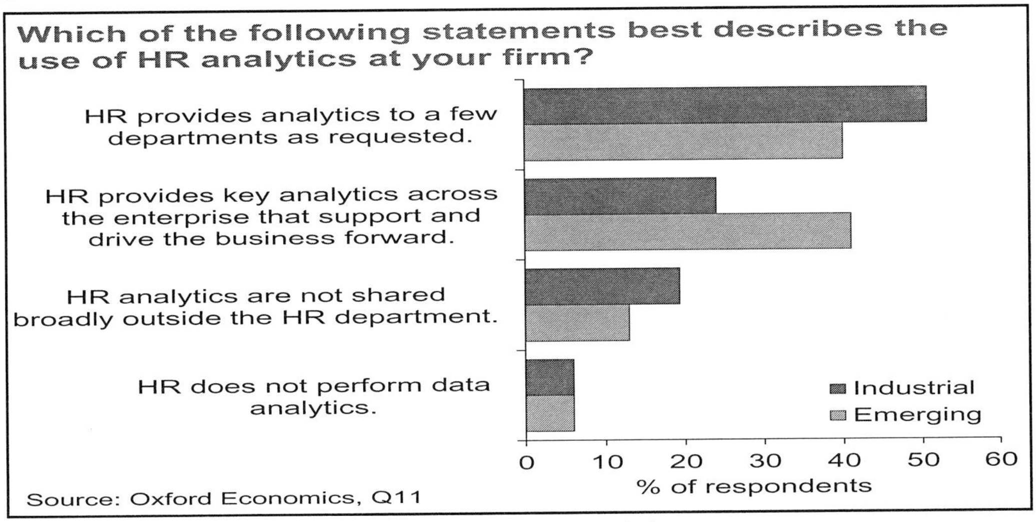

Fig. 4: Uses of HR Analytics

Source: Oxford Economics.

A survey done by Oxford economics showed that use of HR analytics for decision making is comparatively better in emerging market areas as compared to industrial areas, thus imply that emerging market areas are more likely to grow faster and also adapt to need to changing workforce dynamics and thus will be able to remain competitive. Embracing the transition to strategic thinking and driving business results is thus the key to being sustainable in long run. Says Bob Bennett of FedEx Express, "If our HR strategies do not link to that business strategy, then we're not supporting the company the way we need to be supporting it" [13] [14].

CONCLUSION

Predictors that humans come up with inherently embed some kind of a cause-and-effect relationship, our brains are just not equipped to identify and quantify predictors that may not have cause-and-effect synergy. On the other hand, advancements in mathematical sciences and computer science have enabled algorithms to take into account thousands of related and unrelated data points and business rules, process them computationally and come up with far better future decisions than human judgment and traditional methods can and since modern day HR story has definitely developed new dimensions and there is huge paradigm shift in the way HR functions today. The need to maintain global and sustainable organisation has forced HR to strategize on all the fronts to remain competitive. Incorporation of Predictive HR analytics to have a control of many issues like employee retention, development and succession planning through smart decision making drawn using predictive analytics, HR today can hope to be able to create an inclusive and accessible work place.

REFERENCES

[1] Wren, D.A & Bedeian, A.G. (2009). The Evolution of Management Thought 6th Ed, John Wiley & Sons, p. 130.

[2] Santhosh Bagwe (2010). Applying Kautilya's Arthasastra in Human resource management, A research paper.

[3] Joanne Bintliff-Ritchie (2010). Realizing the Full Potential of Workforce Analytics, Industry whitepaper.

[4] Boudreau, J. W., & Ramstad, P. M. (2006), Talentship and HR Measurement and Analysis: From ROI to Strategic Organizational Change, Human Resource Planning, 29(1) pp. 25-33.

[5] Lawler, E. E., Levenson, A., & Boudreau, J. (2004). HR Metrics and Analytics Uses and Impacts. CEO Publication - Working Paper. Retrieved February 23, 2012 from http://classic.marshall.usc.edu/ assets/048/9984.pdf

[6] Levenson, A., Boudreau, J., & Lawler, E. (2005). Survey on HR analytics and HR transformation. CEO Publication - Feedback Report. Retrieved February 23, 2012 from http://classic.marshall.usc.edu/assets/036/8635.pdf

[7] KPMG (2003). People are the real number. Retrived February 1, 2014 from https://www.kpmg.com/GR/en/IssuesAndInsights/ArticlesPublications/Documents/workforce-analytics-download.pdf

[8] IDC (2014). Big Data and Analytics. Retrived Febury 1, 2014 from http://www.idc.com/prodserv/FourPillars/bigData/index.jsp

[9] Harris, J. G., Craig, E., & Light, D. A. (2010), The New Generation of Human Capital Analytics, Accenture - Research Report.

[10] Thomas H. Davenport, Jeanne Harris, and Jeremy Shapiro (2010), Competing on Talent Analytics, Harvard Business Review, October.

[11] The NL HR MANAGER, (2014). Retrieved on 1 February from [http://www.nlhrmanager.ca/index.php?option=com_content&view=article&id=78&Itemid=80&limitstart=1]

[12] Mayo, A. (2008), Financial statements and human capital, ICAEW - Research Report.

[13] Oxford Economics, Spring 2012. The Digital Transformation of People Management.

[14] Paauwe, J. (2004). HRM and performance: Achieving long term viability. Oxford: Oxford University Press.

Challenges of Higher Education and its Role in Social Development: A Case Study of India

Ashish Kumar

University School of Management Studies, Guru Gobind Singh Indraprashtha University, New Delhi

ABSTRACT

Higher education system plays an important role in the sustained development of a nation. The need for the same cannot be ruled out in our country as well. Given the fact that India is adobe to more than 120 crores people and an important economy of the world the creation of a robust higher education system in the country has become a necessity. Besides this, higher education also helps in the social cohesion and cultural development of the nation. Emphasizing more on higher education does not mean that we may neglect basic or primary education as the former is fully dependent on the success of primary education. Therefore, there is a strong need to foster the primary education to increase the literacy level in the country. The higher education of our country is further characterised by lack of resources, government and political intervention, dearth of quality faculty at technical institutions and poor infrastructure etc. The present piece of literature is an attempt to study the problems and challenges in higher education in India. The appreciation of problems will pave the way for overall social welfare and development of the hitherto weaker section of the society.

Keywords: *Higher Education, India, Quality, Economy*

INTRODUCTION

The importance of higher education cannot be negated in any civilised society. It has also been empirically proved that education and growth of the economy have cause and effect relationship (Pradhan, 2004). The higher education system of India is third largest in the world after China and USA when measured in terms of number of students (99.54 lakhs). The harsh reality remains that ever since our independence in 1947 we are not able to install a robust higher education system in our country. Different education policies and systems have been tried to improve the standard of higher education but the results speaks about the success of those. Numerous commissions have been established by the Government of India, e.g. Radhakrishnan Commission (1945), Kothari Commission (1966) and in the recent past National Knowledge

Commission (2007) to observe the status of higher education. Many of the recommendations proposed by these commissions have been considered but the desired results are still awaited. The present global scenario has further created unprecedented challenges before the higher education system. The lack of infrastructure and inadequate research facilities, outdated teaching pedagogy, poor research standards, unmotivated students, non-availability of good faculty, low student enrolment rate and social gap among the students on the basis of income, age, gender etc. further adds to the woes of weak higher education system of our country. The UGC has rightly pointed out that we cannot persist with traditional disciplines in higher education but we will have to make our higher education application oriented and developing its human resource. In the last decade the government expenditure on the development of higher education system has become manifold and serious steps have been taken for the growth of higher education in the country. Despite all these efforts the position of higher education in the country is not very encouraging. In a country of over 1.2 billion population we have only 227 government recognised universities including 20 central universities. Apart from this, IITs, IIMs, NITs and other private institutions are also contributing their bit to the development of higher education in our country. At present we have nearly 17000 colleges out of which 2000 are exclusively for women, 460000 teachers and 1 crore students. Despite this mammoth system none of the university in India has come to top 100 universities of the world as per ranking conducted by various institutions worldwide. The best of the institutions in our country are ranked over 220 [IIT, Kanpur -237, IIT Madras – 284 and IIT Delhi at 291]. The apex regulator of education in India UGC along with other regulators is taking hard measures to improve the academic and research atmosphere in all educational institutions. As per UGC by the end of the year 2020 India need more than 1800 universities equipped with adequate research and infrastructure facilities to compete with best of the institutions in the world. Besides this there is also a need to increase the gross enrolment ratio in higher education. At present this ration stands at 11 per cent only and there is a need to take it to over 20 in next 10 years or so which is still very low in comparison to 83% GER of USA and 91% of South Korea. Another hurdle which may come in between is non-availability of quality faculty, research facilities and aptitude for research. There is a need to bridge this gap urgently before India may dream of bringing its educational institutions at the level of top institutions in the world.

LIMITATIONS OF INDIAN EDUCATION SYSTEM

Inadequate Resources

The resources at the disposal of higher education institutions are too less and are insufficient for providing viable quality education. In 1950-51 0.64% of GDP was spent on education which gradually rose up to 4.28% of GDP in 2000-01 and was at 3.77% of GDP in 2008-09. These figures are not comparable with developed nations and most of the developing countries as well.

Non Availability of Quality Faculty Members

Most of the faculty positions in higher education institutions are lying vacant as after passing out students do not prefer to work as faculty or to enroll for Ph.D. but to work for pocket friendly MNC jobs. As a result of this the quality of education at these institutions is not as per global standard and is persistently falling.

Government Control and Political Intervention

Another hiccup in the growth of higher education is the too much government control and too many regulations for setting up a higher education institution. As a result of this the right numbers of higher education institutions are not coming up. Besides this because of government and political interference government policies and programmes are not implemented in the desired manner, which further defeat the very purpose of such programmes. Political interference is also responsible for the low quality of the education institutions.[1]

Separation and Fragmentation of Education and Research

Indian universities and research organizations have been highly resistant to change and innovation. The course contents of most of the courses in Indian universities are not in tune with the industry requirements. They include subjects which do not have any real life application. This is the reason why even after completing technical education most of the students are still unemployed.

Profit Motive

Most of our higher education institutions are working like an industry in which they produce graduates and postgraduates which are not salable. Education has become a business for them and profiteering is their only motive. It has also resulted in the increase in the cost of higher education.

Undemocratic Structure of Educational Institutions

The authoritarian system and undemocratic structure is still prevalent in most of the educational institutions in the country. In most such institutions students and teachers are never asked for their opinion.

---

1 Our university system is, in many parts, in a state of disrepair.... In almost half the districts in the country, higher education enrollments are abysmally low, almost two-third of our universities and 90 percent of our colleges are rated as below average on quality parameters.... I am concerned that in many states university appointments, including that of vice-chancellors, have been politicised and have become subject to caste and communal considerations, there are complaints of favouritism and corruption. Manmohan Singh, Prime Minister of India (2007).

CHALLENGES FOR HIGHER EDUCATION IN INDIA

Given the peculiar position of our country, i.e. High degree of social diversity, high population, low literacy ratio, high rural population and lower literacy rate of women and minorities and so forth, providing access to education is the greatest responsibility of the government. After reviewing the bottlenecks in front of higher education in India following are the challenges which the government will have to embrace to attain a foothold with its global peers in the field of higher education.

Providing Resources for Higher Education

Lack of adequate resources and funds is one important concern for the government. Higher education is very expensive and it is the onus of the central and state governments to provide access to higher education for all its citizens. Given the constraints of fiscal deficit it is becoming increasingly difficult for the government to mobilise resources for higher education.

Increasing Literacy Level

A huge portion of country's population is still illiterate despite the best efforts of the government to increase the literacy level of the citizens as nearly 38% of our population is still finds it difficult to play with letters and figures. The problem is more severe when it comes to female population. Until the basic literacy rate of the country is increased the premise of a robust higher education system cannot be built. Right to Education is an important scheme launched to increase the literacy rate in the country.

Modernization of Education System

Along with the aim of providing basic education to the last man of the country there is a strong need of modernising our present education system as well so as to make it competitive given the environmental challenges. There is a need to emphasize to strengthen technical education so as to create large population of technology sound people which will further take the growth of the nation to the next level.

Emphasizing on Research and Quality of Education

A strong higher education can only be created on the basis of strength in research and good quality. For this purpose incentive should be provided to capable students to execute Ph.D. Programs and carry out researches in science and technology. It will further meet the requirement of quality teachers at the higher level.

Social Gaps

Yet another characteristic of our country is that there is a big difference between have and have not's. The biggest challenge in front of the government is to provide equal opportunity to people from all the strata of the society. It is through higher education and providing access to modern technology only that the status of the hitherto deprived section of the society can be lifted.

CONCLUSIONS

Indian government has taken large number of steps to establish a strong higher education system in the country. Given the quality of research and level of students produced at IITs and IIMs is indicative of the fact that today our higher education system is not much behind that of developed nations. The measures taken by the government has resulted in the creation increased number of higher education institutions which is really a commendable job. But along with the growth in numbers there is a serious need of quality education in these higher education institutions to keep pace with the competitive world. India is one of the fastest developing nations in the world and to sustain the growth rate of 8% or more there is still a need to establish more number of higher education institutions with focus on research and quality. For this purpose there is an urgent requirement to invest huge amount in higher education so as to provide access to right amount of resources at the right time and attract global talent at our technical education institutions. If the report of the National Knowledge Commission is taken up and implemented in letter and spirit it will catapult the fate of higher education in our country. To become a developed nation in the time to come there is an urgent need of highly educated technically sound people who can carry our country on the path of growth and prosperity. For this purpose there is an earnest need of modern and tech savvy educational system which can cope up with the challenges of the global world and contribute to the sustain growth of the country. Besides this it will also help in bridging the gap between rich and poor in the Indian society and provide equal opportunity to everyone to excel their social status in the society.

REFERENCES

[1] Agarwal, Pawan (2006), Higher Education in India: The Need for Change (ICIER Working Paper No. 180). New Delhi: Indian Council for Research on International Economic Relations (http://www.icrier.org/publication/working_papers_180.html).

[2] Altbach, Philip G. (2006), The Private Higher Education Revolution: An Introduction. University News. January 2-8, 2006. Vol. 44, No. 01.

[3] Anandakrishnan, M. (2006), Privatization of higher education: Opportunities and anomalies. 'Privatization and commercialization of higher education' organized by NIEPA, May 2, 2006, New Delhi.

[4] Hans, V. Basil, Higher Education in India – Assailing Challenges; Assuring Quality (August 6, 2013). Available at SSRN: http://ssrn.com/abstract=2306842 or http://dx.doi.org/10.2139/ssrn.2306842.

[5] Jandhyala B.G. Tilak, Absence of Policy and Perspective in Higher Education. Economic and Political Weekly Vol. 39, No. 21, 2159-2164 (http://www.epw.org.in/epw/uploads/articles/7650.pdf).

[6] Kayte et al, Higher Education Reforms and Challenges in India, Lokavishkar International E-Journal, ISSN 2277-727X, Vol. II, Issue I, Jan-Mar 2013, 27-31.

[7] Misra S.P., Higher Education: New Challenges and Emerging Roles. *Odisha Review*, July 2012, 39-43.

[8] Sanat Kaul, Higher Education in India: Seizing the Opportunity (ICIER Working Paper No. 179). New Delhi: Indian Council for Research on International Economic Relations, May 2006 (http://www.icrier.org/pdf/WP_179.pdf).

[9] Singh, J.D. , Higher Education in India – Issues, Challenges and Suggestions, http://www.gvctesangaria.org/websiteimg/publications/jdarticle.pdf, accessed on 8.2.14.

[10] Stella, Antony (2002) External quality assurance in Indian higher education: Case study of the National Assessment and Accreditation Council (NAAC). International Institute for Educational Planning. Paris.

[11] http://www.ugc.ac.in/ugcpdf/208844_HEglance2012.pdf on 8.2.2014.

Flexi Work: A Welcome HR Initiative in Creating an Inclusive Workplace for Techie Moms – A Case Study

Y. Lakshmi Prabha

Department of Home Science, St. Joseph's College for Women (A), Visakhapatnam

ABSTRACT

Women's participation in varied segments of job market has increased tremendously and this has resulted in an increase in their visibility and financial status. However, this has not changed the concept of gender based division of labour at home. More over, women experience an acute time lag during their child bearing phases. Child care being considered the primary duty of a woman, it leads to career breaks and often, women stretch themselves to extreme levels trying to cope with work and family life. Many women take a break from their careers or shift jobs to lessen job stress or leave their jobs once for all. This causes a loss of committed and dedicated work force in the job market. Women become wary of taking up full time jobs demanding their full attention and time, for fear of being labeled as 'selfish' or 'less family oriented'. In this context, 'flexi work' option addresses most of these issues. It not only gives a woman time to be with her young babies, but also satisfies her career ambition in that it guarantees her return to job market and also enhances her work life balance, thereby, leading to an increased turnover of work and greater employee satisfaction. Case studies of two women employed in Information Technology (IT) sector are presented to illustrate this argument.

Keywords: *Women's Work, Work life Balance, Flexi Work, Satisfaction*

INTRODUCTION

The Indian software industry is creating new sources of employment which are breaking traditional social barriers of gender. The entry of women into the industry has become vital for both the corporate sector and the state, as a symbol of modernity, attracting foreign multinationals and justifying a neoliberal reform agenda (Mukherjee, 2008). Although the IT industry is marketed as being gender-friendly with no overt bias exhibited, it has been observed by many researchers that the numbers of women come down as one goes up the seniority chart or organizational hierarchy. It has been substantiated by various studies conducted in the west, and also in India, in metros like Bangalore, Chennai, that there is a predominance of women in the entry level programming positions (Fuller and Narasimhan, 2008). The industry has also brought about a visible change in the lifestyles of its employees. IT industry carries a reputation of paying its employees 'very handsome' salaries, thereby kick starting new trends in consumption behaviour and family management patterns, indicating an increased affluence and compulsive consumption.

The emergence of urban married women as a workforce has been rightly viewed by sociologists as heralding a profound change in all the vital aspects of Indian society. Many studies on working women in India have found that in the middle classes of metropolitan cities, important changes are taking place in the attitudes of working women, their husbands, their parents, and society in general (Sidramshettar and Punit, 1999). Reinforcing the growing independence of women in India, a survey by market research firm IMRB says the income level of urban Indian women has doubled in the last decade, which has also led to the average urban household income doubling. The urban Indian woman who earned Rs. 4.492 per month in 2001 took home Rs. 9457 as of 2010. As per the survey, the rise in income is directly reflected in the average monthly household income of urban India going up from Rs. 8242 to Rs. 16, 509 in 2010 (*The Times of India*, 2011). Rai (2002) asserts that economic independence has brought marked attitudinal change in the working women. However, the degree of change depends on the level of education, the profession they hold and the attitude of the family members towards them. By and large, employment has brought a sense of confidence among the working women and they are now in a position to think about their independent existence without depending on husband and other family members. Women's income determines, in a significant way, her status in the household, community and society. Factors such as caste, class, cultural practices, marital status and educational status influence her participation in work. Women's work participation rates, occupational distribution and shifts are often taken as indicators to assess the impact of economic development.

Sidramshettar and Punit (1999) and Mishra (2006) state that a married woman professional has to meet many requirements and expectations of the family from social, obligatory, emotional and psychological point of view and she works day in and out to maintain both the fronts. She may not be able to give up her profession due to the fact that, she adds to better economic and social status of the family, she may be aware of her capability and potential and wants to develop herself for her better career prospects, and she may aspire to achieve some excellence and contribute to society and nation as a whole. A job-family balancing exercise is crucial in the managerial function of every gainfully employed woman.

REVIEW OF RELATED LITERATURE

Information and Communication Technology Industry in India has tremendously influenced women's employment and is believed to be contributing to social equity. A favorable work environment that is gender neutral and requires skilled labour has led to the emergence of a new work place that is 'de-gendered'. Women now comprise about 21 per cent of the manpower in the industry. The IT companies are considered to be less bureaucratic, with an emphasis on open management structures, transparency and people development (Shanker, 2008).

Women, being about 50 per cent of the global population, constitute only about 25 per cent of the global IT workforce despite government and industry backed efforts to attract them into these fields. These skewed percentages suggest that in terms of women's participation, the IT workforce is missing significant numbers of potentially valuable human resources for the information age. "Feminine" or "relational" strengths such as intuition, empathy, relationship building, and collaboration skills are now assets in instrumental, "masculine" organizational context, such as IT companies, for gaining a competitive edge in the global economy. Such skills are particularly valuable in ICT – mediated distributed work teams or virtual teams involving "boundary less collaboration" where work is increasingly co-coordinated through trust based relationships (D'Mello, 2006).

Globally, women comprise around 10 per cent of senior management positions in Fortune 500 companies. In India, their presence is known to range between a high of 5.8 per cent to a low of roughly 3 per cent of all administrative positions. They can be seen mainly in HR, IT and servicing activities. Their presence in hard-core production or marketing is much less and still lower at strategic policy influencing levels. Women are playing a significant role in the expansion of the Indian Software Industry and they constitute 45 per cent of the high-tech workforce. A high concentration of men exists in export software firms whereas women are present in a higher proportion of domestic low-end and IT-enabled services (Suriya, 2003). This implies that at the entry level itself there is a marked gender differential in access to employment in this sector. Thus, while there is an argument in favour of women in the Indian IT sector, research indicates that women professionals are still in the minority in this sector with a clear trend towards clustering at the lower ends of the job hierarchy leading to feminization of certain service activities (Budhwar et al., 2005).

Kelkar (2007) quoting a study undertaken by UNDP (2004) states that on an average, of the IT professionals, there is one woman employee for every seven men employed in the IT Industry in India. Women professionals constitute 12.5 per cent of the IT Industry. Women constitute over 19 per cent of the total workforce at lower levels (up to 3 years experience). The percentage drops to 6 in the senior workforce (10 years experience).

Padmanabhan (2011) in a study of the gender equality issues in IT Industry in Kerala quoting ILO (2001) says that the development of IT sector in general was prophesied to open new windows of opportunity for women, since work in the knowledge based sector was viewed as less physically tough and amenable to flexible hours. It was perceived to have the potential of initiating fundamental changes in gender relations through the large scale entry of women into decent jobs. A trend of increasing female representation in software industry with entry of women in larger numbers over the years was reported. Analysis revealed a steady decline in the presence of women as one moved up the ladder, with the decline being most remarkable at the strategic decision making level. While around 36% of professionals at the bottom operations level were observed to be women, they constituted only 21% of the professionals at the middle management level. The figure decreased to around 11 per cent at the level of operations manager, delivery manager and similar senior management category which further declined to 6 per cent at the corporate management level which included top managerial posts such as Chief Executive Officer, Chief Operating Officer, Chairman, etc. According to the Gender Diversity Benchmark for Asia, 2011 study, in India the greatest leak in the pipeline takes place early on in a woman's career- from junior to middle level positions (48.07 per cent). This means the leaking pipeline in India is in fact more severe than in the other Asian geographies as the pool of women is highly diminished at an earlier stage (*The Times of India*, 2011).

METHODOLOGY

Women employees working in different IT companies were identified as 'typical' cases, from the information gathered through a questionnaire. After seeking their consent, in-depth interviews were conducted with these women by the investigator to gain an insight into their issues and concerns pertaining to work and family domains.

Two case studies are presented here. One case illustrates the effectiveness of offering flexi work option as a HR initiative to counter the increasing attrition rate of women employees. The second case presents the choices made by a senior software woman employee to balance her work and family responsibilities. While the earlier case showcases the ingenuity of the HR initiatives in promoting inclusivity, the second one reflects the situation in many firms/ organizations, where women are forced to be satisfied with less challenging roles in order to have a little more time for children and family.

Preet Khanna* was a 26 year old post graduate in Natural Resources Management, employed as an executive in a leading Indian IT company, earning a monthly income of Rs.25,000. Her husband who was an M.C.A. degree holder was also working in the IT sector and was earning Rs.90, 000 per month. She had twin children, a boy and a girl, both aged 18 months and was living in a nuclear family. She joined duty after her maternity leave when the babies were six months old. As both her mother and mother-in-law were unable to come and stay with them, she engaged a full time paid servant to take care of the babies. She introduced formula feed in the fifth month itself as she would not be available to breastfeed the babies once she joined back, and wanted them to get used to it before she rejoined. They were living in a rented three-bedroom flat, which was in the same locality as her company.

"Joining back work was a tough decision, and life was hectic. The house was in a mess, and pending things kept building up." She was back at work and was entrusted a responsible role at work. She received support from her team mates and her work environment was definitely positive. Preeti was able to manage her profession and felt grateful that her employer facilitated her resumption of career. However, on the home front she was losing patience, and was showing it on the babies. Her job was demanding and she had to spend long hours at work. She was not getting enough time to spend with the children and life seemed 'very out of control'. She was finding it very taxing to balance her dual responsibilities. She then decided to give in her resignation as she was not able to spend time with her children. Her husband left the decision to her. She almost made up her mind and spoke to her HR executive about it.

Preeti's HR executive counseled her and convinced her to avail of the part time work option instead of resigning. She was not aware that such an option was available. She applied for it and her application was processed and she had to attend a series of interviews to present her case, before it was finally approved and she was given the part-time work option. She had been working part-time for the past two and a half months. The flexi work option made it possible for Preeti to continue in her job and achieve a semblance of work life balance.

"I don't feel so stressed out, as I am able to spend time on myself and with my children. There is a feeling of relaxation."

She had been working since four years with the same company, which she said was gender-friendly and the management was understanding. "Responsibilities have increased of-late and work is more fast-paced. Every time a challenge is faced, it builds up my confidence and decision-making abilities. I am happy and feel confident now. With the part-time work and adequate support system at home and the day-care which is good, I am able to handle my life and my kids with confidence."

Amala* was an M.C.A. graduate, aged 34 year old and employed as a Quality Manager in an American IT company with a work experience of 12 years, earning a monthly income of Rs.45, 000. She was living in an extended family. Her husband, also an M.C.A. graduate, was employed in the same company, and was earning Rs. 55,000 per month. Her mother-in-law, a retired professor, was staying with them, for most part of the year. Amala had two daughters aged 10 years and 5 years. The younger daughter was in L K.G. class and the elder one was in class four. They were living in their own house, which was an independent duplex house. Her parents and her siblings also lived in the same city, at about a distance of 8k.m.

"When my elder daughter was born, I took leave for six months and then I could manage my job and home because of my parents' help." They were at that time living in a rented house near her parent's house. But when her second daughter was born, who was more demanding and attention-seeking by nature, there were many changes. A full time servant, who was with them since the birth of her elder daughter took care of the children. Besides, she also had a cook who came in the morning and evening, a servant for the cleaning and washing of clothes and also a driver.

Amala was in a technical and demanding role in her work place. It involved working for late hours and being available online 24 × 7. It was very challenging and it gave her a deep sense of accomplishment. Since her husband was also in similar job, they were able to appreciate one another's concerns.

"IT career is very demanding and I am not able to spare time for my kids or for any social obligation. So when my second daughter was born, I opted for a less demanding job shift in the company." She moved to the Quality Assurance section, but even here, she was not able to come home before 8p.m. at the earliest." However late I come home. I have to sit with them and supervise and help their studies. It is just terrible during their exams and monthly tests. Even if my husband comes home early, he plays or watches T.V. along with them, but does not bother about their home work or studies."

"Eventhough I am happy because of my financial independence, I miss taking care of my parents and also meeting my siblings or other friends. All errands have to be done during weekends only." She had no time to go to the gym also or for any such physical activity because after coming home and finishing with children's studies she was left with no energy to do anything.

Amala was able to balance her work and family satisfactorily as long as they were only two, till the children were born. Once her responsibilities and expectations at home multiplied with the children, she found it difficult to cope with both. Eventhough her employer was reputed to be gender friendly, no relaxation or alternate strategy was available to her. Inspite of being qualified and experienced to be promoted to next level, she had to be satisfied and compromise with a not so challenging role and being sidelined for promotion.

CONCLUSION

From the case study 1 it is obvious that the IT company could ensure that the employee stayed on and her sense of commitment towards the company multiplied. In the second case, the company did not recognize the need of offering flexi work or other such options to her. This could also be attributed to a deficit of dynamic leadership and absence of a mentor, which has resulted in her opting for a less challenging work role, which could have affected her morale and self image. By making options like flexi work and work from home available to women in their mid careers, organizations would render the work environment inclusive and gender friendly.

REFERENCES

[1] Budhwar P.S., Saini D.S. & Bhatnagar J. (2005), Women in Management in the New Economic Environment: The case of India, *Asia pacific Business Review*, Vol. 11, Issue 2, pp. 179-193.

[2] D'Mello, M. and S. Sahay (2008), Betwixt and Between? Exploring Mobilities in a Global Workplace in India, In Upadhya C. and A.R. Vasavi (Eds), *In an Outpost of the Global Economy,* Routledge Taylor & Francis Group, New Delhi, pp. 76-100.

[3] Fuller, C. and H. Narasimhan (2008), Empowerment and Constraint: Women, Work and the Family in Chennai's Software Industry, In Upadhya C. and A.R.Vasavi (Eds), *In an Outpost of the Global Economy*, Routledge Taylor & Francis Group, New Delhi, pp. 190-210.

[4] Kelkar (2007). Women in the Digital Era: Gender, Culture and Technology, IFAD-UNIFEM Gender Mainstreaming Programme in Asia, New Delhi, 4-6 February 2007.

[5] Mishra (2006), Working Women Issues and Challenges, Omega Publications, New Delhi, pp. 70, 72-73, 179-80.

[6] Mukherjee, S. (2008), Producing the Knowledge Professional: Gendered Geographies of Alienation in India's New High-tech Workplace, In Upadhya C. and A.R.Vasavi (Eds), In an Outpost of the Global Economy, Routledge Taylor and Francis Group, New Delhi, pp. 50-75.

[7] Padmanabhan, N. (2011), Understanding Gender Equality in the Software Industry of Kerala through the Capability Approach, EPW March 19, 2011, Vol. XLVI, No. 12, pp. 70-75.

[8] Rai, C.P. (2002), Working Women in India, Vol. 1, Anmol Publications Pvt-Ltd, New Delhi, pp. 30-81.

[9] Shanker, D. (2008), Gender Relations in IT Companies: An Indian Experience, Reprinted from *Gender, Technology and Development*, Vol. 12(2), 2008, Sage Publications, pp. 185-207.

[10] Sidaramshettar, S.C. and A.E. Punit (1999), Married Working Women: Attitudes Towards Work, In Indra R. and D.K. Behera (Eds), *Gender and Society in India*, Vol. I, Manak Publications, New Delhi, pp. 229-246.

[11] Suriya, M. (2005), Employment Opportunities for Women in Business Process Outsourcing in India, In Archibald. J, J. Emms, F. Grundy, J. Payne & E. Turner (Eds), *The Gender Politics of ICT, 6th International Women into Computing Conference*, University of Greenwich, U.K, pp. 485-501.

[12] *The Times of India* (2011), September 28, Ascent Global, p. 4.

Lifelong Learning for Organizations: Managing Inclusiveness and Growth

Vijita S. Aggarwal

University School of Management Studies, Guru Gobind Singh Indraprastha University, Dwarka, New Delhi

ABSTRACT

This paper focuses on applicability of the concept Life Long Learning for organizations. The concept of Life Long Learning has become important as in today's environment organizations have to be continuously evolving. The external challenges of the environment forces organizations to mold themselves placing a premium on information/knowledge intensive work, necessitating continuous retraining and redeployment of the manpower. Knowledge Management also becomes important. The strategy with reference to knowledge creation, management and sharing needs to be clearly conceived, articulated and propagated. Organizations increasingly are part of a global village in their reach, orientation and concerns for this effective and efficient mobilization of knowledge and mix of transmission mechanisms need to be deployed to be effective in organizations continuously changing with the external forces.

Keywords: *Lifelong Learning, Environmental Forces, Global Village*

INTRODUCTION

Lifelong learning as a concept has recently received a lot of attention. It has however been viewed largely in the context of individuals and as to how they need to continuously learn and evolve in a knowledge economy. The concept places value on flexible learning strategies, multidisciplinary and flexible approaches to curricula and up gradation of skills to respond to the demands generated by the external environment. The external environment however affects not only individuals but the organizations as well. And to continue to remain relevant to the external system, organizations need to learn and evolve as much. This essay proposes to discuss issues involved in this phenomenon and possible strategies for the organizations aiming at strategic investments in this direction for their continued survival and growth. The emerging learning society and knowledge economy places a premium on analytical ability, information assimilation, knowledge generation and mobilization Morley, L. (2003). It is felt that these could be indicative of some of the options available to successful organizations of tomorrow. It is also argued that organizations that are successful in responding to this challenge will only be able to meet the test of continued relevance, sustainability and growth. The value in these organizations will be created essentially through intelligent creation, accumulation, management and application of knowledge.

THE EXTERNAL CHALLENGE

Organisations in today's world are faced with two challenges. Firstly the speed and the volume of the interactions and the transactions with the clients are far more intense and varied than ever before (Delors, 1996). This has been enabled by rapid developments in the areas of technology focusing on creation, management, analysis and communication of information. Secondly the world is increasingly a global village where productive assets can be deployed at the most cost effective location to produce a good or a service, which can be utilized at the most relevant or premium location. These two challenges by themselves are placing a premium on information/knowledge intensive work, necessitating continuous retraining and redeployment of the manpower.

Faced with these challenges, different organisations tend to respond differently. There are those that see these challenges as insurmountable hurdles and are not really able to respond to the challenge faced. These organizations simply go under. There is the second category that looks at these as challenges that need to be surmounted to sustain their business and maintain their performance. These organizations are able to adapt to some extent and survive. Then we have the third category, which views these new realities as opportunities. Such organisations ride on the new technologies and the opportunities provided by them to forge ahead of others and build competitive advantage for future. A knowledge-oriented organization that focuses on continuous learning for its people and its stakeholders is better placed to meet the challenges of tomorrow. In these organisations knowledge will increasingly be viewed and managed as a productive asset.

THE ORGANISATIONAL RESPONSE TO THE CHANGED REALITY

An organisation is a complex system, whose particular systems, processes, linkages with its stakeholders, organizational culture, etc., allow it to sustain, survive and grow in a complex socio-economic system. More and more organisations are now discovering that their continued relevance and sustainability depends on organizing a response system to the external stimuli in all its complexity with effective managing of internal variables mentioned above as a systemic whole (Bauman 2000). Thus an organization needs to evolve at all levels, be it technology, culture, systems, processes and people. The basic survival and sustainability of an organisation will depend on its competencies in terms of technology, information and the perceived wisdom regarding how to do things in a particular situation. This notion of evolution of an organization is totally independent of the type of organization it is. It is as much applicable to a business organization as to a non-government organization, a university, a research organization, an association or even organized religion.

While all the components of organizational system remain important to respond effectively to the environment, yet some are more difficult to organize then others. While the hardware aspects of buildings, machines, technology and the like are the easiest to put in place, a little more difficulty is experienced in evolving software aspects like systems, processes and operating procedures. The toughest part however remains in the human and cultural aspects of the organization. A great part of which is organized around organizational accumulated knowledge or generally perceived wisdom. The effective management of this knowledge is what is going to differentiate great organisations of tomorrow from others. All the successful organizations of tomorrow will be governed by what Peter Drucker calls the decisive competitive factor "The decisive competitive factor in the knowledge society will be the capabilities in acquisition and application of knowledge". The business of acquisition and application of knowledge however on the one hand is getting extremely organized on account of technology, yet on the other hand posing challenges on behavioral aspects of sharing knowledge. This is so as the cultural aspects in many societies (for example traditional, feudal and vertically organized societies like India) are not quite in harmony with the culture of sharing knowledge.

Nevertheless it is well recognized today that effective organizational response system to the external dynamics is an integrated value chain dealing with the management of knowledge. It would encompass soliciting, creating, searching, systematizing, storing, retrieving, redistributing, applying and eventually evaluating knowledge. This process however can only add value if it fits in with the overall organisational objectives and a generally agreed strategy to achieve them. Further to be meaningful, this process will need to be a continuous self-correcting mechanism.

KNOWLEDGE MANAGEMENT IN ORGANISATIONS

The knowledge utilization in an organisation is dependent on two factors. These are the extent of knowledge created, collected or acquired and the extent to which it is shared and mobilized across the organization. The effective value is a product of isolated knowledge pools and the velocity of their flow across the organization. Hence a learning organization needs to focus on both the augmentation of the individual knowledge banks and also their sharing across individuals and organizational units.

Technology today has broadly enhanced the access and availability of isolated knowledge resources in the organisations to be pooled and shared across work groups, locations and hierarchies. This has become possible due to enhanced connectivity and data mining tools like search engines and browsers. Propriety databases appropriately utilized with such technology are increasingly becoming a uniquely productive asset for many organizations. However the key determinant of success in all these initiatives is the extent to which such initiatives are manpower oriented. The fact that in any organization it is essentially the people who are both repository and users of the new information, systems need to be designed around people rather than the technology. The systems need to be designed to facilitate as well as encourage documenting and sharing of information, a culture of mentoring and creating an effective organizational knowledge pool.

Development of such systems and culture is critically dependent on the top management support for its nurture and to enable it to take root. Knowledge management can no longer be incidental to evolution of an organization, dependent on personal leadership style or strategic option taken by management at a particular point in time. The strategy with reference to knowledge creation, management and sharing needs to be clearly conceived, articulated and propagated. This can then logically lead to putting in place systems and tools to concretise the strategy adopted. For the system to be really successful it needs to integrate well with the functional and operational aspects of the organization. The system also needs to provide for its evaluation, mid-course correction, reorientation and periodic up gradation. Keeping in view the behavioural aspects, organizations can be well advised to put in place incentive systems to foster a culture of sharing, documenting, seeking and adapting information in their quest to emerge as knowledge based learning organizations.

This notion of knowledge management is quite different from the traditional pyramid oriented flow of information in the organizations. The focus here is clearly on a shift from an intellectual elite oriented organization to continuous development and evolution of manpower at all levels by way of sharing of knowledge. The real truth of the ancient Indian saying that knowledge is the only wealth that increases by sharing is only beginning to be realized today. The adaptive learning in such a system obviates reinventing the wheel from time to time. It can be hypothesized that this by itself should lead to an organization that is able to improve the quality of its response and shorten the response time to its clients and its environment (Schuller et al., 2004). These improvements in turn will provide a strategic advantage for the organizations focusing on the development and adoption of such systems.

GLOBAL VILLAGE AND THE LEARNING ORGANISATION

Organisations increasingly are part of a global village in their reach, orientation and concerns. This implies that these organizations have to increasingly face the challenge of diversity. Diversity however besides being a challenge, with which an organization must cope, also offers a critical resource that the organizations can use to build value for their customers and other stakeholders. Need based location specific innovations represent the creation of new knowledge in an organization. A large part of such adaptive responses can have long term value relevance for the organizations across locations and product offers. However despite an appreciation of the tremendous synergistic energy that can be unleashed by creating and mobilizing such intellectual capital, the operationalizing of such systems remains far below potential in most of the organizations.

Notwithstanding the fact that diversity is of value for learning and managing in today's dynamic and complex environment, it can also be dysfunctional. The diverse learnings and perspectives in an organization can unleash synergic forces only when the elements of diversity can be fused to yield a coherent perspective, vision, decision plan and action set. In the absence of such comprehension and capitalizing on diversity, organizations can only be left with a fractured mandate, compromised decisions, conflicts, delays and frustration. In order to ensure that the organizations can capitalize on diverse knowledge to yield decisions in terms of their quality and timeliness it is necessary that diverse knowledge resource pools are integrated.

Many effective mechanisms can be deployed to drive such integration of knowledge derived from diverse sources and locations. One option can be defining and cultivating a set of core values throughout the organization. Such a strategy can provide a common platform on which a cohesive and productive learning tool serving as a dialogue can be built among people from diverse cultural backgrounds and with diverse knowledge bases. Another integrative strategy can be a widespread distribution of ownership stake on a global basis in the organization. This option however is limited largely to commercial organizations only. A third option can be ensuring upward mobility in the manpower resources driven purely by meritocracy in a global context. Job rotation across geographic regions, functional aspects and product/service offers of an organization could provide the context to support this option. A softer option in building such integrative mechanisms is nurturing social and interpersonal ties among diversely placed people Lifelong Learning in Europe (2004).

The Social Dimensions of the Learning Organisation

The fact that in all organizations most knowledge starts as raw information, very often focus in an organization tends to be oriented towards information management. Very often this tends to place an undue emphasis on installation of ambitious information technology infrastructure as the only investment in a knowledge management and propagation system. However effective knowledge management depends only partly on the information technology based resources such as hardware, databases, search engines and artificial intelligence. Information Technology though important in knowledge management in any organization, represents only a part of the total picture and is far from a complete answer to the problem of knowledge management Halimi, S. (2005).

Though it can not be disputed that while information technology is perhaps the only viable mean to provide a linkage between widely spaced people in their locations or work content, yet it has limitations in its scope. The technology by itself is only a tool capable of being deployed effectively, under deployed or even wrongly deployed. Information Technology by its own market logic is available to all organisations and thus does not really provide by itself a sustainable competitive advantage. Sustainable advantage however can be found in the method of deployment of Information Technology, which could be conceptualized taking in account the logic of other factors relevant to the whole process OECD (1973, 1997).

The most important such factor is the social system of the organization. These social systems are the determinants of the expectations from the individuals (both formal and informal). Social systems shape the behaviour of the people in the system by signaling the desired norms of behaviour and the extent of freedom normally available to people in taking independent decisions. The system also indicates to the people in the organization as to which aspects of their behaviour patterns or work performances are more or less valued by the organization, what kind of people are more or less likely to be recruited or promoted by the organization, what are the expected notions of quality, and the interactive patterns preferred in an organisation Thus by way of its impact on people's motivations, abilities and behaviour the social system becomes critical to the whole learning process.

Various aspects of such a social systems are culture, structure, information systems, reward systems, processes, people and leadership. The systemic aspect of these elements of the social system is that these elements need to be viewed as an integrated package wherein various elements have an interactive dimension to them.

BUILDING AN EFFECTIVE LEARNING ORGANISATION

With the speed of knowledge creation and its redundancy ever becoming faster a learning organization must excel at both creating and acquiring new knowledge coupled with a very quick sharing and mobilizing of the newly acquired knowledge. The knowledge generation is required for preparation of the organizational response to the impinging challenges and its mobilization is required for its most timely and widespread application leading to efficiency and effectiveness.

Some of the tools that the organizations can use for maximizing knowledge generation and accumulation are setting of tough targets that would necessitate innovative thinking by their very definition. This innovative thinking can then be encouraged by generous incentives to compensate for the risk involved in the situation. This innovative thinking needs to be further supported by a system that empowers people to engage in innovative thinking, by provisioning appropriate resources and time. Another enabling aspect that needs to be fostered is a culture that encourages willingness to take risks. This can be done by earmarking well-defined areas of discretion with acceptable levels of risks for the organization. Innovative thinking can further be nurtured by creating a shelf of ideas generated, which even if not found relevant immediately by the concerned part of the organization are still available to other units or functions of the organization for immediate or future exploitation.

While this knowledge generation and accumulation is of value, yet to really unlock its potential it needs to be mobilized across the organization. Some of the strategies that can be deployed to encourage this are firstly providing cultural context that abhors knowledge hoarding and treats knowledge disseminators as stars. Knowledge needs to be treated as an organizational resource and not a proprietary of a fringe unit or a person. Secondly group based generous incentives for innovative thinking are positively correlated with the culture of knowledge sharing and hence need to be encouraged. A third strategy aimed at facilitating knowledge mobilization is the codification and documentation of new knowledge. The fact that star performers and knowledge creators are often not the most willing document writers, specific investments are required to be made in this direction. And lastly to ensure effective and efficient mobilization of knowledge a mix of transmission mechanisms need to be deployed to suit the type of knowledge being mobilised. For example while the codified knowledge can be very efficiently and effectively mobilized by document exchange, people interactive mechanisms are required to be provided for mobilizing uncodified, unstructured or nascent knowledge.

REFERENCES

[1] Baumann, Zygmunt (2000). Liquid Modernity. Cambridge, UK, Polity Press.

[2] Delors, J. (1996). Learning: The Treasure Within. Paris, UNESCO.

[3] Halimi, S. (2005). L'Enseignement supérieur au Royaume Uni [Higher Education in the United Kingdom], Paris, Ophrys et Ploton.

[4] Lifelong Learning in Europe, Journal edited by Kauko Hämäläinin. Helsinki, Finland, KVS Foundation.

[5] Morley, L. (2003). Quality and Power in Higher Eeducation. Maidenhead, UK, Open University Press.

[6] OECD. (1973). Recurrent Education: A Strategy for Lifelong Learning. Paris, OECD. OECD. (1997). Education Policy Analysis 1997. Paris, OECD.

[7] Schuller, Tom et al. (2004). The Benefits of Learning. London, Routledge Falmer.

Empirical Study of Work-Life Balance of Paid Workers in Banking and the Financial Services Sector with Special Reference to Women

Pranava Prakash and Somya Bhargava

IILM Graduate School of Management, Greater Noida

ABSTRACT

In the contemporary ear of industrialization and still further of knowledge economy the individuals roles as employee and family person has taken a huge shift. The line of separation between job and personal life has blurred to an extant that it has become extremely difficult for work force to manage the both leading to increased absenteeism and reduced productivity. The situation of women is even worse considering her traditional role of an house wife with the newly induced role as a bread earner. This paper explores the situation of paid workers in banking and financial sector with reference to work-life balance. It brings to fore an urgent requirement of intervention to address the work life balance in women.

Keywords: *Paid Workers, Banking Sector, Finance Sector, Work Life Balance, Women Workers*

INTRODUCTION

Since the end of hunting and fruit gathering as the only source of survival and emergence of animal rearing and agriculture work started to emerge as separate from life. It emerged as an activity in which people engaged themselves so that they can earn enough food and meat to eat and share with family, friends and the tribes men. It was a point of separation of livelihood from job. A man was working till the end of the day to spend his after work hours at leisure. It was a great source of development by providing luxury of time, security of food and physical safety which allowed men to indulge in higher order desires and a host of self actualization needs came out.

This separation of work from life further increased in the era of industrialization where gradually human physical effort was transferred to various machine through the use of power generation and harnessing of power through various means like steam engine to start with and most sophisticated computer controlled automated machines running on fossil fuel, renewable fuels and nuclear power. This development worked in multiple ways. It provides people with means to earn and contribute to social well being through different ways and spend, splurge and consume more and more which require him to earn evermore. The rise of standard of life quietly raised the number of hours to maintain and funds that life style.

Since the time of world war two women joined the industrial work force with great zeal and élan but that also meant that they had to work harder to manage their traditional role as home maker and newer roles as career women. They reacted to this situation in two ways. Some choose to join the work force in what was considered to be softer jobs like shop assistance, education and banking and manage their life with support of additional income to their house hold without too much of sacrifice from their regular call of duty as mother, wife and home maker. Some other women chose slightly difficult world of manly jobs which required them to travel extensively, toil hard in office and slog no less than their male counterpart to earn respect, admiration and desired growth at the work place. This did not mean they freed themselves form household chores. This raised the image of super moms who were stretching themselves impossibly to achieve best work as well as home. This gave rise to immense stress to manage and balance the work and life.

This situation applies on both men and women but definitely more to women than men, which prompts to do research to find out the impact of job related demand and work life balance on women.

LITERATURE REVIEW

Diverse countries like India, Japan, the Netherlands, Norway, South Africa, the UK and The USA – the issue faced is same and the challenge, how to create a balance between work space requirements and the requirements of employees role as a family person is equally daunting everywhere. The way out is not to provide a short term solution but to create a lasting long term solution a multi stakeholder approach needs to be built based a whole relook into the situation of paid work and the perceived need of economic competitiveness to be achieved (Gamble, Richenda, 2006). It has been reported that overwork causes stress related absenteeism, reduced creativity, lowered retention level, apathy towards customer service leading to reduced customer satisfaction and a tendency in employees to ignore ethical conducts. These factors add up to create a working environment which is less than adequately productive and the friction between the relationship of employee and employer is forever on rise. Increased thrust on understanding the need of engaging employees and managers and creating right template is being felt (Clutterbuck, David, 2003). Another view point to emerge from academia as is highlighted in the blog on Harvard business Review by Prof. Riordan of University of Kentucky is that it is no longer important just to achieve the work life balance but now it is imperative to achieve an effectiveness in both work and life. She strongly advocates defining success in all category of life to achieve a well rounded set of accomplishment. Her strategy include building high level of control in all the activity, be it paid work or work done for pleasure and family. (Riordan, 2013) In India the status of work life balance is equally grim. A study conducted among university students in down south Karnataka found that the balance of work and life is completely skewed with students finding it increasingly difficult to balance and achieve a satisfactory growth. (Kumar, Paramashivaiah, 2011) Some study based on the research by London School of Economics done in Australia employees when compared between the employees who are techno-enthusiast and those who are technophobe, suggests that internet helps employee striking a right balance between paid work and home responsibilities easier. They found that people use technology to better their life and create better adaptability. (Coget, Jean Franco, 2011) The research conducted in India to compare the work life balance in Indian companies to the American and European companies found out that Indian companies rank lower in the work life balance. Their attention to the need of work life balance is not pronounced in their HR policies. It also concluded that even government consideration towards employee working hour is on harsher side in India as compared to Western countries when compared on parental leave parameter (V. Chandra, 2012). Another study conducted in America focuses on creating work life system and how this helps achieve work life balance. It finds that creating a meaningful work for all employees is essential to solve the issue of work life balance by creating better employee engagement (Munn, Sunny L., 2013). From real estate environment the research suggest that setting goal, keeping a structured plan to spend time with family and creating a to-do list helped the employees. It also suggests that there is a great variation in the effective techniques in managing work and life according to uses by individual employees (Burg-Brown, Stephanie, 2013). A study among IT and ITES employees in India found that the strong feeling about work, the dependents in the family and being absent from work are among the factors which contribute towards strong feeling of having a balance between work and life yet they failed to find any relation between work environment and work-life balance (Pandu A, 2013). A study which focused on finding out relationship between individuals' privacy orientations within their families and their experience in their home and work place concluded that these are closely linked and it was positively linked with work life balance as well (Carmon, Anna F., 2013). A study which explored the psychological factors of remote e-workers' who were most off from the physical space of their deposal of work, job effectiveness, well-being and work life balance found that there is a adverse impact on employee well being because of excess work and relatively less time to recuperate. It was also found that increasingly the line between work and family life blurred in those workers which led to a continuous work pressure on the employee affecting even health and causing emotional stress (Grant, Cristine A., 2013). A research was conducted in Australia to assess the influence of several social factors on the perception of work life balance of employees. This research studied the role of child care, the care of elderly, the role of gender and part time work. This found that compared to women the contemporary men workforce is finding is difficult to manage the balance between the work and family life (Hayman, Jeremy, 2013).

There are also some researches which report that employees perceive gender sensitive policies as special treatment meted out to parents and women at the cost of employees who do not come in these categories (Smithson, Janet, 2005). Rise of opportunities in the sector of new media has raised hopes among the parents and care providing people to take up paid work and get evolved meaningfully. It reasserts that though new media has created opportunities to extend the scope of work the gender divide still remains and work environment is still not so favorable to women paid workers (Perrons, Diane, 2003).

OBJECTIVE OF THE RESEARCH

This research studies the challenges faced by women paid workers in Indian context in the Banking and financial service sector to understand the gender dimension of work life balance. The research also wants to measure the extent and ease of women in handling the balance between work and life and the strategies which are emerging in their course of action to adjust their life according to the professional requirement of continuous challenge to compete and concern for family in the different stages of marriage, spouse and parenting and being a care provider to elderly parents.

METHODOLOGY

The study was made using a questionnaire. The content validity and internal consistency of the questionnaire was checked by senior HR professionals of vice president level in banking and academicians training banking professionals. The 456 paid workers in Banking and financial service sector were administered a questionnaire. It had questions related with work life balance. A separate detailed interview was undertaken to probe deeper into the strategies used by women workers to cope with the challenges of work life balance.

DISCUSSION ON SAMPLE

The research was conducted by non probability snow ball sampling spread over seven cities, Delhi, Lucknow, Patna, Jaipur, Mumbai, Goa and Chennai. HR department was requested to recommend employee and then referrals of those employees were taken. Their response rate was 78 percent. Out of 456 workers Male 289 and Female 167.

Profile of Respondents who Participated in the Research			
Variable	*Modality Variable*	*Absolute Frequency*	*Percentage*
Gender	Male	289	63.37719
	Female	167	36.62281
Social Origin	Urban	315	69.07895
	Rural	141	30.92105

Profile of Respondents who Participated in the Research			
Variable	*Modality Variable*	*Absolute Frequency*	*Percentage*
Family stage	Parents	236	51.75439
	Married non parents	117	25.65789
	Unmarried	103	22.58772
Care Status	Living with parents	187	41.00877
	Living without parents	269	58.99123
		(N= 456)	

ANALYSIS AND KEY RESULTS

On Ability to do Justice to Kids

Majority of paid workers feel they are not able to do justice to kids.

Highly satisfied	52
Satisfied	87
Do not know	117
Dissatisfied	143
Highly dissatisfied	57
	456

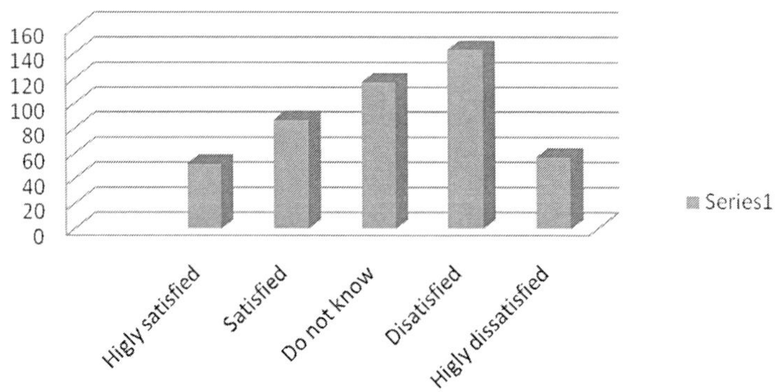

Fig. 1: Ability to do Justice to Kids

Ability to Get Quality Time to Sleep

Result clearly show paid workers are over worked. They are not getting enough sleep which can ultimately lead to reduced productivity.

Highly satisfied	31
Satisfied	103
Do not know	87
Dissatisfied	167
Highly dissatisfied	68
	456

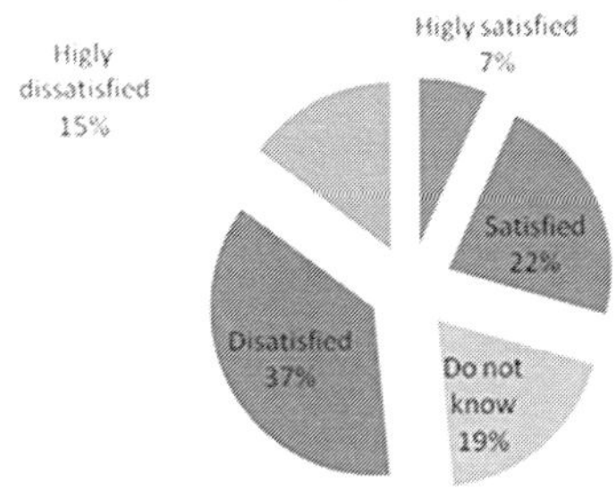

Fig. 2: Ability to Spend Quality Time to Sleep

On Being Forced to Take Work, Back Home

This clearly again show how overworked the employees are. Most of them have to take their work back home.

Highly satisfied	30
Satisfied	63
Do not know	76
Dissatisfied	172
Highly dissatisfied	115
Total	456

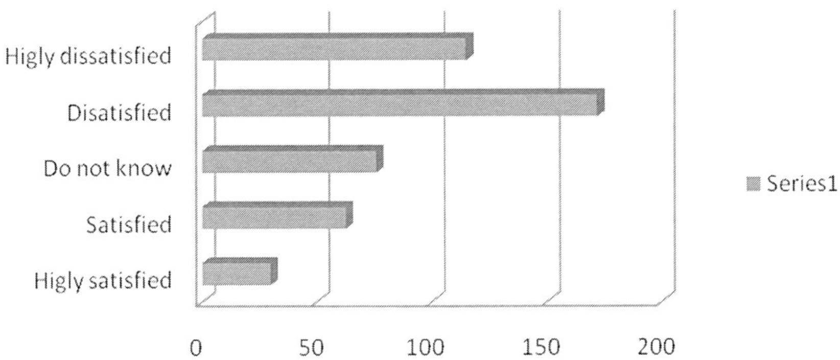

Fig. 3: On Being Forced to Take Work Back

On Ability to Take Care of Elderly Parents

Most of the employees feel they are unable to take care of their parents, which leads to dissatisfaction, annoyance and absenteeism.

Highly satisfied	57
Satisfied	89
Do not know	32
Dissatisfied	187
Highly dissatisfied	91
	456

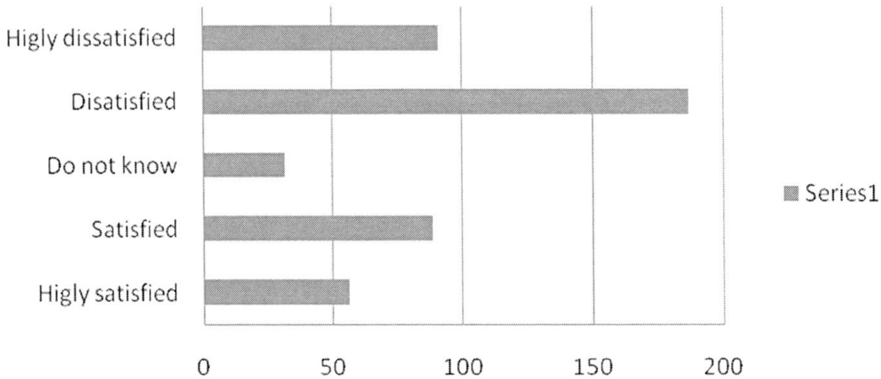

Fig. 4: On Ability to Take Care of Elderly Parents

On the Ability to Spend Time Socially

This again comes as a shocker. Most employees are unhappy with their role as a member of society which implies that social support system is on decline which will lead to increased employee vulnerability.

Highly satisfied	23
Satisfied	45
Do not know	125
Dissatisfied	165
Highly dissatisfied	98
Total	456

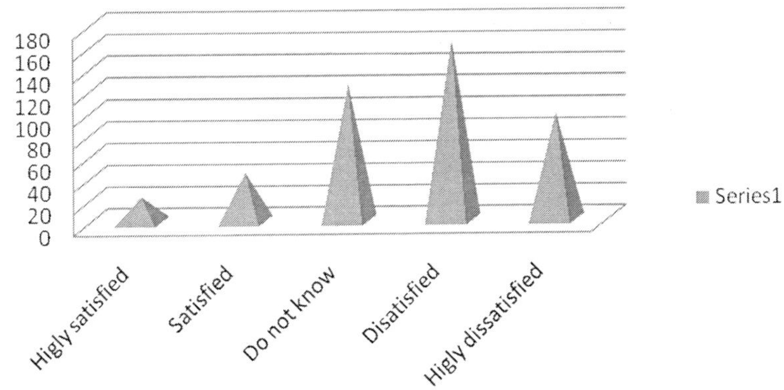

Fig. 5: Ability to Spend Time Socially

This research tests three hypotheses. First there is no significant difference between genders regarding work-life balance. Second hypothesis says there is no significant difference between different stages of family. Third hypothesis says there is no significant difference between the paid workers in different care status.

H1: There is no difference between gender regarding perception towards ability to balance work and life

H2: There is no difference between workers coming from different stages of family regarding ability to balance work and life

H3: There is no difference between workers coming from different care status

T- test for independent means was conducted for the entire hypothesis. H1 and H3 were rejected. H2 was accepted.

Detailed interview with the workers revealed that for women it is increasingly being difficult to balance work and life. They are outsourcing the house hold chores as possible. Their sleep hours have significantly reduced. Though they feel competent enough to progress in career they feel their family responsibility is somehow a hindrance in their professional growth. They stretch themselves between family and work and most of them feel they do not get enough time to take care of their body.

DISCUSSION

Result suggests gender has a role to play when ability to balance work and life is concerned and same is true when a worker has to care for his parents. But rearing a child has no such difficulty. It may be due to age factor because worker is relatively young when he has to raise a child as compared to when his parents are old enough to be cared about.

LIMITATIONS

The study used non probability snow ball sampling due to time constrains. Many interviewees dropped due to their professional requirement. Some women employees were not forthcoming in sharing their experience for the fear of disciplinary action. These things make the research difficult to generalize to pan India.

REFERENCES

[1] Gambles, Richenda, The Myth of Work Life Balance: The Challenge of Our Time for Men, Women and Society, Richenda Gamble, Suzan Lewis and Rhona Rapoport, Jon Wiley & Sons, 2006.

[2] David Clutterbuck, Managing Work-life Balance: A Guide for HR in Achieving Organisational and Individual Change, CIPD Publishing, 2003, London, 1e.

[3] Blogs.hbr.org/2013/06/work-life-balance-isnt-the-poi/

[4] A Research Study on Managing Work-Life Balance, Kumar, Aravind S., Shivakumar, P. Parmeshshivaiyah, *International Journal of Knowledge & Research in Management & E-Commerce*, Vol. 1, No. 2 (2011).

[5] Technophobe vs. Techno-enthusiast: Does the Internet Help or Hinder the Balance Between Work and Home Life?, Coget, Jean Franco, *Academy of Journal Perspectives*, Feb 2011, Vol. 25 Issue 1, pp. 95-96.

[6] Work-life Balance: Eastern and Western Perspectives, V. Chandra, *The International Journal of Human Resource Management*. Vol. 23, No. 5, March 2012, 1040-1056.

[7] Unveiling the Work-Life System: The Influence of Work-Life Balance on Meaningful Work, Munn, Sunny L., *Advances in Developing Human Resources*, Nov 2013, Vol. 15 Issue 4, pp. 401-417.

[8] Work-Life Balance, Burg-Brown, Stephanie, *Journal of Property Management*, Jul/Aug 2013, Vol. 78 Issue 4, pp. 48-53.

[9] Assessing Work-Life Balance among IT & ITeS Women Professionals, Pandu A., Balu A., Poorani, K., *Indian Journal of Industrial Relation* , Vol. 48, No. 4, April, 2013.

[10] Privacy Orientations: A look at Family Satisfaction, Job Satisfaction, and Work-Life Balance, *Communication Reports*, July Dec 2013, Vol. 26 Issue 2, pp. 101-112.

[11] An Exploration of the Psychological factor Affecting Remote E-worker's Job Effectiveness, Well-being and Work-Life Balance, Grant, Christine A., Wallace, Louise M., Spurgeon, Peter C., *Employee Relations*, 2013/ Vol. 35, Issue 5, pp. 527-546.

[12] Gender, Caring, Part Time Employment and Work, Life Balance, Hayman, Jeremy; Rasmussen, Erling. *Employment Relations Record.* 2013, Vol. 13 Issue 1, pp. 45-5.

[13] Discourses of Work-Life Balance: Negotiating 'Genderblind' Term in Organizations, Smithson, Janet, Stokoe, Elizabeth H., *Gender, Work & Organization* Vol. 12, Issue 2, pp. 147-168, March 2005.

[14] The New Economy and the Work-Life Balance: Conceptual Explorations and a Case Study of New Media, Diane Perrons, Gender Work & Organization, Vol. 10, Issue 1., pp. 65-93.

An Inclusive and Accessible Workplace – HR initiatives at Wipro

Manisha Vijayran

Era Business School, Dwarka, New Delhi

> *"A great place to work is where you trust the people you work for, have a pride in what you do, and enjoy the people you work with."* – *Robert Levering*

> *"In order to meet the needs of customers, employees and stakeholders in today's business environment, diversity and inclusion efforts must be integrated into overall business strategy."*
> – *Ronald E. Harrison, retired senior Vice President of PepsiCo & Chairman of the Diversity institute*

ABSTRACT

Globalization, rapid change in technologies, demand for skills, talent and ethnic diversifications have changed the workforce employment scenario of today's era. That is why; organizations have started realizing the significance of creating an inclusive and accessible workplace than ever before. As per experts say, in IT sector, approximately 30% of the whole working population is consisted of women, which is way ahead than that of other industries as far as the gender neutrality and sensitivity is concerned.

For the purpose of study, Wipro, an organization that values diversity and incorporate inclusiveness in its culture is selected.

This article highlights inclusive workplace initiatives taken by Wipro for People with Disabilities(PwD) and women and enabling it to receive "15th Hellen Keller Award" by NCPEDP, "2013 ESCAP-Sasakawa Award" and NASSCOM Corporate Award for Excellence in Diversity and Inclusion 2012.

Keywords: *Constitutionalism, Social Integration, Manpower Acquisition, Workplace Design, Flexible Work Schedules*

INTRODUCTION

An inclusive workplace is one where employees from different generations, gender, nationalities and cultures work together in the same organization.

It is a place where the basic principles of human rights, i.e. principles of respect, dignity, fairness, participation, autonomy, transparency and non-discrimination are encouraged and are very much a part of the organization culture.

Here, everyone is treated equally irrespective of whatever is their nationality, place of residence, sex, national or ethnic origin, colour, religion, language, or any other status.

Benefits of Inclusivity in an Organization

- Organizations enhance their brand image/reputation
- Able to attract best talent in the industry.
- Employees become more committed, motivated and engaged.
- Enhance job satisfaction of employees.
- Improve physical and psychological health of employees which generates positive feeling
- Build environment of openness and trust.
- Retain staff
- Reduction in turnover of employees.
- Increase in the productivity, profitability and success of the organization.
- Enhance the potential and performance of employees and appreciates the differences between them.

Initiatives/Activities: that can be undertaken by an organization for creating an inclusive workplace:

- **Management Commitment-** Top management should depict commitment, accountability for building inclusive workplace and communicate its significance.
- **Manpower acquisition:** The recruitment should focus on equality and no discrimination is to be made on basis of caste, creed, religion and sex.
- **Workplace activities:** Activities based on common interests like sports, hobbies, etc., should be organized that enables interaction between employees of different profiles and departments.
- **Workplace design:** Create open office environment and spaces for employees to meet informally (e.g. Common rooms, pantries) so as to facilitate interaction between employees.
- **Flexible work schedules:** Flexi time, flexi place, compressed work week, telecommuting, job sharing, part-time employment and other types of work schedules can be followed to provide freedom to employee in prioritizing their work schedules.
- **Buddy system:** The existing job holders can help the new employees to settle down in the organization by providing necessary information, guidance and responding to their queries/questions.
- **Employee networks:** Help the employees to connect, receive support and career guidance by making resource groups and mentorship program.

- **Awards and recognition:** Recognize the efforts of high performers to create positive attitudes and behaviors in other employees.
- **Manage employee grievances:** Establish grievance handling mechanisms/procedures so that the discontents, dis-satisfaction and problems of employees could be redressed as soon as they arise.
- **Active involvement, participation and consultation of employees:** Everyone in the organization from top level to junior level management should be treated with respect and dignity. An equal opportunity should be provided to them to present their ideas, opinions and suggestions before taking any final decision or drawing up a plan of action so that they feel valued.
- **Safe and healthy working conditions:** Adequate attention should be paid by an organization for making healthy and safe work environment that helps in the smooth functioning and increasing productivity of employees.
- **Training, development and growth:** Chalk out suitable training and development programs, career paths and advancement opportunities for entire workforce without any partiality.
- **Social integration in the work organization:** Employees of all classes, religions, races and designations must be treated equally on a social platform as relationships between and among the employees is an indicator of healthy work organization. Hence, opportunities must be given for formal and informal interactions so that egalitarian/democratic environment can persist.
- **Constitutionalism:** It relates to organizational framework of norms that influence the freedom of an individual employee. The norms and tradition of an organization must maintain freedom of speech, equity and freedom to disagree of on certain issues of an employee.
- **Work and the total life space:** Working continuously for erratic long hours causes psychological and physiological strains in employees. Thus, they should not tax their systems for long hours at a stretch and organization should think of the ways to make a balance between personal and professional life of their employees.

WIPRO

Wipro Ltd. is a leading Information Technology, Consulting and Outsourcing company which offers solutions to facilitate its clients to carry out business in a better and improved manner.

Wipro welcomes diversity and inculcate the environment of the area/geography/location it works in. This logic of inclusiveness creates an environment of creativity and innovation. Diversity is a basic mantra that Wipro observes and disseminates it transparently to the numerous global markets, wherever it is operating and their efforts clearly depict this.

- Gender
- Nationality
- People with Disabilities
- Underprivileged

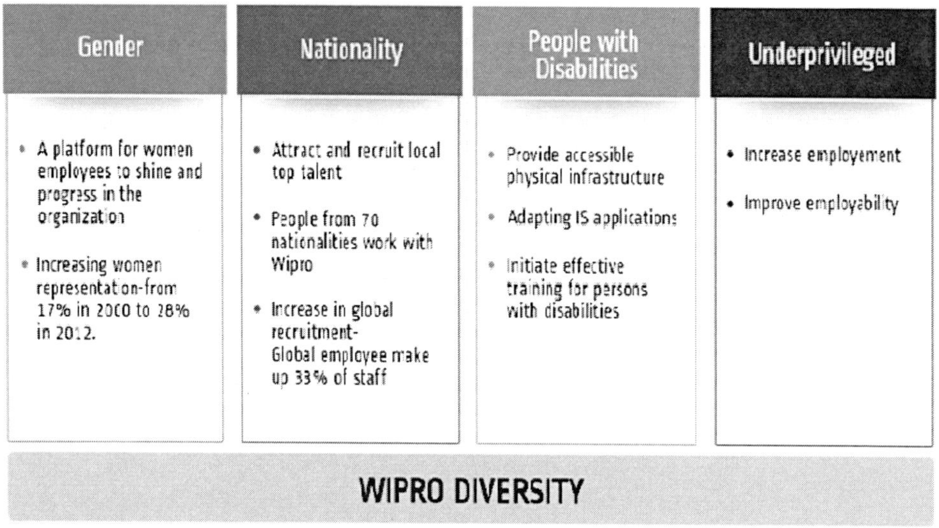

Source: http://careers.wipro.com/hotjobs/diversity_drive.htm

Initiatives Taken by Wipro as a Part of its Diversity Drive

1. **People with Disability (PwD) Hiring Event:** Wipro provide equal opportunities to all candidates. It take pleasure in making certain that the talent they consider for employment is purely on the basis of their knowledge, skills, qualifications and competencies. As part of its diversity initiative, Wipro is going a step further by not only providing employment opportunities to deserving individuals with disabilities but also urging them to maintain long term careers with it.
2. **Special Hiring Drive for Women:** Wipro also encourages women candidates who are looking forward to rejoin IT industry after a career break.

Initiatives Taken by Wipro for Making it Accessible Workplace for People with Disabilities (PwD)

1. **Accessible Physical Infrastructure:** Wipro has benchmarked its various campuses with global guidelines for barrier-free access and is making changes to its facilities. It has included the UN standards in determining that its infrastructure is accessible for the physically challenged.
2. **People Policies:** Its people policies were audited by experts to encourage inclusivity and to communicate relevant information to people with disabilities. In all, 56 policies were audited and many were modified to provide reasonable accommodation.
3. **IS:** It has adapted IS applications to connect with typical software used in the organization so that IT resources and information are made easily available to the

physically challenged. It is transforming its applications, websites and career portals based on the WCAG 2.0 guidelines to provide complete accessibility to persons with special needs.

4. **Talent Transformation:** It has trained its trainers and library staff to be inclusive in instructor led programs, streamlined its administrative processes to enable specific accommodation where required, and developed curriculum that would help induct and assimilate people with disabilities .
5. **Talent Acquisition Process:** It has streamlined its processes to be more inclusive as it interface with prospective employees with disabilities.

Source: http://www.wipro.org/ecology/diversity/people-with-disabilities.html

Wipro's Achievements for Being an Inclusive and Assessable Workplace

Wipro Receives 15th NCPEDP-Shell Helen Keller Awards

Wipro Ltd. declared that it has been recognized as a role model organization by the Helen Keller awards. The National Centre for Promotion of Employment for Disabled People (NCPEDP) also conferred the 15th Hellen Keller Award to Wipro employee, Ankit Rajiv Jindal.

Instituted in 1999, every year the NCPEDP-Shell Helen Keller awards honors individuals or organizations who are working towards helping people with disabilities find positions of equality and dignity in the workplace.

Wipro has been hiring persons with disabilities and providing them with necessary support on an individual basis to help them realize their potential, for many years now. The company has also supported employees who may have sustained disability during the course of their employment and provided them with necessary support to enable them to continue their work adequately. Inspired by the UN/DPI theme "Nothing about us without us", Wipro is now consciously involving persons with disabilities in reviewing, re-designing and sustaining the company's "Persons with Disabilities" charter.

Ankit Rajiv Jindal is the first marketing manager with visual impairment at Wipro and was hired from Faculty of management Studies, Delhi University in 2011. Technology has been a great enabler and equalizer for Ankit who leverages it extensively to perform his work and personal tasks.

Isaac George, Vice-President and Human Resources Head, Wipro InfoTech said, "It is a matter of immense pride that Wipro has won the NCPEDP-Shell Helen Keller Award under the Category: Role Model Companies/Organizations. Wipro currently employs over 450 persons with disabilities. Many functions have collaborated to create the opportunity for them to pursue mainstream careers through a supporting framework of accessible software applications, physical infrastructure, policies, training and culture building initiatives. This reflects the importance that Wipro accords inclusion, and this award recognizes the spirit of all Wiproites who joined hands to create a more inclusive workplace."

Source: http://www.wipro.com/newsroom/Wipro-receives-15th-NCPEDP-Shell-Helen-Keller-awards

Wipro has received the '2013 ESCAP-Sasakawa Award for Disability-Inclusive Business in Asia and the Pacific', in the category 'Disability-Inclusive Multinational Enterprise'.

The award for Disability-Inclusive Business was established by ESCAP in cooperation with The Nippon Foundation (TNF) and the Asia-Pacific Development Center on Disability (APCD) to recognize and honour companies that have made a significant breakthrough in engaging and hiring people with disabilities in their daily operations. The award is an initiative that views persons with disabilities as an untapped workforce.

Wipro was identified amongst nominations from across 62 countries for its initiatives in including employees with disabilities in its business model, enabling mainstream careers for them and for supporting them through accessible software applications, according to a company statement. **Isaac George, Vice-President and Human Resources Head, Wipro InfoTech said:** "We currently employ over 450 persons with disabilities. They have the opportunity to pursue mainstream careers through the supporting framework of accessible software applications, physical infrastructure, policies, training and culture-building initiatives."

Source: http://www.thehindubusinessline.com/industry-and-economy/info-tech/wipro-wins-award-for-disabilityinclusive-hr-policy/article5451647.ece

Wipro Wins NASSCOM Corporate Award for Excellence in Diversity and Inclusion 2012

The NASSCOM Corporate Awards for Excellence in Diversity and Inclusion honors IT and BPO organizations that have made a significant breakthrough in promoting inclusion. This award creates a platform for organizations to share their experiences and initiatives in enabling employment opportunities for the disabled.

Isaac George, Vice President - HR and Head, Persons with Disabilities (PwD) Initiatives, Wipro Ltd. said, "This award is a reflection of our sustained efforts in making Wipro more inclusive and creating meaningful careers for persons with disabilities. It also recognizes the contribution of many people, and we hope that this would spur us on to even greater accountability and momentum."

Wipro has introduced several initiatives to support the careers of persons with disabilities. These include making physical and IT infrastructure accessible, transforming software applications to suit people with disabilities, designing more inclusive training programs and building awareness through campaigns.

Wipro constantly works towards creating an inclusive environment at the workplace, which helps and supports persons with disabilities to take on a wide variety of roles.

Source: http://www.wipro.com/newsroom/Wipro-Wins-NASSCOM-Corporate-Award-for-Excellence-in-Diversity-and-Inclusion-2012

Initiatives Taken by Wipro for Making it Gender Balance Organization

According to Sunita R. Cherian, Vice President – Human Resources, Head - Gender Diversity, Wipro, "Diversity and Inclusion is a key pillar at Wipro and is evident by the way of life and work at Wipro: A diverse workforce is a reflection of a changing world and marketplace. A true celebration of diversity can best happen in an environment that allows for the expression of individual talents. Gender Diversity is a key chapter of our Diversity & Inclusion charter and initiatives. It ensures that women get equal opportunity to compete, perform and a choice of roles; nurture careers and thus actively build this pool. While Wipro believes and promotes a culture of meritocracy - this focus particularly helps new comers understand how a process of merit works as well. Over the years, our women employee population has seen an increase and is now almost 30% of our total employees. While this has helped create more opportunities for women, we believe this is not enough. It's important to enable them to grow and build meaningful and enduring careers in the organization.

Women of Wipro

On the basis of the experience of dealing with thousands of women employees, their exit interviews and the findings of this survey, Wipro evolved a gender inclusivity program called Women of Wipro, or WOW as it is popularly known. The "Women of

Wipro" program aims to bring together women executives from across Wipro and channel their passion for personal and social transformation towards building sustainable careers. WOW's philosophy on gender inclusivity is simple – aspire to create a sensitive organization where men and women alike can flourish and grow in their careers with a holistic approach towards performance and work.

WOW has crafted a segmented approach towards Gender diversity focusing on 3 major themes according to the life-stage of the employee – Wipro's Women Focused Initiatives 2012:

- **Exposure (early career stage):** Initiatives to encourage and inspire women to "conquer the world" e.g. Fuelling ambition in women through "WOW Speaker Series", structured job rotations and networking opportunities.
- **Flexibility (mid-career stage):** Initiatives to ensure women can balance work and personal lives with an opportunity to grow with the organization. E.g. extended maternity leave, transfers to ensure family stays together, on-ramping and off-ramping (women leaving and coming back from maternity leave), working from satellite offices and telecommuting.

- **Empowerment (advanced career stage)** – Initiatives to make work more meaningful and making a difference. E.g. Leadership grooming and formal mentoring with top management, Succession planning on women talent pipeline, Women in Leadership workshops and the recently launched "Career Conversations"

Governance

The diversity council begun in 2008 has now evolved to be part of the organization's sustainability council, thus driving the focus on gender diversity imperative. The diversity council meets every quarter where all diversity and inclusion initiatives are tabled and discussed for further action.

Women of Wipro Micro Site

The Women of Wipro micro site is a treasure trove of information pertaining to Women @ Wipro, their achievements and thoughts. There are 4 sections to it – WOW Soar Higher, Juggle Better, Reach Further and WoW Is Healthier, where articles and initiatives are showcased. There is a dedicated WOW bloggers community today, passionate Wiproites who blog about gender issues and challenges around. Discussion boards on topics like Career, Parenting and Hobbies have seen an overwhelming participation from women and men employees.

Mentoring for Women

A mentoring program for high-potential women in middle management, this program has been instrumental in grooming several key women leaders in the organisation to take up senior management positions. The program focuses on overall development - especially perspective development, networking, creating visibility and impact for the organisation. The mentors and mentees in this program have undergone a dedicated training – "Mentoring for Success", which helped in setting the context and expectations with the participants. They were also empowered with a "Mentoring Toolkit" to supplement their learning experience during the program.

Women in Leadership Workshop

These workshops were based on the inputs from the research study undertaken to understand the issues/dilemmas often faced by successful career women, by interviewing women leaders across industry and geographies. While women executives are busy gaining skill and expertise, we have simultaneously organized exclusive workshops for developing sensitivity among managers covering middle and senior management so that there is a greater receptivity towards gender balance.

Career Conversations

The recently launched Career conversations is aimed at creating awareness on different career paths and setting holistic goals which will enable women to take right career decisions if at cross-roads. The self-awareness and self-confidence it builds helps women take ownership of their careers

Diversity Education

Diversity appreciation workshops, gender inclusion talks, WOW speaker series, the IWD celebration globally has helped raise awareness among Wiproites. "Xperience

Wipro" over Facebook and Twitter has these celebrations to the world outside. An e-Module to help understand diversity at the workplace and what constitutes inclusive behavior was designed and is now a mandatory course for all employees to ensure sensitization at all levels in the organization.

Source: http://www.indousstf.org/pdf/Wipro.pdf

CONCLUSION

There is an increase in knowledge of people about inclusive and accessible workplace, the benefits it offers and means for accomplishing it. Wipro completely realize the significance of providing equal opportunities to all the people without partiality of any type. Its manpower requisition policy ensures that it "hires employees without regard to their race, color, religion, national origin, citizenship, age, sex, marital status, ancestry, physical or mental disability, medical condition, socio-economic background or sexual orientation."

REFERENCES

[1] http://www.mom.gov.sg/Documents/employment-practices/WDM/Managers_Guide.pdf

[2] http://www.indousstf.org/pdf/Wipro.pdf

[3] http://www.wipro.com/newsroom/Wipro-Wins-NASSCOM-Corporate-Award-for-Excellence-in-Diversity-and-Inclusion-2012

[4] http://www.thehindubusinessline.com/industry-and-economy/info-tech/wipro-wins-award-for-disabilityinclusive-hr-policy/article5451647.ece

[5] http://www.wipro.com/newsroom/Wipro-receives-15th-NCPEDP-Shell-Helen-Keller-awards

[6] http://www.wipro.org/ecology/diversity/people-with-disabilities.html

[7] http://careers.wipro.com/hotjobs/diversity_drive.htm

e-HR: Towards Accessibility and Creating HR Value

Puja Sareen

Ansal University, Gurgaon

ABSTRACT

Human Resource Management function has undergone an immense transformation in the last decade. The prime reasons for this transformation include globalization of economy, emphasis on product and service quality, workforce diversity, outsourcing trends and inexorable power of technology to transform the Human Resource function in an organization. To meet the growing demands of their profession, the Human Resource (HR) professionals need to be strategic business partners, lead change in the organization, teach HR competencies to line managers and most importantly, leverage technology in the delivery of HR services to employees. They must quickly respond to changes in business by making workforce related decisions based on real-time information, decisions that align corporate strategies with team and individual goals, supporting employees in all phases of the employee lifecycle. In the present times, the HR professionals are looking to technology and the information it provides, to help them empower employees, make HR data accessible and available to employees in a real-time environment, drive decisions that will lead to success of the organization and create value for the HR function as a whole. The combination of the need to work more efficiently, on one hand, and the possibilities of technology on the other, has resulted in the swift development of e-HR systems. This paper gives a background of HRM, the journey from traditional HR towards e-HR and integration of HR and technology in current scenario. The paper highlights the essence of e-HR, which lies in the devolution of HR functions to management and employees.

Keywords: *Organisation, Employee, Accessibility, Management, Technology, Decisions, Transformation, Professional*

INTRODUCTION

The Human Resource Management function in any organization is most important as well as challenging, because it deals with a very important and difficult to manage resource: human capital. Employees are unlike other leverage points, which may include financial capital, machinery, patents and so on. They make the organization work (Laumer, Eckhardt, & Weitzel, 2010).

HRM involves all management decisions and practices that directly affect or influence the people or human resources, who work for the organization (Fisher, Schoenfeldt, & Shaw, 2007). Over a period of time, People and the management of People are increasingly seen as key elements of competitive advantage (Boxall & Purcell, 2003; Gratton, Hailey, & Truss, 2000).

Today's HRM follows an organization science approach which focuses more on the 'total organization' and less on the 'individual' centric policies. So, HRM, as practiced today, grew out of organizational science trend and combines learning from previous movements namely, scientific management and human relations, with current research in various behavioural sciences (Fisher et al., 2007). HRM now partners with various business functions and is gradually accountable to cultivate the indispensable culture that is conducive of required behaviour. HR leaders have become the change agents in the growth of competitive organizational systems.

According to Singh (2006), the function of HR management is increasingly held responsible for its involvement in business strategy, overall managerial efficiency, employee contribution and bringing around change. All these are accomplished through various HR activities like staffing, development, compensation, benefits, communicate organization design and develop high performing teams and so on. According to Armstrong (2010), the practice of HRM is concerned with all aspects of how people are employed and managed in organizations. It covers activities such as: Strategic HRM, Human Capital Management, Knowledge Management, Organization Development, Resourcing (Human Resource Planning, Recruitment and Selection, and Talent Management), Performance Management, Learning and Development, Reward Management, Employee Relations and Employee Well-Being.

HUMAN RESOURCE (HR) ROLES

Over a period of time various researches have been done on the roles of HR. Dave Ulrich gave the four HR roles which have been widely used in literature. In Figure 1, the Ulrich (1997) model is represented.

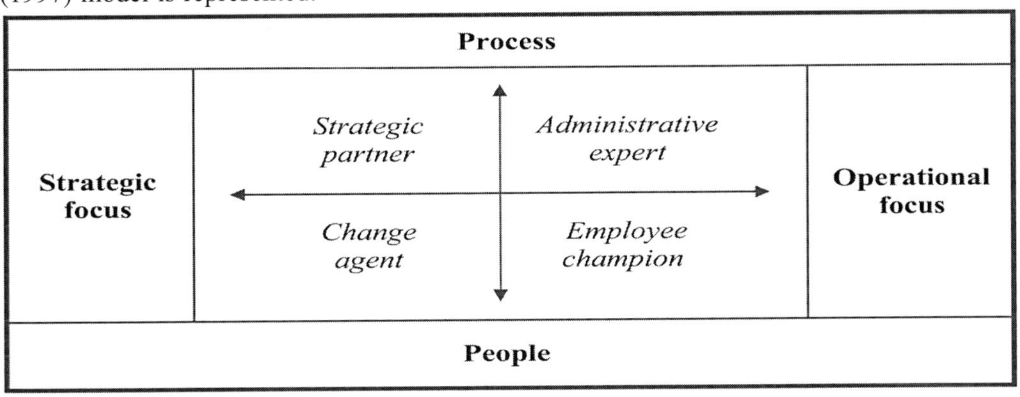

Source: Ulrich (1997)

Fig. 1: HR Roles: Ulrich (1997) Model

1. As a *"strategic partner"*, HR should ensure that its overall practices, policies and processes are aligned with organization's policies.
2. As a "change agent", HR helps the organization to change in line with long term targets and assists in developing and facilitating change management.
3. The role of "administrative expert" is the sum of transactional processes with regard to the personnel and the administrative support needed by the organization in these transactions.
4. In the role of *"employee champion",* HR focuses on operational, short-term problem solving and support to employees and managers in day-to-day matters. The HR should know the employees well and must promote communication in the organization.

Lengnick-Hall and Lengnick-Hall (2003) take the view, that in the knowledge economy, organizations will need HRM that is characterized by a new set of roles that can assist in generating and sustaining organizational capabilities. These HRM roles are as follows:

1. *Human capital steward:* HR should act as a leader as well as a key facilitator in partnership with employees and should aim at attaining maximum return on the investment made by an organization in its human resources.
2. *Knowledge facilitator:* In this role, HR should facilitate both knowledge capital and knowledge flows in an organization.
3. *Relationship builder:* Build better relationships between individuals and groups both within and outside the organization to enhance the social capital across the total value chain.
4. *Rapid deployment specialist:* HR should assume the responsibility for evolving human resources with an importance on adaptability, forbearance and learning capabilities.

The challenges facing HRM has been changing and so is the role of HR managers. The challenges include increasing globalization of economy, competitive work environment, prime focus on product and service quality, growing workforce diversity, outsourcing trends and inevitable power of technology to transform HRM (Bernardin, 2007). To meet the growing demands of their profession, the HR professionals need to be strategic business partners, lead change in the organization, teach HR competencies to line managers and more importantly, leverage technology in the delivery of HR services to its internal customers, i.e. employees. To facilitate these roles, moving towards e-HR (integrating technology in HR functions) is the most apt solution.

EVOLVING ROLE OF e-HR

Towards the end of 1980's, academicians deliberated the varying role of HR. They projected that ultimately many HR officialdoms would convert from a 'Police and Polite' administrator role into an increasingly 'Strategic role'. It was being increasingly realized that employees were most important resources and therefore should be taken care of so as to improve their role in business. Porter (1990) highlighted that management of the people is the most important of all the three resources, i.e. physical, organizational and human.

Towards 1990's, the bound of competition continued to hasten as customers became more demanding and internet technologies emerged and tear down the barriers to entry for competition. There was a decentralization of management functions in manufacturing and services organizations; also there was an attempt to maintain a centralized control through consistent processes. The researchers have observed HR roles as transitioning from operational, secretarial, functionally oriented and reactive; in the direction of more strategic, consultative, business oriented and proactive, respectively (Ulrich, 1997).

HRM has been at the proverbial crossroads since long. Walking the fine line between demonstrating strategic value and providing traditional HR services, the industry remains stuck, as the business environment around it grows increasingly global and complex. It's a known fact that the pressure on organizations to excel, has resulted in organizational introspection to identify the keys to excellence and developing HRM is one such key. The emergence of the global economy, over capacity in many industries, monumental improvements in the power of computers and telecommunication tools, and the emergence of the knowledge economy are among the forces that resulted in a fundamental change in the design of HR arena of activities. A whole constellation of organizational features such as vertical integration, managerial control, stability and two-way loyalty between organization and employee, that fit in a benevolent, relatively stable environment have been giving way to new organizational designs for competitiveness, flexibility, continuous improvement, and self-management (Khan & Chahar, 2010).

Progressively, corporations began to clinch telecommuting or virtual work as part of everyday operations. With a largely diversified workforce in terms of location, gender, race, talent, career aspirations and culture, corporations not only required better, more dynamic insight into personal data, but also outfits through which employees be empowered and connected (Fletcher, 2005). This was the HR 'Transformation age'; the change from the Personnel department to Human Resource (HR) department. The department which had long been viewed as an 'expense' was under pressure to justify its position as a business partner.

The hope for HR was that by automating the non-value-added processes, the HR workforce could concentrate on providing key services to executives, managers and employees. Since, employee empowerment was such a critical concern for the workforce and because the war for talent included the need to retain staff, HR knew that it had to deliver better services to the workforce. Many HR executives began to understand that the best way to be seen as a valued member of the management team was to partner with the key business executives and managers (Fletcher, 2005). To improve effectiveness and efficiency in terms of service delivery, cost reduction and value-added services, HR professionals were under force to hitch technology that was becoming powerful (Kavanagh & Thite, 2009).

On the technology front, during 1980-1990's, the payroll vendors began to emerge, offering technology and in some cases the possibility to outsource the personnel function and promoting Enterprise Resource Planning (ERP) solutions which could combine personnel data and payroll applications (Ball, 2001). In the late 1980's, small and medium-sized firms could start to afford computer-based HR processes which were run by microcomputers which were quite cost-effective. Magalhaes and Ruel (2007) described the automation of HR tasks and processes during the mid-1980, as being the first steps which attracted the attention among HR scholars. To gain insight into even the most seemingly basic information about the workforce in the late 1980's more and more companies were beginning to embrace a more comprehensive approach to HR automation through which disparate systems and broken processes would be replaced with a Human Resource Information System (HRIS). During this time, most of the large business organizations embraced an HRIS strategy that enabled them to replace outdated, time-consuming personnel processes with streamlined automated processes. HRIS applications enabled operational efficiency, cost reductions and control.

By the mid-1990, the internet, or the worldwide web, had made its presence felt. According to Magalhaes and Ruel (2007), the growth of internet, as the main technological development of this era, opened the way to connect computers across countries and ERP created the opportunity to integrate databases into a 'seamless whole' for real-time transaction processing and decision making. In the late 1990's, vendors began to offer basic HR portal solutions which would bring together in one place the tasks relating to career decisions, personnel information and personnel development. Many businesses had branded corporate intranets that provided information to their employees, virtual bulletin boards for information ranging from internal job postings to a calendar of events. In a time when the buzzword for employees was 'empowerment', the focus of HR professionals was on deploying applications that could give employees all the tools and information they needed to perform their jobs and make better decisions (Fletcher, 2005). The period from 1990 to 2000 has been described as the era of technological advancement and the emergence of 'Strategic HR' (Kavanagh & Thite, 2009). The companies were going in for re-engineering their HR processes so as to replace non-value-generating, extremely labour-intensive and expensive processes, like payroll, benefits administration, and employee data capture, etc., with efficiently streamlined back-office solutions which required very less human interaction. Finally, from the year 2000 to the present, the beginning of the 21st century; the purpose of HR has been to create value for key stakeholders. This would mean that employees have right set of competencies; employees are committed to organization and communities in which organizations participate and have more confidence in the organization's ability to deliver on its social responsibilities (Ulrich, Younger, & Brockbank, 2008). In terms of HR, this is described as 'Player phase' as aiming for creating strategic value (Evans, 1997).

In the current scenario, there has been a tremendous change all over the globe with respect to the HR function. Continued globalization, rising customer and shareholder expectations, corporate scandals and the resulting rise of corporate governance issues, downsizing, off-shoring, and a 'job-less economic recovery' around the globe have combined to create tremendous pressure on HR professionals.

To sum up the changing role of HR; to survive, HR department has to prove its value time and time again and technology can be its best partner in doing so. HR must also possess technology acumen like never before. HR professionals must recommend and provide the right tools that not only give access to personal information but also aid in workforce productivity and value creation. They must quickly respond to changes in business by making workforce related decisions based on real-time information, decisions that align corporate strategies with team and individual goals, supporting employees in all phases of the employee lifecycle. It is evident that electronic human resource management is gaining importance in today's business (Cedar Crestone, 2005) and the use of web-based technologies for HR practices, policies and processes is enhancing within organizations. Literature uses the terms electronic Human Resource Management (e-HRM) or electronic Human Resource (e-HR) both referring to technology integration into the HR function. e-HR is concerned with the application of the internet, web-based systems and mobile communications technologies to change the nature of interactions among HR staff, line managers and employees from a pure face-to-face relationship to a technology-mediated one (Ruel, Bondarouk, & Looise, 2004). The concept of e-HR has also been defined in several ways: from the 1980's, "specialized information system within the traditional functional areas of the organization, designed to support the planning, administration, decision-making, and control activities of human resource management" (DeSanctis, 1986, p.18) to a more frequently used definition, "planning, implementation and application of information technology for both networking and supporting at least two individual or collective actors in their shared performing of HR activities" (Strohmeier, 2007, p. 20). Armstrong (2003) states that e-HR provides the information required to manage various HR processes. These systems could be web-based, which enable access to remote or online and at any point of time.

An interesting phenomenon in the present century is the redistribution of conventional HR functions in the hands of line managers. HR has begun to evaluate self-service applications to help streamline business processes, capture better data and most importantly put information into the hands of those who need it the most: managers and employees. The impetus for this change can in part be attributed to the fact that there are benefits like cost efficiencies among many others which are being offered by high end HR technologies. Interestingly, many of the traditional HR functions have changed into a new set of competencies altogether as many of these can be enhanced or performed using technology (Waddill & Marquardt, 2011).

TECHNOLOGY AND HR INTERFACE: CURRENT SCENARIO

As discussed above, in today's scenario, HR professionals need not only master traditional HR skills and knowledge but should be effective in applying that skills and knowledge through technology. Technology is an independent variable having a range of effects at different levels of analysis (individual, group, enterprise and inter-organizational) on multiple organizational outcomes as the dependent variable (Orlikowski & Scott, 2008). Information Technology (IT) is designed and implemented to meet organizational goals in various business functions.

According to Johnson and Gueutal (2011), HR is evolving into a technology-driven process due to the following reasons:

- To streamline HR processes and reduce administrative burdens.
- Reduce HR administration and compliance costs.
- Compete more effectively for global talent.
- Improve service and access to data for employees and managers.
- Provide real-time metrics to allow decision-makers to spot trends and manage the workforce more effectively.
- Enable HR to transform so it can play a more strategic role in the business.

Organizations are seeking possibilities to run HR operations more efficiently and effectively. The combination of the need to work more efficiently, on one hand and the possibilities of current information and communication technology on the other, have resulted in the swift development of e-HR systems (Stanton & Coovert, 2004; Fletcher, 2005). Mayasoman (2007) stressed on the fact that leveraging of technology for HR would result in digitizing the routine and mundane HR activities and powering the back office and transactional activities which are associated with recruitment, selection, performance management, career planning, training and development and so on and so forth.

Through technology-integration, e-HR has begun to replace or complement face-to-face relationships and HRIS with a 'smart self-service relationship', customized content and greater individualization of services. e-HR has been able to create a parallel internal HR virtual value chain, complementing the existing physical internal HR value chain. Drawing from literature, a lot is expected of e-HR systems in areas of improving the quality of HRM and growing its contribution towards making HR as a strategic partner. Organizations are making high investments in adoption of e-HR systems and these are justified as well given the reasonable expectations that e-HR will enhance HRM quality in organizations. This will be done by releasing staff from administrative loads. These views are a result of ideas about the infinite potentials of IT in facilitating HR practices and about the endless capacity of HR to adopt these technologies. Surveys of top HR consultants propose that the number of organizations adopting e-HR as well as the depth of applications within the organizations will constantly be increased (Cedar Crestone, 2005). According to Esen and Erdogmus (2011), using information and communication technologies in human resource services has become an important strategy to achieve competitive advantage for organizations.

Although IT has been widely used in HR function since the 1980's, this application of technology has to be distinguished from e-HR. The earlier usage of technology has been in the form of Human Resource Information Systems (HRIS) which were focused on automating the systems used by the HR function itself. 1990's have seen a significant increase in the number of organizations gathering, storing and analyzing human resources data using HRIS (Ball, 2001; Barron, Chhabra, Hanscome, & Henson 2004; Ngai & Wat, 2006). However, in case of HRIS, its main 'customer' has been HR staff rather than employees or managers. It has been typically used in automating systems such as payroll and personal information, often with little or no attempt to make such data interactive or available to staff outside of HR.

Today, internet is entering our everyday lives and is being incorporated into business strategies in an unprecedented manner. 'Internet' simply means a 'network of networks', and is defined as a network of interlinked computers throughout the world operating on a standard protocol which allows data to be transferred between otherwise incompatible machines (Hamill, 1997). Such networks link a wide range of participants (like individuals, companies, organizations, governments, education and research institutions) and support the transfer of a wide range of data (text, graphics, audio, video and software). With the ever-increasing usage of information technologies in the HR function, planning and delivery, the way in which employees look at the nature and role of HR has drastically changed (Roehling, Boswell, Feldman, Graham, & Guthrie, 2005). In the present times, organizations have increasingly been using web-based applications for HRM purposes and are moving fast in their e-HR journey.

There is an increased usage of new social media such as blogs, wikis, media sharing sites, social networking and the like, which are collectively known as Web 2.0. These media are becoming more widely used by organizations to increase knowledge sharing, improve collaboration and employee voice as well as connect with new generations of employees (Martin & Reddington, 2009). At large, companies in the 21st century have adopted at least one of the following e-HR technologies: HR Functional Applications, Integrated HR Suite Applications, Interactive Voice Responses, HR Intranet Applications, Employee Self-Service and Manager Self-Service portals, HR Extranet Applications or HR portals (Florkowski & Olivas-Lujan, 2006).

The influence of internet and browser technology has seen the growth of self-service applications. These are internet based solutions providing employees with a browser interface to relevant HR data and transactions, enabling real time access to their data without leaving their desktop. Employees are able to update their personal details, apply for leave, view their pay details and associated benefits, view internal job vacancies and book training and travel. The tangible and intangible benefits of these solutions have been well documented (Alexander, 2002; McKenna, 2002; Webster & Buchanan, 2002) and include reduced administrative overheads, freeing up HR staff for more strategic activities, improved data integrity and empowerment of employees.

Stone (2005) suggests technological changes influencing e-HR during the end of this decade will include intelligent self-service systems, interchangeable devices, cognitive software, nanotechnology and the convergence of the internet, digital TV and the wireless technology communication into a vibrant network.

ERP AND HRM

The arcade of HR technology is swamped with a range of stand-alone applications as well as high end ERP systems. ERP is well defined as "a packaged business software system that enables a company to manage the efficient and effective use of resources by providing a total, integrated solution for the organization's information-processing needs" (Nah & Lau, 2001, p. 285). This software facilitates, if well implemented, the integration of all the functional information flows across the organization into a single package with a common database. Therefore, it lets easy and instant access to information regarding inventory, product or customer data and prior history information (Shehab, Sharp, Supramaniam, & Spedding, 2004). In other words, ERP is an integration of all data and processes of an organization interlaced together in an intelligent manner using technology into a single unified system. Although the acronym ERP coined in the manufacturing environment, today's use of the term ERP systems has much broader scope. ERP systems endeavour to include all basic functions of an organization, regardless of the organization's business or charter. With ERP, organizations have a single enterprise wide application including modules within, which are capable of absorbing all business functions under a unique umbrella structure where these could co-exist without any hostile impact on their working and efficiency. However, according to Kroenke (2008), in practical terms, the entire process of moving from functional applications to an ERP system is not only difficult but challenging as well. Additionally, the switch to ERP system is expensive and it requires development of new procedures, training and converting data (Zhang et al., 2005).

On the other hand, some organizations may not invest in ERP for the HR function and use stand-alone applications for HR activities. The key difference between the ERP version and the stand-alone versions is integration. The ERP applications share the same technical architecture, database, look and feel, and processing standards. Major ERP vendors like Infor HCM (Human Capital Management), Microsoft Axapta Human Resource Management III, SAP HCM, Oracle HRMS, Peoplesoft, Adrenalin and others; now offer organizations HR modules that help automate an array of tasks while generating crucial data for enterprise planning and optimization.

Today, the HR function has an opportunity to influence from some of the best IT solutions which have been developed precisely keeping in view the strategic role played by every single HR process.

e-HR MODULES

After a comprehensive study of the various ERP and stand-alone e-HR applications available in the market, the researcher has summarized below, how these e-HR tools and applications have standardized, digitized and automated the key Human Resource functions and given a whole new perspective to the outlook of business and industry towards human resources. These e-HR applications have not merely brought technology into the human resource function but have challenged the function to be more strategic and process oriented. The e-HR applications have been developed for key areas of HR functions:

Talent Acquisition/Recruit Workforce

Hiring workers and employees has always been critical to the success of an organization. Amalgamation of technology with a process oriented approach has changed the way employees are recruited. It has streamlined the complex task of recruiting for recruiters and also hiring professionals. In a single online location, recruiters can create and post job requisitions, search the talent pool existing within or in the market, screen applicants, perform background checks, hire and on-board the most suitable candidate for the job. It has transformed the paper based processes related with recruiting into a better and more modernized electronic system. The key outcomes include:

- Administering and posting job requisitions on company's intranet and internet portals.
- Managing applications received online or from other sources.
- Scheduling and organizing interviews.
- Managing employee referrals in the organization.
- Optimum utilization of social media for recruitment.

Workforce Administration

This is the foundation on which the entire organization structure will be built and needs to evolve over the years as the organization grows. The HR department, today, wants new tools and processes which can enable the shift from an administrative role to a strategic one. This has been made possible by e-HR applications, which provide solutions which are malleable and also help to connect human capital processes with business results. By automating administrative tasks, these enable HR managers to focus on managing the most important asset: People. It helps in reducing costs and increasing efficiency, in the long run, throughout the employee lifecycle. It helps to automate the activities, such as:

- Manpower database maintenance, that includes recording employee personal data, organizational data and dependent data.
- Setting up different employee categories (could be: Temporary, Full-Time, Part time) and assigning them into distinct categories.
- Setting up the organizational hierarchy by configuring the basic framework for enterprise application to operate.
- Maintain a chronological history of every milestone, step or event in an employee's tryst with organization.

Enterprise Learning/Training Administration

With the war for talent increasing by the day, one of the key differentiators for employees is to see if organization is willing to invest in enhancing the skills and abilities of its workforce. e-Learning is one such measure that organizations are investing in. It's defined as an online method of evolving skills and knowledge across the employees. The online trainings can be made available in various ways: self-paced courses, live virtual classrooms or even an informal learning driven by the user. Today, e-Learning is used across a spectrum of HR processes, from training new hires, tracking employee certifications, business skills, leadership, computer skills.. The e-HR solutions in this space generally include:

- Designing training courses and programs.
- Managing course sessions.
- Registering or wait listing students.
- Tracing employee training and certifications.

Competency Management/Career and Succession Planning

This forms a major part of Organizational Development in an organization. All processes under the function have a level of inter-dependency and relatedness on other HR functions like Learning or Training and Development. These e-HR applications help assimilate all these functions as well as guide the management with a clear picture of existing talent, skills available, which skills are in short supply and so on and so forth. These applications help in managing the processes in the following ways:

- Defining key competencies for the various roles existing in the organization.
- Categorize and associate competencies with individuals, jobs and teams.
- Identify developmental needs of employees as well as enrol them in various training programs.
- Trace leadership and talent gaps in the organization, and identify and follow up on employees who have potential.

Time and Labour/Absence Management

If one was to ask HR managers working in any large organization to name one key pain area; almost every response would have some relation with the transactional and administrative tasks and activities. These are non-value adding but at the same time integral to any HR function. One such area where technology has helped HR managers is in keeping a track of employee's leave records and tracking their actual time spent on productive output. At present, most of the activities under this function have been automated as well as pre-built in HR modules. These HR modules are configured to route transactions related to following components:

- The different kind of leave and absence plans offered by organization.

- Define eligibility conditions for leave and absence plans.
- Developing a flexible standard 'work schedule' for all employees.
- Define holiday schedules governed by regulatory and/or legislative guidelines.
- Tracking the actual time spent by employees on productive work.

Monitor Workplace/Occupational Health and Safety

This application provides organizations with the tools and processes to help them track health and safety information, design and manage a health and safety program, and conform to governmental regulations and standards. It also helps to meet human resource reporting requirements of various countries, by generating reports which are specific to a country's requirements. There are various tools available which can help in the following ways:

- Trail health details of the employees as well as their families.
- Manage the health claim schemes.
- Track injuries or any workplace incidents.

Plan Salaries/Administer Compensation/Base Benefits

Compensation management is one of the most critical processes in the HR function. e-HR applications have configurable options to define what kind of compensation grades, compensation bands and salary plans would suit the organization's structure, how different type of employees can be assigned to different compensation plans and so on. Having a flexible tool to change the compensation structure in response to the changes in external or internal factors means less of data entry or transactional job and overall satisfied workforce. Some of the other options these applications provide are:

- Help develop organization wide departmental salary budgets and create salary plans.
- Creating standard salary matrices and review rating scales with salary grades.
- Web based salary modelling for department managers.
- Managing variable compensation plans, different incentive plans, including how they are valued and vested.
- Build a set of plan types, design calculations, eligibility criteria and specify pay-out amounts.

The calculation of award amounts can then be connected to Payroll for final payment to the employee and to Stock Administration for the processing of employee stock options.

Payroll Solutions

Today ERP applications such as SAP and PeopleSoft provide organizations with computerized and highly flexible solutions which take care of meting out salaries after taking into account all essential factors which have an impact on employee monthly pay out. These could be leave balance, actual hours spent on work, any deductions on account of benefits, retirement contributions and so on. Most of the ERP vendors now offer options which are all-inclusive set of payroll solutions and which can be added on top of organization's existing application. e-HR system records all compensation changes to employee records and push the monthly pay out for each employee over to the payroll applications which automatically validate data, calculate their gross earnings and then deduct a specific amount as per the policy and finally deduct the 'Income Tax' to arrive at their net earnings. Different kind of payroll solutions available in the market can be categorized under the following:

- A cloud based payroll processing system.
- A rules-based global payroll system.
- A payroll for purpose of outsourcing or integrating third-party payroll systems.

SELF-SERVICE APPLICATIONS: EMPOWERING EMPLOYEES

All ERP applications available in the market today have an integrated self-service collaborative application, which enable the employees, managers and HR professionals to act in diverse dimensions and have different level of power to operate these systems. These self-service applications fall under either of the following two categories:

Employee Self-Service (ESS)

This provides every employee in an organization ability to view and update their own personal information/details anytime they want and in a way most suitable to them. After the system validates their credentials, employees can easily view, add or update their personal information online, which is critical for any organization to track and record. For instance, updating their residential address when they move from one location to another, recording their emergency contact information, recording and updating their educational qualifications, languages and any other professional qualifications they have, all with click of a button anytime. These applications have an inbuilt mechanism for approvals anytime employee initiates an update to specific set of data.

Manager Self-Service (MSS)

These are a group of transactions bundled together which are similar to how ESS operates but are available to only those individuals within an organization who are managing teams directly. These applications provide an opportunity to the managers, to view and update the details to their team member records at click of a button from anywhere they want. Transactions which earlier used to take days and involved many round of discussions and meetings with HR managers are now available at hand and do not require any face-to-face or long discussions or personal visits.

There are a variety of collaborative applications available today for HR management systems, some of which cater only to the employee and some supporting only managers. The manager desktop applications work with the employee self-service applications to support transactions specific to managers and supervisors.

CLASSIFICATION OF e-HR APPLICATIONS

Cedar Crestone (2008-2009) HR Systems survey divides e-HR activities into the following categories:

- *Administrative applications:* Core HR management, payroll, and benefits record keeping systems.
- *Workforce management:* Time management and absence management that enables labour forecasting, planning, budgeting and task scheduling.
- *Employee and manager productivity applications (service delivery):* Self-service transaction services that improve service delivery, reduce administrative costs, and enable employees, HR, and managers to spend less time on administrative tasks.
- *Strategic HCM applications:* Talent management applications that enable an organization to plan, attract, develop, and retain key talent.
- *Business intelligence applications:* Applications and technologies that when combined enable an organization to move towards metrics-based management.

IMPROVING ACCESSIBILITY AND CREATING VALUE

Today technology underpins all the HR functions and can increase their effectiveness. Technology can be used to make HR accessible to employees, empower them with real-time information, enhance performance, quicken decision making, enable exchange of knowledge, provide cost savings and offer learning to a broader audience (Gueutal & Stone, 2005). Value for the HR function can be defined as "the strategic benefits achieved from a particular HR activity relative to the costs associated with its deployment" (Lepak and Snell, 1998, p. 222). After an in-depth study of the journey of traditional HR towards e-HR, it can aptly be said that e-HR helps to empower line managers and enable them in team management by providing real time HR information related to their team, create competitive advantage and align the HR function more closely with business or corporate strategy and can achieve the long-term branding and reputational objectives of organizations as well. Gradually as e-HR develops and becomes more and more entrenched in an organisation's culture, the benefits will become more apparent.

REFERENCES

[1] Alexander, S. (2002). HR e-power to the people. *Infoworld.* Retrieved August 07, 2002 from http://staging.infoworld.eom/articles/ca/xmll

[2] Armstrong, M. (2003). *A Handbook of Human Resource Management* (9th ed.). London: Kogan Page.

[3] Armstrong, M. (2010). *Armstrong's Essential Human Resource Management Practice: A Guide to People Management.* London: Kogan Page.

[4] Ball, K. S. (2001). The Use of Human Resource Information Systems: A Survey. *Personnel Review, 30* (6), 667-693.

[5] Barron, M., Chhabra, D., Hanscome, R., & Henson, R. (2004). Exclusive Panel Discussion: Tips and Trends in HRIS. *HR Focus, 81,* 6-7.

[6] Bernardin, H. J. (2007). *Human Resource Management: An Experiential Approach.* New York: McGraw-Hill.

[7] Boxall, P., Purcell, J., & Wright, P. (2007). *The Oxford Handbook of Human Resource Management.* Oxford: Oxford University Press.

[8] CedarCrestone. (2004). *Workforce Technologies and Service Delivery Approaches Survey.* Retrieved August 12, 2009 from http://www.cedarcrestone.com/ whitepapers.ph

[9] CedarCrestone (2005). *HCM Survey: Workforce Technologies and Service Delivery Approaches–Eighth Annual Edition.* Retrieved May 16, 2008 from *http://www.cedarcrestone.com/serv_research_pr-100912.php*

[10] CedarCrestone. (2008-2009). *HR Systems Survey: 1st Survey Focused on Asia and Australia.* Retrieved June 21, 2010 from www.cedarcrestone.com/ *CedarCrestone _2008-2009_APAC_WP.pdf.*

[11] DeSanctis, G. (1986). Human Resource Information Systems: A Current Assessment. *MIS Quarterly, 10,* 15-27.

[12] Esen, M., & Erdogmus, N. (2011). An Investigation of the Effects of Technology Readiness on Technology Acceptance in e-HRM. 7th International Strategic Management Conference. *Procedia Social and Behavioural Sciences,* 24, 487-495.

[13] Evans, C. (1997). The use of consensus methods and expert panels in pharmacoeconomic studies. *Pharmacoeconomics,* 12, 121-129.

[14] Fisher, C.D., Schoenfeldt, L.F., & Shaw, J.B. (2007). *Human Resource Management.* Boston: Houghton Mifflin Co.

[15] Fletcher, P.A.K. (2005). From Personnel Administration to Business-Driven Human Capital Management: The Transformation of the Role of HR in the Digital Age. In H. Gueutal, & D. L. Stone (Eds.), *The Brave New World of E-HR: Human Resources in the Digital Age.* San Francisco, CA: Pfeiffer.

[16] Florkowski, G.W., & Olivas-Lujan, M.R. (2006). The diffusion of human resource information technology innovations in US and non-US firms. *Personnel Review, 35* (6), 684-710.

[17] Gratton, L., Hailey, V.H., & Truss, C. (2000). *Strategic Human Resource Management.* New York: Oxford University Press.

[18] Hamill, J. (1997). The Internet and International Marketing. *International Marketing Review,* 14 (4/5), 300-323.

[19] Johnson, R.D., & Gueutal, H.G. (2011). *Transforming HR through technology: The use of E-HR and HRIS in organizations.* Society for Human Resource Management Effective Practice Guidelines Series. Alexandria, VA.

[20] Kavanagh, M.J., & Thite, M. (Eds.). (2009). *Human Resource Information Systems: Basics, Applications & Directions.* Thousand Oaks, CA: Sage.

[21] Khan, S., & Chahar, B. (2010). Future of HR management in Indian scenario: Issues & Challenges. *Asian Journal of Management Research,* 1, 40-48.

[22] Kroenke, D. (2008). *Experiencing MIS.* Upper Saddle River, NJ: Prentice Hall.

[23] Laumer, S., Eckhardt, A., & Weitzel, T. (2010). Electronic Human Resource Management in an E-Business Environment. *Journal of Electronic Commerce Research,* 11 (4), 240-250.

[24] Lengnick-Hall, M.L., & Lengnick-Hall, C.A. (2003). *Human Resource Management in the Knowledge Economy: New Challenges, New Roles, New Capabilities.* San Francisco: Berrett-Koehler Publishers.

[25] Lepak D. and Snell S. (1998). Virtual, HR: Strategic human resource management in the 21st century, *Human Resource Management Review,* 8 (3), 215-234.

[26] Magalhaes, R., & Ruel, H. (2007). *Studying Human Resource Information Systems from an Integrated Perspective: A Research Agenda.* Proceedings of the 1st international workshop on Human Resource Information Systems. Fucnhal (Portugal).

[27] Martin, G., & Reddington, M. (2009). Reconceptualising absorptive capacity to explain the e-enablement of the HR function (e-HR) in organizations. *Employee Relations,* 31 (5), 515-537.

[28] Mayasoman, T. (2007). *Performance Management.* Citation: Paper Presented in Bangalore HR Summit 2007 on Dec. 7 & 8, 2007 at Le Meridien, Bangalore, India.

[29] McKenna, E. (2002). *Empowering employees.* Retrieved August 05, 2007 from http://www.fcw.com/fcw/articles/2007/0107

[30] Nah, F., & Lau, J. (2001). Critical factors for successful implementation of enterprise systems. *Business Process Management Journal,* 7 (3), 285-296.

[31] Ngai, E.W.T., & Wat, F.K.T. (2006). Human Resource Information Systems: A Review and Empirical Analysis. *Personnel Review*, 35 (3), 297-314.

[32] Orlikowski, W.J., & Scott S.V. (2008). Sociomateriality: Challenging the separation of Technology, Work and Organization. *Academy of Management Annals*, 2(1), 433-474.

[33] Porter, M. E. (1990). *The Competitive Advantage of Nations*. Boston: Free Press.

[34] Roehling, M.V., Boswell, W. R., Caligiuri, P., Feldman, D., Graham, M. E., Guthrie, J.P., Morishima, M., & Tansky, J.W. (2005). The future of HR Management: Research needs and directions. *Human Resource Management,* 44 (2), 207-216.

[35] Ruel, H.J.M., Bondarouk, T., & Looise, J.C. (2004). E-HRM: Innovation or Irritation. An explorative empirical study in five large companies on web-based HRM. *Management Review,* 15 (3), 364-381.

[36] Shehab, E., Sharp, M., Supramaniam, L., & Spedding, T. (2004). Enterprise Resource Planning: An Integrative Review. *Business Process Management Journal,* 10 (4), 359-386.

[37] Singh, S. (2006). IT for Organizational Excellence. *Articles on Management.* Retrieved May 08, 2008 from http://www.indianmba.com/Occasional_Papers/ OP119/ op119.html

[38] Stanton, J.M., & Coovert, M.D. (2004). Turbulent Waters: The Intersection of Information Technology and Human Resources. *Human Resource Management,* 4 (2/3), 121-125.

[39] Stone, R. (2005). *Human Resource Management* (5th ed.). Milton: John Wiley & Sons.

[40] Strohmeier, S. (2007). Research in e-HRM: Review and Implications. *Human Resource Management Review,* 17, 19-37.

[41] Ulrich, D. (1997). *Human Resource Champions: The Next Agenda for Adding Value and Delivering Results*. Boston MA: Harvard Business School Press.

[42] Ulrich, D., Younger, J., & Brockbank, W. (2008). The twenty-first century organization. *Human Resource Management, Winter,* 47 (4), 829-850.

[43] Waddill, D. & Marquardt, M.J. (2011*). eHR Technologies at Work: The Complete Handbook for Technology-Enabled Human Resources.* Boston: Nicholas Brealey Publications.

[44] Webster, & Buchanan. (2002). *HR self-service - The practitioners' view.* Retrieved August 16, 2009 from http://www.websterb.com

[45] Zhang, Z., Lee, M., Huang, P., Zhang L., & Huang, X. (2005). A framework of ERP systems implementation success in China: An empirical study. *International Journal of Production Economics,* 98, 56-80.

Towards Inclusiveness at the Workplace for the Differently Abled: Issues and Challenges

Meenakshi Handa and Jyoti Kukreja

University School of Management Studies, Guru Gobind Singh Indraprastha University, Dwarka, New Delhi

ABSTRACT

Although the efforts to diminish and abolish discrimination of all types has yielded results in some measure, workplaces still harbor discrimination on innumerable criteria, some evident some implied. There is still a long struggle ahead for ensuring that persons with disabilities are provided the necessary support to enable them to be an important part of the workforce and contribute their best to the organization. This paper begins with highlighting the major barriers to inclusiveness of the disabled into the workplace It then traces the disability laws in several countries such as the US, UK and India which are aimed at protecting and promoting the rights of the disabled. Further, measures for enhancing the participation of the disabled at the workplace are presented along with inclusive practices by Indian IT organizations.

Keywords: *Disability, Inclusiveness, Laws, Rights Movements*

INTRODUCTION

A successful organization is not only an assortment of different individuals but also represents a range of skills set. A policy of inclusion of people from minority zones or those who are different is very vital for ensuring that the talents and capabilities of these stakeholders can be harnessed towards helping organizations achieve their goals. Persons with disabilities constitute a significant group which has the potential to contribute in a meaningful way to organizational performance if the right opportunities are made available. They can be reliable and productive employees who have the ability to acquire the necessary training, skills and expertise to perform a variety of jobs. A policy of including persons with disabilities in the workforce enables organizations to add to the diversity and creativity at the workplace. Besides contributing towards enhancing employee morale it is also a means for the organization to discharge its social responsibility.

The World Health Organization defines Disability as follows:

"Disabilities are an umbrella term, covering impairments, activity limitations, and participation restrictions. Impairment is a problem in body function or structure; an activity limitation is a difficulty encountered by an individual in executing a task or action; while a participation restriction is a problem experienced by an individual in involvement in life situations. Thus disability is a complex phenomenon, reflecting an interaction between features of a person's body and features of the society in which he or she lives." (www.who.int/topics/disabilities/en/)

Tables 1 and 2 present data on the disabled population in India as per the 2011 Census of India according to which there are almost 27 million disabled persons constituting 2.12 percent of the total population in India. However, according to a World Bank Report (2007) there is growing evidence that people with disabilities comprise between 4 and 8 per cent of the India population (around 40-90 million individuals)".

According to World Health Organization and the World Bank, *World Report on Disability*, 2011 persons with disabilities comprise about 15 per cent of the world's population of which about 785 million to 975 million are of working age (15 years or older) and most live in developing countries.

Table 1: Disabled Population by Sex and Residence India, 2011

Residence	*Persons*	*Males*	*Females*
Total	26,810,557 (2.21)	14,986,202 (2.41)	11,824,3559 (2.01)
Rural	18,631,921 (2.24)	10,408,168 (2.43)	8,223,753 (2.03)
Urban	8,178,636 (2.17)	4,578,034 (2.34)	3,600,602 (1.98)

( ) In Brackets: Percentage of disabled to total population

Source: Census of India 2011.

Table 2: Decadal Change in Disabled Population by Sex and Residence, India, 2001-11

	Absolute Increase			*Percentage Decadal Growth*		
Residence	*Persons*	*Males*	*Females*	*Persons*	*Males*	*Females*
Total	4,903,788	2,380,567	2,523,221	22.4	18.9	27.1
Rural	2,243,539	997,983	1,245,556	13.7	10.6	17.8
Urban	2,660,249	1,382,584	1,277,665	48.2	43.3	55.0

Source: C-Series, Table C-20, Census of India 2001 and 2011.

According to the Annual Report of the United Nations High Commissioner for Human Rights (2012), persons with disabilities are more likely to be find employment in low-paying jobs, at lower positions and with lower career development prospects and poor working conditions. They are also more likely to be working at part-time or temporary jobs.

INCLUSION IN THE WORKFORCE: ISSUES AND CHALLENGES

Persons with disabilities risk being passed over in the competition for jobs and avenues for livelihood. In the face of negative attitudes and lack of access to proper education, transportation and financial resources, they are often in danger of living out a negative cycle wherein the low expectations from them are in danger of becoming self-fulfilling prophecies.

There are several sets of challenges which hamper the rights of the disabled to have access to meaningful employment of which some of the major ones are highlighted in the ensuing paragraphs.

Inadequate Access to Education and Training

The barriers to employment start early for the disabled in the form of unequal access to education and training opportunities. Often there is a lack of proper transportation facilities for the disabled to conveniently commute to educational institutions. Further, the educational institutions are not disabled friendly and it becomes difficult to navigate within the premises. Also, in the absence of special teaching methodology, it can become difficult to keep up with the learning pace of other students in the class. As a result the entire learning experience becomes extremely challenging and there is a higher likelihood of dropping out from the traditional educational system.

Social and Psychological Barriers

There may also be prejudice and stereotyping about the capabilities of the disabled. The disabled person may himself or herself experience low self-esteem and lack of confidence in their capabilities. Sometimes over-protective families are not willing to allow them to venture out thereby adding to the lack of confidence. Also, at the workplace, acceptance from fellow-workers may be slow in coming.

Discrimination in Hiring and Promotions by Employers

The disabled may be subjected to various forms of discrimination in hiring, working conditions, and advancement opportunities. They may be hired at lower paying jobs or may even be offered lower payment for the same work. They may be expected to work on lower positions and in poorer working conditions. In the absence of limited bargaining power, the disabled may be compelled to accept these terms. Also, promotional avenues may not be very much available to them because of attitudinal and perceptual barriers on the part of the employers.

Inadequate Accessibility to Workplace

Lack of adequate and appropriate public transport facilities to the workplace may pose a major challenge for the disabled. Also the workplace design may not be adequately sensitive to the needs of the disabled. Although the law requires employers to ensure that workplaces are disabled friendly, the compliance may not be forthcoming in letter and spirit.

DISABILITY LAWS IN DIFFERENT COUNTRIES

In the USA the Americans with Disabilities Act (ADA) was passed in 1990 under which disability is defined as "...a physical or mental impairment that substantially limits a major life activity." The ADA prohibits disability discrimination by all public entities at the local (i.e. school district, municipal, city, county) and state level. Public entities must comply with the relevant regulations by the U.S. Department of Justice which cover access to all programs and services offered by the entity. Access includes physical access described in the ADA Standards for Accessible Design and programmatic access that might be obstructed by discriminatory policies or procedures of the entity. Further no individual may be discriminated against on the basis of disability with regards to the full and equal enjoyment of the goods, services, facilities, or accommodations of any place of public accommodation by any person who owns, leases (or leases to), or operates a place of public accommodation.

As result of sustained activism, the Disability Discrimination Act 1995 (DDA 1995) was passed in the United Kingdom whereby it was unlawful to discriminate against people with disabilities for employment, the provision of goods and services, education and transport. The Equality and Human Rights Commission provides support for this Act. In Northern Ireland to there exists an equivalent legislation which is enforced by the Northern Ireland Equality Commission. In 2010 DDA 1995 was repealed and replaced by the Equality Act 2010.

In Israel too, since 1988 employers were prohibited by law from discriminating between employees or prospective employees on the basis of gender, sexual orientation, attitude, whether they have children, age, race, religion, nationality, country of origin, viewpoint, political party. In 1998, with the passing of the Equality at Work Law people with disabilities were granted equal rights.

In Australia,the Disability Discrimination Act 1992 (DDA) is aimed at providing Australians with disabilities the right to equality of opportunity in employment, education and the provision of goods and services. According to an Australian Government Productivity Commission Inquiry Report (2004) the DDA has been reasonably effective in reducing discrimination. However much more needs to be achieved. For example, disabled there has been greater improvement in access to public transport and education for the disabled as compared to employment opportunities.

Disability Laws in India

In 1995, the Government of India passed the Persons with Disabilities (Equal Opportunities, Protection of Rights and Full Participation) Act (PwD Act). As per Section 2 (I) of the Act, Disability is defined as:

(i) Blindness;
(ii) Low vision;
(iii) Leprosy-cured;
(iv) Hearing impairment;
(v) Loco motor disability;
(vi) Mental retardation;
(vii) Mental illness;

Further, according to Sec 2(t) of the Act, 'persons with disability' means a person suffering from not less than forty percent of any disability as certified by the medical authority. (http://www.socialjustice.nic.in/policiesacts3.php)

According to the PwD Act in order to prevent the occurrence of disabilities, governments and the local authorities shall promote research on the cause of occurrence of disabilitie and various methods of preventing disabilities; They shall also create awareness and educate the public through mass media nd other methods about the causes of and preventive measures for disabilities.

The Governments and the local authorities shall also ensure that every child with a disability has access to free education in an appropriate environment till he attains the age of eighteen years and endeavour to promote the integration of students with disabilities in the normal schools. Also special schools in Government and private sector should be set up for those in need of special education where vocational training facilities are also available. The PwD Act also provides for transportation facilities, books and other material for children with disabilities along with disabled friendly school environments.

The PwD Act further requires the government to identify posts, in the establishments, which can be reserved for the persons with disability and provide in every establishment a minimum of three per cent of posts for persons disability

RECOMMENDATIONS

In order to ensure that the disabled have equal opportunities and enjoy fair and equal rights at the workplace, several sets of issues need to be addressed. These issues could be broadly classified in to legal aspects, physical barriers and attitudinal barriers. The focus needs to be on addressing these disabling aspects of the environment which add to the challenges of people with disabilities and deny them equal opportunities.

- **Infrastructure Upgradation:** For people with physical disabilities, accessibility and safety are major issues. Access to public areas such as city streets and public buildings and restrooms are some of the more obvious changes required. The installation of elevators, automatic doors, wider doors and corridors, transit lifts, wheelchair ramps, curb cuts, and the elimination of unnecessary steps where ramps and elevators are not available, allowing people in wheelchairs and with other mobility impairments to use public sidewalks and public transit more easily and more safely. These infrastructure upgradations must be expedited in India for the ease and accessibility of a section of the work force. The impact of more accessible transportation and infrastructure facilities will positively impact the access in other areas such as education and employment.

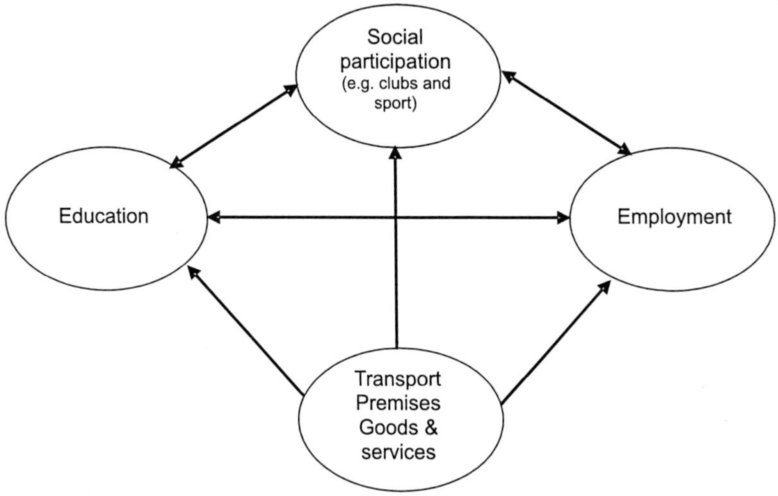

Fig. 1: Discrimination in One Area has Flow-on Effects

Source: Productivity Commission Enquiry Report 2004, Review of the Disability Discrimination Act 1992, Australian Government

- **Access to Education and Skills Training:** In order to ensure the employability of persons with disabilities, their education and skills training is imperative. There are several organizations in India offering special education and skills training for persons with disabilities. The Ministry of Social Justice and Empowerment, Government of India has established or sponsors various institutions and programmes for providing specialized education and vocational training to persons with different types of disabilities as well as for training of trainers. Thus in order facilitate delivery of various services to persons with disabilities by voluntary organizations, the Ministry grants-in-aid to NGOs for setting up and running Vocational Training Centres, Sheltered Workshops, Special Schools for the Persons with Disabilities, Project for Pre-School and Early Intervention and Training etc. Institutions established by the Ministry include Pandit Deen Dayal Upadhyaya Institute for the Physically Handicapped, New Delhi, the Rehabilitation Council of India, National Institute of Visually Handicapped, Dehradun, etc.
- **Change in Attitudes of Employers**: Employers and prospective employers must believe that a person with disability may be able to deliver the same results in many

jobs as the person without disabilities but may need some initial assistance for example a special workstation. Employers may need to provide training opportunities which are inclusive. For example for a person with visual impairment, material may be provided in Braille or in an oral form and for a person with a hearing impairment, communication via a sign language could be arranged. Employers can also provide flexible working hours and some work-form-arrangements to persons with disability.

- **Enabling Attitude of Fellow Employees:** Co-workers also need to be sensitized about displaying the right behavior so that persons with disabilities can give their best at the workplace. Thus the colleagues must learn to respect the person with disability for what they can contribute rather than underestimating them. The fact that he or she has been hired by the organization indicates that he/she possesses the necessary qualifications and skills and would have the capability to deliver what the job requires. Other employees must understand the pace and method of working of their colleagues with disabilities and provide the necessary enabling support. At the same time they must be encouraged to be accountable for the work assigned to them and colleagues must avoid the inclination to b unduly overprotective. Disability awareness workshops can be conducted by organizations so as to encourage employees to develop the right attitude towards colleagues with disabilities.
- **Creation of an Overall Inclusive Environment:** It is necessary to create accessible physical infrastructure at the workplace. This includes lifts, ramps, and accessible restrooms for the disabled and office space which is organized in such as way as to make it easier for the disabled to navigate. Other aspects such as outings and off-site activities can be planned at venues which are accessible to persons with disabilities and the activities themselves planned in a manner that enables the participation of persons with disabilities.
- **Maintaining a Dialogue and Open Channels:** It will help to maintain open communication within the organization regarding concerns that employees may be having regarding working along with people with disabilities. The employees may be holding some misconceptions and these would require to be cleared before they are comfortable in their team roles. Only when there is a dialogue can the issues be discussed and addressed in an open manner.
- **Reservation:** for differently able must be made in the private sector too. This is section is an important employer in the economy and reservation in employment will expand the opportunities for people with disabilities. The government has set up various incentives for employers in the private sector for providing regular employment to persons with disabilities. Thus under a Central Sector Scheme of providing one-lakh jobs per annum to the persons with disabilities, the Government will make payment of the employer's contribution to the Employees Provident Fund and Employees State Insurance for the first three years, as an incentive, in return of employment of persons

with disabilities with monthly wage up to Rs 25000/- per month (www.socialjustice.nic.in).

Organizations like Wipro, Infosys have been recognized for their implementation of inclusive practices at the workplace. Wipro has introduced several initiatives to support the careers of people with disabilities within the company (http://www.wipro.com/newsroom). These include:

- Building infrastructure benchmarked against UN guidelines to provide barrier-free access
- Auditing of people policies to build a culture of inclusivity and to communicate relevant information
- Transforming applications, websites and career portals based on the WCAG 2.0 guidelines to provide complete accessibility
- Training trainers and library staff as well as developing curriculum that will help induct and assimilate people with disabilities
- Streamlining administrative processes to include prospective disabled employees
- Wipro encourages disabled employees to take on a wide variety of roles across businesses depending on their skill and experience. (http://www.wipro.com/newsroom).

Vindhya E-Infomedia located in Bangalore "recruits mainly the disabled for all its operations in data management, data entry, data processing, data conversion, etc. While companies are still deliberating the employment of PWDs, eVindhya has set a path breaking example by designing their business model around employing primarily persons with disabilities; as many as 95% of their workforce is disabled. Further, most of their employees are school and college dropouts who are given relevant training for jobs in the company. Not turning away any disabled person who applies is their motto and if candidates are found to be lacking in job skills, they are referred to relevant skill training programs and absorbed on completion of the training. Their attrition rate is minimal, employees' productivity is at par with any able bodied person and the company still runs a sustainable business model. The 5% of their workforce who are not disabled are hired based on their sensitivity to and understanding of persons with disability". (http://www.nasscom.in)

MindTree, candidates with disabilities are encouraged to apply for all available posts that they may be qualified for. "The objective here was to get rid of stereotyping where it is believed that a person with a certain kind of disability will only be able to effectively perform certain kinds of jobs" (http://www.nasscom.in). The company conducts diversity sensitization trainings for new hires and also informs them of relevant Government schemes and benefits. It conforms to physical accessibility norms and has undertaken an accessibility audit for some of its buildings to ensure that they adhere to international standards.

The belief that those who have disabilities add to the diversity of skills available in the organization and their higher retention rates has made many BPOs and IT firms take a serious look at this talent pool.

CONCLUSION

Although the legislation aimed at protecting the rights of the disabled have been enacted in India, much more needs to be done to ensure that it is implemented in letter as well as spirit. Both the government and the private sector need to go that extra mile to ensure diversity through inclusion at the workplace Increasingly organizations are appreciating the fact that persons with disabilities can deliver the desired results and contribute to organizational performance.

REFERENCES

[1] Annual Report of the Office of the United Nations High Commissioner for Human Rights (2012) *Thematic study on the work and employment of persons with disabilities.*

[2] Australian Government Productivity Commission Inquiry Report (2004) Review of the

[3] Davis Ken, (1996), 'Glascow Centre for Inclusive Living: The Social Model of Disability-Setting the terms of a new debate', accessed on http://www.gcil.org.uk/FileAccess.aspx?id=59http://www.disabled-world.com/definitions/disability-definitions.php

[4] Disability Discrimination Act 1992, Report No. 30, Volume 1.

[5] http://www.nasscom.in/sites/default/files/awards/inclusivity_at_workplace.pdf

[6] http://www.ohchr.org/EN/Issues/Disability/Pages/ThematicStudies.aspx

[7] http://www.skillsforemployment.org/wcmstest4/groups/skills/documents/skpcontent/mdaw/mdix/~edisp/fm11g_021829.pdf

[8] http://www.socialjustice.nic.in/policiesacts3.php

[9] http://www.undp.org/content/dam/india/docs/pub-povertyreduction/livelihood-opportunities-for-persons-with-disabilities.pdf

[10] http://www.wipro.com/newsroom/Wipro-selected-as-Indias-Role-Model-Organization-for-the-NCPEDP-Shell-Helen-Keller-Awards-2012

[11] https://www.humanrights.gov.au/our-work/disability-rights/guides/brief-guide-disability-discrimination-act

[12] Jausovec Tim, (October, 2007), 'Positive Discrimination in regard to disabilities'.

[13] Sian Moore, Tessa Wright and Hazel Conley, Working Lives Research Institute, London Metropolitan University Queen Mary, University of London (September, 2011), 'Addressing discrimination in the workplace on multiple grounds – the experience of trade union Equality Reps'.

[14] World Bank Report (2007) People with Disabilities in India: From Commitments to Outcomes.

[15] World Health Organization and the World Bank (2011), *World Report on Disability*, p. 261, available at http://whqlibdoc.who.int/publications/2011/9789240685215_eng.pdf.

Gendered CSR: An Initiative Towards Creating an Inclusive Workplace

Prachi Jain and Vijita Singh Aggarwal

University School of Management Studies, Guru Govind Singh Indraprastha University, Dwarka, New Delhi

ABSTRACT

India has been on the path of economic growth for over a decade now.India is one of the fastest growing economies in the world, but it has not been able to make it inclusive.The concept of the inclusive workplace(Mor Barak, 2000b, 2005, 2011) refers to a work organization that accept and utlizes the diversity of its workforce. While also being active in the community and in state and federal programs that support immigrants, women, the working poor, and other disadvantaged groups.The developed countries are already facing scarcity of human resources and they need the developing countries to be their markets. Hence, upliftment of women through CSR initiatives can prove to be a step forward towards creation of an inclusive workplace.This article explores the link between CSR initiatives and its impact on the journey towards inclusive growth by focussing on the gender perspective of CSR. (CSR, 2013) (More women leaders, means higher levels of Corporate Social Responsibility, 2011)

Keywords: *Corporate Social Responsibility, Inclusiveness, Gender-Perspective*

INTRODUCTION

Corporate social responsibility (CSR) is increasingly important for the competitiveness of companies, as it brings benefits in terms of risk management, cost savings, access to capital, customer relationships, human resource management and innovation capacity (European Commission, 2011).

Corporate social responsibility (CSR) is a form of corporate self-regulation integrated into a business model. CSR policy functions as a built-in, self-regulating mechanism whereby a business monitors and ensures its active compliance within the spirit of the law, ethical standards, and international norms. CSR is a process with the aim to embrace responsibility for the company's actions and encourage a positive impact through its activities on the environment, consumers, employees, communities, stakeholders and all other members of the public sphere who may also be considered as stakeholders (From Wikipedia).

Although, the concept's application is essentially contested (Moon et al, 2005), it has been defined as business responsibility for its economic, legal, ethical and philanthropic activities (Carroll 1999).

In simple words, CSR is a concept whereby organizations consider the interests of society by taking responsibility for the impact of their activities on customers, suppliers, shareholders, communities and the environment in all aspects of their operations. In other words, CSR focuses on main elements: the workplace, the community, the marketplace and the environment Implementing CSR principles implies that the organization acts consciously and actively considers gender, amongst other topics, when taking business decisions that affect its employees and society. In the context of the current crisis, corporate social responsibility (CSR) becomes a key tool as it enables enterprises to better anticipate and take advantage of fast changing societal expectations and operating conditions, therefore driving the development of new markets and creating opportunities for growth (European Commission, 2011).

CSR AND GENDER

Women and men, girls and boys share life in the society. However, in most societies women and men, as well as girls and boys have different opportunities and possibilities, as well as restrictions for what they can do and not. Women and men have different experiences, due to their different roles, to different expectations and opportunities. Gender refers to these differences. Gender differences exist everywhere there is human interaction. It affects the economy and health of individual persons, it affects productivity, development and economy for business enterprises, and it affects the education and health systems of societies as well as their economy and development. Gender relations are further intertwined with other diversity aspects, such as differences in age, ethnicity, social class, culture, sexual identity, etc.

Gender equality should be included more explicitly among the CSR priorities for several reasons: first, because these principles constitute compelling moral claims; secondly, because there are systemically biased business models that create advantages for men and disadvantages for women, and finally, because corporations, as moral agents, have the duty to adopt gender equity as a priority of social responsibility (Thompson, 2007). Besides, corporations can benefit economically from the promotion of gender equality (Catalyst, 2007; Carter et al., 2003; Erhardt, et. al., 2003; European Union, 2010). Therefore a new management trend is emerging which involves the incorporation of gender variable in CSR's management (Grosser, 2009; Grosser and Moon, 2006). The so called Gendered Social Responsibility considers the existing relations among the company and the stakeholders under the gender perspective (Torre and Maruri, 2009).

GENDER BIAS AT WORKPLACE

Since independence, the government of India has brought in many laws to protect women's rights. The constitution prohibits discrimination on many grounds, including gender, and recognizes the principle of equality for all before the law and of opportunity in matters relating to employment (Articles 14 to 16 of The Constitution of India, as modified 1 December 2007). However, according to the **ILO's Global Employment Trends 2013 report**, India's labour force participation rate for women fell from just over 37 per cent in 2004-05 to 29 per cent in 2009-10. Out of 131 countries with available data, India ranks 11th from the bottom in female labour force participation."Despite very rapid economic growth in India in recent years, we're observing declining female labour force participation rates across all age groups, across all education levels, and in both urban and rural areas," said ILO economist Steven Kapsos during a presentation of the report in India.As per the 68th Round of the National Sample Survey Women make up just a fifth of the organised sector workforce. The latest data shows that of the total organised sector employment in the country in 2010, women accounted for 20.4 per cent of the total workforce.Even within the organised sector, most women are located in the lower steps of the hierarchy (Joseph and Prasad, 1995; Srivastava, 1997). Very few are managers, bosses or decision-makers (Agrawal and Rao, 2004; Menon-Sen and Kumar, 2001). In Kerala, women constitute 39 per cent of all organised sector workers (DGE&T). The States with a low share of women's employment in organised sector jobs are Bihar, Uttar Pradesh, West Bengal, Jammu and Kashmir and Orissa.

There is a scarcity of women among highly qualified professions.This has many consequences, such as: long working hours with fierce resistance to any reductions; unpaid overtime; high management expectations of employee flexibility to meet unanticipated client demands; and the need for employees to negotiate flexible working arrangements on a case-by-case basis with a project manager, who often has much discretion on whether to accommodate such requests. The study declares that women are particularly disadvantaged in such a system, which could partly explain their under-representation in such jobs (Stéphanie, 2010).

Amartya Sen, Indian author and winner of the Nobel Prize in economics, discusses gender inequality in his book *The Argumentative Indian: Writings on Indian History, Culture and Identity.* He points out that the social movement for Indian women had been, until recently, primarily focused on achieving better treatment and well-being for women: "In the course of the evolution of women's movement [...] women are not passive recipients of welfare-enhancing help brought about by society, but are active promoters and facilitators of social transformations. Such transformations influence the lives and well-being of women, but also those of men and children—boys as well as girls. This is a momentous enrichment of the reach of women's movement" (Sen, A.2005).Khandelwal, in his study on *Gender Stereotypes at Work:*

Implications for Organizations notes that stereotypes and perceptions of Indian women in the workplace appear to have a significant negative impact on the position of women managers. The study suggests that male Indian managers are viewed, stereotypically, as working in the areas of sales, marketing and production; being good leaders, decision makers and bosses; and handling challenging assignments. On the other hand, Indian women are viewed as working in HR and administrative positions at low to junior levels, and in fields such as fashion and beauty. Women in Indian organizations felt that such stereotypes result from not being given challenging assignments. Yet, male managers saw women as being treated more leniently than men when making mistakes (Khandelwal, 2002).Women are paid especially little in "women's jobs" such as those in cleaning and child care (ILO, 2003). During the last decade an increasing number of studies have indicated adverse health consequences of sexual harassment at work (Kauppinen, 1998). In short a gender based CSR takes into account the perspectives of women and men, boys and girls, strengthening the strategic value of the CSR instrument. A recent study on public reporting by CSR gender group on gender equality concluded that the reasons companies give for taking action on gender and diversity may be divided into the following areas:

Recognition of the importance of intangible assets, including human capital management

Reputation, brand management and increased stakeholder interest in gender and diversity issues Monitoring, once in place, drives further action,Regulation to report to government values and the emergence of CSR.

IMPORTANCE OF GENDERED CSR

A recent newspaper article reported that the representation of women on Indian boards is just around 5.3%. In comparison USA is 14.5%, Canada is 15%, Britain 12.2 and hongkong about 8.9%.Why is this figure so abysmally low, especially in India?Focussing specifically on how women leaders might impact CSR, researchers from Harvard Business School and Catalyst conducted follow up analysis. Compared to companies without women executive leaders, research found that companies with gender inclusive leadership teams contributed, on average, more charitable funds.Companies with more women corporate officials donated significantly m(csr-gendergroup.com)ore funds between 1997 and 2007, and for each percentage point increase in women corporate officers, yearly donations increased by $5.7 million, report says. A large body of literature indicates that men have many more occupational accidents than women, in all working jurisdictions where data is available (Islam et al. 2001; Laflamme and Lilert-Petersson, 2001). Men die at work much more often than women, from violence as well as accidents (Helmkamp *et al*, 2000). The idea that the gender makes men more likely to be exposed to many risks at work has been raised by several authors (Cru and Dejours, 1983; Loukil, 1997; Kjellberg, 1998). In some countries, tensions may arise if men feel they are asked to do harder jobs (Messing and Elabidi, 2003).

WHAT BASIS COULD GENDER DIVERSITY OPERATE? INEQUALITY OF REPRESENTATION IN THE WORKPLACE

Gender inequality can be attributed to two main factors: (i) external factors such as legal framework, social and cultural perceptions: and (ii) internal factors that reinforce gender inequalities such as corporate culture, values, human resources structure and CSR application.

External Factors

Legal Framework

The industries and economic activities that are prohibited for women workers, as well as the hours during which women are not allowed to work.

Work at night for women is limited thus depriving women from increased income through overtime work. In reality, these restrictions serve to limit the competition between men and women in favor of men.

For example, women have specific protections in the workplace, including the right to a 10-week maternity leave for the purpose of childcare, of which 6 weeks must be allowed immediately following the birth of the child.

Social Perceptions and Interference

Society, in addition to the legislative framework, directly and indirectly enforces certain practices and "acceptable" standards, i.e. the role of women, the time women can work, priorities for women, etc.

Internal Factors

In addition to the external factors that influence women in the workplace, there are internal factors that reinforce social perceptions and play on the gender inequalities, either by increasing them or marginalizing them.

Corporate Culture and Values

The corporate culture and values influence the overall situation of women and gender dynamics in a direct way; namely :through the mental models, informal culture, recruitment policy and promotion policy of the organization.

Mental Models

Social perception and interference create or reinforce within companies certain mental models that dictate the role of women in the workplace

The "traditional" role of women: it was out of social consideration for the "traditional" role of women, as the housekeepers and child bearers. In company women should not take on late night shifts so they can be home for their husbands when they return from their work and have the opportunity to look after their children before or as they come back from school.

The "appropriate" role of women:women could take on certain posts whilst other posts were inaccessible to them. In principle this was related to the physical nature of the job or post; however, the physical labor required by these posts today has been substantially reduced enabling women to perform such tasks. Regardless, the "traditional" stereotype remains.

The "priority" for women:women were clearly tagged as individuals with a

social role to play i.e. housewife, child bearer, and that a job in essence may not be acceptable – but if necessary the job is a secondary role. Also, there was clear skepticism of women's commitment to their jobs because of the social role they play or are expected to play. This skepticism resulted in the perception that to women the job will never be their priority (and should not e), and as such they are temporarily in the workplace making focus or attention on their role in the workplace unnecessary.

Policy Versus Practice

Some of the companies have strict policies aligned with international standards with respect to women in the workplace. However, it was clear in many cases that such policies, although well written and in some cases even effectively communicated, were not necessarily translated into practice or embedded within the company culture

Recruitment Policy

Recruitment policy at best is gender blind i.e. criteria for employment is a set qualification without consideration of social, culture or gender issues. In implementation, this leaves much room for an informal culture to dictate the applicability of social, cultural or gender norms, making the recruitment policy a mere guideline but not a process or practice.

For example if a woman wanted to work as a technician, whose job description is gender neutral, the application may not be considered because of the stereotypical mental model and the resulting informal culture and perception that it is inappropriate for a woman to work as a technician.

It appears that a recruitment policy that was gender blind is disadvantageous to women because it enables an informal culture to dictate their inappropriateness for particular posts.

Furthermore, there is no audit of process and practice to monitor how mental models and informal culture affect the interview and recruitment process.

Job Description Policy

Men and women performing the same jobs don't in actual fact have the same responsibilities. For example, men and women with the same job title and position will perform different responsibilities because of stereotypes and gender differentiation.

For Example male accountants are expected to perform out of office work whilst female accountants are not. By policy their job descriptions are identical; yet in practice they are not because of the informal culture that dictates it is inappropriate for women to undertake out of office work since it entails dealing with governmental officials that are usually men.

Promotion Policy

Policies and practices, as they relate to promotion, are difficult to ascertain since they reflect on a conglomerate set of actions.

For example, all companies were clear in that promotions are directly tied to defined criteria based on performance. However, performance is based on being able to effectively perform ones responsibilities. This may require out of office work for the female accountant, late night shifts for the female manager or experience and know-how in non-traditional female posts, all of which are activities women have limited access to because of the informal cultures.

Therefore, although policy and practice may be aligned in the technical sense, it is unjust to base the same performance criteria on men and women without taking into account factors that have a direct impact on women's ability to perform effectively.

HUMAN RESOURCE MANAGEMENT

A key asset to any business is their human asset. It would be difficult to ascertain growth, success or sustainability without good human resources and effective human resource management. Accordingly, it is important to review human resource management as it may influence gender roles, rights and opportunities in the workplace.

The key issues identified in the study are summarized as follows:

1. Existing gender blind policies are often neither effective nor sufficient to ensure gender equality in the workplace. Without an accountability structure and effective supervision to avoid gender biases gender blind policies, in general are not effective in promoting women advancement and gender equality. The existing mental models within the companies tend to play a role in the application of such policies, rendering them subject to personal stereotyping, perceptions and biases.
2. Positive discrimination towards female empowerment needs to be revisited. Initiatives and practices in place to support female empowerment or employment often hinder the development, growth and advancement of women as they are often based on positive

discrimination; such initiatives and practices need to be revisited to ensure they are in fact supportive and are without any negative impact on women's career choice and development.

3. Education, training and awareness are required to effectively implement gender equality in the workplace.
   - Education is key to creating a balanced workplace in terms of gender equality, and to build awareness of its importance and value to the companies and society.
   - In general, the understanding of gender equality in the workplace is limited to female employment; education is required to enhance companies' understanding of gender equality and broaden the scope and effectiveness of related policies.
   - Enhancing gender equality within the work place requires a practical approach from management that indeed requires executive training on how to identify issues and address them.

More awareness is needed for both men and women, especially in manual and blue – collar jobs, on the value of women's participation in the workplace and in some cases their ability and capacity to engage effectively.

CONCLUSION

Organizations are becoming more aware of their responsibilities as CSR accountability becomes more accepted globally. As this awareness evolves organizations will begin to look differently inside their own organizations and see a need to extend CSR to employees who may have been undervalued in the past. An increased value on CSR internally, as well as externally will become a competitive advantage for the recruitment and retention of future employees.

Today, businesses succeed based on engagement of their employees. By engagement of employees we mean the two-way conversation with employees addressing their needs and the needs of the business. CSR is a key tool to facilitate such engagement.

HR has a key role in making CSR work, and CSR without HR runs the risk of being dismissed as PR or shallow "window-dressing". As such CSR is an opportunity for HR to demonstrate a strategic focus and act as a business-focused department as opposed to simply managing human resources.

CSR needs to be embedded in an organization's culture to change behaviors and attitudes, and the support of the top team is critical to success. To be effective CSR should be integrated into processes such as recruitment, appraisal, retention, motivation, reward, internal communications, diversity, coaching and training.Placing an increased value on CSR internally and externally will result in a competitive advantage for the recruitment and retention of employees. Education, training and awareness are required to effectively implement gender equality in the workplace. Education is key to creating a balanced workplace in terms of gender equality, and to build awareness of its importance and value to the companies and society.In general, the understanding of gender equality in the workplace is limited to female employment; education is required to enhance companies understanding of gender equality and broaden the scope and effectiveness of related policies. Enhancing gender equality within the work place requires a practical approach from management that indeed requires executive training on how to identify issues and address them.

More awareness is needed for both men and women, especially in manual and blue – collar jobs, on the value of women's participation in the workplace and in some cases their ability and capacity to engage effectively.The above key findings of this study demonstrate that although female employment may be increasing in India, female empowerment and the role of women in the workplace remains limited as a result of gender stereotyping, mental models and social conditioning.

e.g. :In 1992, a female government official in rural Rajasthan, India, was gang raped by 5 men whom she tried to refrain from marrying off a girl (less than a year old) from their family. The demon of sexual harassment of women and automatic discrimination of women at work hit Indian society very hard. It was not people were unaware of these sorts of incidents but it was an eye opener. There have been several instances in the past which have necessitated more policy directives and adherence to the principles of gender equality.

The latest govt ruling has mandated the corporate to spend 2% of their profit on CSR.P. Chidambaram said in a report in 2013 that such ruling will have a great multiplier effect in bringing out much greater inclusiveness. However, it is not only the business community that bear the responsibility for correcting inequalities. There is a need for policies that promote women's agency, opportunities and rights in the workplace. Policies that empower and enable the entire workforce, both men and women, to participate and contribute with their capacity.

Thus, more stringent policies must be framed in favour of women so as to create a more sustainable and inclusive workplace.

REFERENCES

[1] Agrawal, R. & Rao, B.V.L.N. (2004). *Gender Issues. A Road Map to Empowerment.* New Delhi: Shipra Publications.

[2] Alison McKewen Scott, 'Informal sector or female sector? Gender bias in urban labour marketmodels', in Diane Elson (ed), Male Bias in the Development Process, Manchester: Manchester University Press, 1995.

[3] Angela Hale & Jane Wills (eds), Threads of Labour: Garment Industry Supply Chains from the Workers'Perspective, Oxford: Blackwell for WomenWorking Worldwide, 2005.

[4] Bonde, J.P. & Storgaard, L. (2002). How work-place conditions, environmental toxicants and lifestyle affect male reproductive function. *International Journal of Andrology*, Vol. 25(5):262-8.

[5] Brighton: IDS, 2006, at www.ethicaltrade.org.

[6] CAFOD, 'Clean up your computer: working conditions in the electronics sector', 2004, at http://www.cafod.org/uk.

[7] Cru, D. & Dejours, C. (1983). Savoir-faire de prudence dans les métiers du bâtiment. *Cahiers médicaux-sociaux, Vol. 27, 239-247.*

[8] Esther Schipper & Irene de Hahn, 'CSR issues in the ICT hardware manufacturing sector', SOMO ICT Sector Report, Amsterdam: Centre for Research on Multinational Corporations (SOMO), 2005, at www.somo.nl.

[9] European Commission (2011) A renewed EU strategy 2011-14 for Corporate Social Responsibility. Communication from the Commission to the European Parliament, the Council, the European Economic and Social Committee and the Committee of the Regions, COM(2011) 681 final.

[10] Habtu, R. (July 2003). Information technology workers: Perspectives on labour and income, 4(7), 5–11. Retrieved from http://www.statcan.gc.ca/pub/75-001-x/75-001-x2003007- eng. pdf.

[11] Helmkamp, J., Lundstrom, W. & Williams, J. (2000). Work-related fatalities in West Virginia. A summary of surveillance, investigation, and prevention activities, July 1996-December 1999. *Annals of Epidemiology,* Vol. 10 (7), 478.

[12] Jennifer Hurley with Doug Miller, 'The changing face of the global garment industry', in Hale & Wills,Threads of Labour, pp. 16–39.

[13] Khandelwal, P. (2002, April-June). Gender stereotypes at work: Implications for organizations. *Indian Journal of Training and Development,* Vol. XXXII(2), 72-83.

[14] L Brill, 'Can codes of conduct help home-based workers?', in Jenkins et al, Corporate Responsibility and Labour Rights

[15] Marina Prieto, 'Corporate social responsibility in Latin America: Chiquita, women banana workers and structural inequalities', *Journal of Corporate Citizenship*, 21, 2006, pp. 85–94.

[16] Menon-Sen, K. & Shiva Kumar, A.K. (2001). Women in India: How Free? How Equal? Report commissioned by the Office of the United Nations Resident Coordinator in India. New Delhi: UNDP.

[17] M Prieto, A Hadjipateras & J Turner, 'The potential of codes as part of women's organisations' strategies for promoting the rights of women workers: a central American Perspective', in Jenkins et al., *Corporate Responsibility & Labour Rights*, p. 153.

[18] R Pearson, 'Gender perspectives on health and safety in information processing: learning from international experience', in Swasti Mitter & Sheila Rowbotham, *Women Encounter Technology: Changing Patterns of Employment in the Third World*, London: Routledge, 1995.

[19] Sally Smith & Catherine Dolan, 'Ethical trade: what does it mean for women workers in African horticulture?', in Barrientos & Dolan, *Ethical Sourcing in the Global Food System.*

[20] Sen, A. (2005). The argumentative Indian: Writings on Indian history and culture and identity. New York: Farrar, Straus and Giroux.

[21] Stephanie Barrientos & Sally Smith, The ETI Code of Labour Practice: Do Workers really Benefit?

[22] S Razavi & R Pearson, 'Globalization, export-oriented employment and social policy: gendered connections', in S Razavi, R Pearson & C Danloy (eds), *Globalization, Export-oriented Employmentand Social Policy: Gendered Connections*, Basingstoke: Palgrave, 2004

[23] Stéphanie, C. (2010). *Canadian Journal of Administrative Sciences Revue canadienne des sciences de administration,* Vol 27: 236–248.

[24] Thompson, L. (2008) "Gender equity and CSR in a post-feminist era". Business Ethics: A European Review, Vol. 17(1), pp. 87-106.

[25] 'Women and men in the informal economy', available from www.idrc.ca.

[26] World Health Organization, "Health Topics: Gender," (2010). online: WHO, <http://www.who.int/topics/gender/en/index.html>. Assessed 2 February 2012.

A Study of Employee Wellness Programs in IT Companies in India

Gunjan Mathur and Deepali Dabas

Ansal University, Gurgaon

ABSTRACT

Wellness is defined as a life- long process by which an individual is able to achieve balance in his physical, social, environmental and intellectual, well being. Thus it is state of balance of the mind, spirit and body. Wellness ensures that the individual maximizes his potential. Organizations are working on emotional, environmental, occupational, intellectual, social, physical and spiritual wellbeing of their employees.

A number of employee wellness programmes are being used by organizations to prevent the occurrence of chronic diseases among employees. The business houses are running these programmes to improve productivity and reduce healthcare costs .The results of wellness initiatives are manifold, it is believed that it improves morale among the employees, and there is a higher job satisfaction and better team work.

Indians are becoming more and more conscious about their health, but due to a number of reasons like stress, long working hours and family commitments, it becomes difficult for finding time to satisfy their wellness goals. Workplace wellness programs are very important as the major part of an individual's time is spent working.

The current study focuses on wellness initiatives taken by IT companies in India. The high stress levels, poor nutrition, physical inactivity, smoking and long working hours are resulting into reduced productivity and chronic diseases, all this is reflected in the high number of deaths caused by the chronic diseases. The current paper attempts to highlight some major companies who have sophisticated wellness programmes in place.

Keywords: *Wellness Initiatives, Indian IT Companies*

INTRODUCTION

According to the World Health Organization (WHO), close to 60% of deaths in India could be attributed to chronic diseases, including cardiovascular disease (stroke and heart disease), cancer, chronic respiratory diseases and diabetes. The estimated deaths from chronic diseases will register a sharp increase from 3.78 million in 1990 to 7.63 million in 2020 accounting for 66.7% of all deaths and that is the reason why the wellness programmes are very essential in the Indian context.

India stands to lose on average International$ 200 billion in national income due to deaths from heart disease, stroke and diabetes from 2005 to 2015. This is illustrated in the figure below.

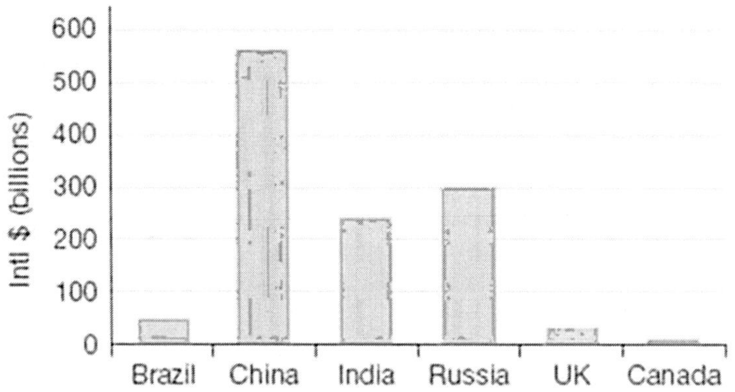

Source: An estimation of the economic impact of chronic non communicable diseases in selected countries, World Health Organization, 2005

Fig. 1

THE NEED FOR WELLNESS PROGRAMMES

Organizations invest in wellness programmes because they want to:

- Improve their productivity.
- Become more socially responsible which helps to build their corporate image.
- Become a very attractive organization for employees to work.
- To cut-down the cost of healthcare of employees.

It is very crucial for an organization to look after the well-being of their employee in today's competitive business environment. Organizational prosperity is directly influenced by the well-being of its employees. With innovative and creativity planning the management can look after the well-being of their employee which in turn would benefit them and enhance the performance of employees.

One of the best ways to develop competitive advantage for an organization is to enhance the well being of an employee. Employee health status has a direct influence on the performance, productivity, profitability and reduced absentees Boles, M., Pelletier, B., & Lynch, W. (2004)

An equation between well-being of an employee and high performance can only be understood by high-performance companies. Management at these high performing companies are often lead by functional team which foster a culture of health which becomes a competitive advantage, this is put into practice by involving employees, creating management for innovative practices, offering meaningful incentives, supporting employees, motivating to do the best in life Meyer, L., & Parton, R. (2011).

Before planning any wellness program companies need to focus on some major areas which are discussed:

- *Be Innovative:* Corporate wellness should be powerful and unique rather than boring one to ensure success and wellbeing of employees. Employees need to be challenged in different ways to create change. Improving employee wellbeing can create significant benefits to the organization.
- *Compromising on Health Care Cost:* Year after year health care cost has been increasing rapidly. Employees of small company cannot take this burden any more. However, through higher deductibles they are passing the cost on to their employees. Healthier employee can actually contribute to the productivity and profitability of the organization. Some employers these days lower the employees' contribution with rebates if they are willing to participate in wellness programmes.
- *Corporate Wellness is Complicated:* A unique strategy is involved when we talk about the success of corporate wellness which comprises a framework of short term goals and long term goals for the employee. Corporate wellness needs leadership, co-operation, support and commitment from employees which involves education, communication, incentives, rewards and physical activities.

Healthy work place enhances the well being of an employee while enhancing the organizational performance which benefits employers as well as the organization. Improving well being of an employee create significant business benefits. Employees who have a positive well being are more energetic, focused, resilient and positive than the employees who have a negative wellbeing. Higher level of well being predicts the higher level of performance of employees.

For creating a Healthy work place, practices can be grouped into following categories:

- *Employee Involvement:* Employees should be involved in decision making; problem solving and a level of freedom should be allowed to the employee which increase employee involvement.
- *Balance between Work-Life:* Programs and policies should be made for employee to balance their work life as well as personal life which help them to manage multiple demands such as Benefits for family members, flexible work arrangements and flexible leave options.
- *Growth and Development:* Favorable circumstances for growth and development help employees to expand their skills, abilities and knowledge such as career development, skills training, opportunities for promotions and developing leadership skills.
- *Health and Safety:* This help employee to improve their mental and physical health through encouraging a healthy lifestyle and behaviour. Some of the workplace practices are: Counselling, efforts to develop healthy life style, training, health screening.

- *Employee Recognition:* Employee in an organization should be recognized for his contribution to the organization. Ways of recognizing are: competitive benefit packages, acknowledging their contribution, employee awards and ceremonies for recognising work of an employee.

Work related well being can be studied in three types: Health (psychological and physiological health); Happiness (subjective experiences of an employee) (Danna & Griffin, 1999); relationship well-being (quality of relation between employee and their employer) (Grant, Christianson & Price, 2007). A healthy work environment has a direct effect on the performance of an employee. A high level of awareness is an important factor to success. Americans are very much conscious about their health and due to high level of stress they no longer work days and multitasking. Creating an on-site wellness programs is very essential because employee spend most of their time at the workplace.

REVIEW OF LITERATURE

The workplace is an important part in an individual's life which affects his or her well-being and the well-being of the society. The average adult spends most of his life working for an organization. The nature of work such as complexity and supervision has been found to be linked with individual sense of depression and control (Kohn & Schooler, 1982). It has been recognized that depression is the disease which contributes to reduction of healthy years of life (Murray & Lopez, 1996). It has been found that employees of recent generation want to work with an organization which contributes to a meaningful development in their life (Avolio & Sosik, 1999; Wrzesniewski, McCauley, Rozin, & Schwartz, 1997).

Researchers have studied a positive relationship between well-being of an employee to work performance (Iaffaldano & Muchinsky, 1985; Judge, Thoresen, Bono &Patton, 2001). Spector's (1997) suggested that employees who are more satisfied with their work perform better as compared to dissatisfied ones and are more likely to be associated with their organisation. Employee who experience positive well-being in work place is more likely to be hardworking and action oriented. Work is one of the most dominant factors which play an important role in an individuals and community's well-being. It can affect the well-being of an individual resulting in loss of the entire communities. Employees' well-being can be linked with the outcome of business such as productivity, employee turnover and profitability.

Lyubomirsky, King, & Diener, (2005), Found that people who are positive in their approach and happy have a better mental and physical outcome when compared to the people who were negative. Lyubomirsky (2008, p. 25), in a recent update it was concluded that people who were happier and positive in their approach were more resilient and physically healthier and have a stronger immune system. Happy people live their life happily.

Studies have clearly shown that there is a link between happiness (Graham, Eggers, & Sukhtankar, 2004), positive emotions (Ostir, Markides, Peek, & Goodwin, 2001), life satisfaction (Mroczek & Spiro, 2005), and positive self-perceptions (Levy, Slade, Kunkel, & Kasl, 2002) and mental and physical health outcomes. Wright (2003, p. 441) suggested that positive well-being at workplace is essential to increase the productivity which contributes to the organization. Experimental studies have shown that positive state of an employee reports higher efficacy and self-perception (Baron, 1990; Schuettler & Kiviniemi, 2006), have optimistic approach (Brown, 1984) and set higher goals themselves (Baron, 1990; Hom & Arbuckle, 1988). In Occupational Health Psychology it has been demonstrated that well-being is impacted by hope (Snyder, Lehman, Kluck, & Monsson, 2006), self-efficacy (Axtell et al., 2000; Bandura, 1997; and Meier, Semmer, Elfering, & Jacobshagen, 2008), resiliency (Britt, Adler, & Bartone, 2001; Ferris, Sinclair, & Kline, 2005; Keyes, 2007; Williams & Cooper, 1998) and optimism (Carver et al., 2005). Seligman's cited that optimism is one of the primary factor which leads to the well-being of an employee (Quick, 1999).

Recently employee well-being has gained attentions from management and psychologists all over the world. Many researchers have concluded that organisations should adopt a healthy practices at workplace for their employees which not only focus on the profitability and productivity of an organization but also look after the well-being of an employee (Grawitch, Gottschalk, & Munz, 2006; Grawitch, Trares, & Kohler, 2007; Russell, 2008; Wright & Cropanzano, 2004). The normal notion is that the worker who is happy delivers a greater performance which results to the productivity and profitability of an organization. The well-being of an employee is related to numerous outcomes of an organization such as: work involvement, enhanced job performance, job satisfaction, commitment, increased profitability, competitiveness and reduced employee turnover (Grawitch et al., 2006; Keyes, Hysom, & Lupo, 2000; Russell, 2008; Spector, 1997; Warr, 2005; Wright & Bonnet, 2007). Researchers have found that positive well-being leads to higher performance and high level of commitment towards the organization Grawitch et al., 2007; Warr, 2005; Wright & Cropanzano, 2004) on the other hand many researches argued that organizational commitment and work performance leads to better well-being of an employee (Begley & Czajka, 1993; Meyer & Allen, 1997). (Wright & Cropanzano, 2004; p. 343) Found that employees who are more passionate towards their work are more committed and deliver higher performance. Grawitch and colleagues (2006) suggested that organizations should focus more on positive health of employees rather than on preventing the negative outcome of poor health. Grawitch et al. (2006) identified five major practices which organization should adopt for maximizing the well-being of employees. (1) Growth and development of employees; (2) Balance between work-life; (3) Health; (4) Involvement of employee; (5) Recognition. Grawitch and colleagues (2007) showed that employee satisfaction with their workplace which uses healthier practices enhances their well-being and work performance.

OBJECTIVES

- To identify the importance of Wellness in the development and sustainability of the Organizations.
- To identify the Wellness initiatives by IT companies in India

FINDINGS AND ANALYSIS

The wellness initiatives taken by some of the Indian IT companies to make their workplace more attractive and build a healthy global community are discussed in detail.

DELL

At Dell multiple programmes are launched to help employees to keep themselves and their families healthy. Programs are monitored for effectiveness and conformity. Global Benefits, Regional programmes and Environmental Health and Safety teams engage employees through site which offer medical screenings, smoking cessation, stress management programs, time management programs and personality development programs.

Global Benefits

Dell's employee benefit programs are designed in a way that helps employees and their family members to plan their major life events such as Disability, retirement and death.

They have a program Well at Dell which enhances employee well being, health and provide health management assistance. Some of Well at Dell activities are:

- On-site wellness centre where employee can exercise and receive information regarding staying health.
- Health Screening including blood pressure and breast cancer.
- Seminars which cover topics such as nutrition and excise, smoking cessation.
- Seasonal Flu vaccines for employees and their family members.
- Medical insurance of employees and their family members
- Events for home safety fairs.

Regional Program

In India Dell regional team developed programs to meet the needs of their employees. This program included:

- A regular Health Check up (Dental checks, Blood pressure check, Body mass index measurement).
- Events creating awareness about Cardiac

- Seminars Healthy Meal choices

India's corporate world is facing challenges of mental stress and burnout. The body and mind of an employee are unable to keep pace with their goals due to the level of stress at work place. The organizations have realized if the well being of an employee is not taken care then the organization may experience loss of productivity, may not achieve targets on time, Absenteeism, Increasing health expenses on employees, large insurance premiums which in turn will affect the revenue of the company. After looking at these factors companies realize that there is a great importance for health care programs in the organizations. Promoting well being at work place helps in building healthy team spirit, enhancing profitability and productivity. At workplace people are affected by Anxiety, Depression, Stress burnout, Obesity, addiction, Backaches, neck pain and life style diseases such as Diabetes, Hypertension, etc.

WIPRO

At Wipro wellness programs are running in both IT as well as BPO sector to enhance the well being of employees. The key components of their program are

- Counselling center
- Medical Camps
- Nutrition Consulting
- MITR (Counselling Initiative)
- Events focusing on well being of employees
- Offering low calorie food at their cafeteria.

The MITR Initiative (Counselling)

MITR is one of the most successful wellness programmes running at WIPRO. The highlights of program are:

- Counsellor work with full commitment.
- The team goes through a careful selection process
- Precise training is given to them
- Make them aware about the programmes and ask them to reach as many as people possible and help them to deal with their level of stress related to both personal and professional life.
- Only when the employees feel confident and ensure that he can cope up with the issue himself the help is discontinued.
- Suggestions are taken from both counsellor as well as the subject who has been counseled.
- The program is conducted in office premises by WIPRO employees for WIPRO employees.

Key component of the wellness programmes are:

- Involving key people in the programmes.
- Use of tools such as corporate intranet
- Commitment from high management
- Sustainable model of wellness
- Continuous interaction with public health agencies

Infosys Technologies

Infosys developed a holistic approach towards the well being of their employees. After recognizing that most of their employees range between 25 to 30 years who spend a quality amount of time outside their home, Infosys decided to ensure a quality well being to its employees focusing on physical as well as mental health. The company provides in-house doctors for regular check-ups and a counsellor offering psychological wellbeing to its employees.

The "Health Assessment Lifestyle Enrichment" (HALE) program is one of the most successful programmes launched by Infosys. The main components are:

- Safety
- Health
- Stress
- Leisure
- Team Building
- Fun at work

For Health and Safety various awareness programs have been put together.

For Leisure, the focus is to enrich the lifestyle of employees which is done through seminars.

For Stress, HALE online tool and a HALE Hotline is available 24*7, 365 days a year.

For Fun and Team Building, planned interventions are organized to ensure wellness at work.

Major components of the programmes are as follow:

- Holistic approach to increase productivity, profitability and health.
- Reduced Absenteeism and turnover.
- Ensure in-house feedback
- Interaction with public health agencies

DISCUSSION AND CONCLUSION

Private organizations in India have a very important role to play in preventing the occurrence of chronic diseases. The main reasons identified for chronic diseases are unhealthy diet intake, excessive use of tobacco and physical inactivity and sedentary lifestyle.

With the commitment from leaders, organization based wellness programmes and involvement of public-private partnerships, the large scale epidemic of chronic disease can be prevented and employers can enhance the productivity of the workforce and reduce the burden of healthcare costs.

All these initiatives can make an organization sustainable. Some Indian organisations have been prominent in promoting wellness programmes for preventing chronic diseases and bring about behavioral change to the benefit of themselves, their employees and all other stake holders. These organizations like Dell, Wipro and Infosys have used a sophisticated approach to persuade their employees to participate in the wellness initiatives for mutual benefit.

These organizations have come to realize that a healthy workplace provides number of benefits to employee such as high job satisfaction, better mental and physical health, high level of motivation, positive approach towards work, high morale, improved ability to deal with stress which in turn benefits the organization such as reduced absenteeism and turnover, improved satisfaction of customers, improved quality, productivity and profitability.

REFERENCES

[1] Avolio, B.J., & Sosik, J.J. (1999). A life-span framework for assessing the impact of work on white-collar workers. In S.L. Willis & J.D. Reid (Eds.), Life in the middle: Psychological and Social Development in Middle Age pp. 251-274, San Diego, CA: *Academic Press.*

[2] Axtell, C., Holman, D., Wall, T., Waterson, P., Harrington, E., & Unsworth, K. (2000). Shopfloor innovation: Facilitating the suggestion and implementation of ideas. *Journal of Occupational and Organizational Psychology,* 73, 265–285.

[3] Baron, R.A. (1990). Environmentally induced positive affect: Its impact on self-efficacy, task performance, negotiation and conflict. *Journal of Applied Social Psychology,* 20, 368–384.

[4] Begley, T.A., & Czajka, J.M. (1993). Panel analysis of the moderating effects of commitment on job satisfaction, intention to quit, and health following organizational change. *Journal of Applied Psychology*, 78(4), 552-556.

[5] Boles, M., Pelletier, B., & Lynch, W. (2004). The relationship between health risks and work productivity. *Journal of Occupational nd Environmental Medicine,* 46, 737-745.

[6] Brown, J. (1984). Effects of induced mood on causal attributions for success and failure. *Motivation and Emotion,* 8, 343-353.

[7] Britt, T.W., Adler, A.B., & Bartone, P.T. (2001). Deriving benefits from stressful events: The role of engagement in meaningful work and hardiness. *Journal of Occupational Health Psychology,* 6, 53–63.

[8] Carver, C.S., Smith, R.G., Antoni, M.H., Petronis, V.M., Weiss, S., and Derhagopian, R.P. (2005). Optimistic personality and psychosocial well-being during treatment predict psychosocial well-being among long-term survivors of breast cancer. *Health Psychology,* 24, 508–516.

[9] Danna, K. & Griffin, R.W. (1999). Health and well-being in the workplace: A review and synthesis of the literature. *Journal of Management,* 25, 3, 357-384.

[10] Ferris, P.A., Sinclair, C., & Kline, T.J. (2005). It takes two to tango: Personal and organizational resilience as predictors of strain and cardiovascular disease risk in a work sample. *Journal of Occupational Health Psychology*, 10, 225–238.

[12] Graham, C., Eggers, A., & Sukhtankar, S. (2004). Does happiness pay? An exploration based on panel data from Russia. *Journal of Economic Behavior and Organization,* 55, 319–342.

[13] Grant, A.M., Christianson, M.K. & Price, R.H. (2007). Happiness, health, or relationships? Managerial practices and employee well-being tradeoffs. *Academy of Management Perspectives*, 21, 51-63.

[14] Grawitch, M.J., Gottschalk, M., & Munz, D.C. (2006). The path to a healthy workplace: A critical review linking healthy workplace practices, employee well-being, and organizational improvements. *Consulting Psychology Journal: Practice and Research*, 58(3), 129-147.

[15] Grawitch, M.J., Trares, S., & Kohler, J.M. (2007). Healthy workplace practices and employee outcomes. *International Journal of Stress Management*, 14(3), 275- 293.

[16] Hom, H., & Arbuckle, B. (1988). Mood induction effects upon goal setting and performance in young children. *Motivation and Emotion*, 12, 113–122.

[17] Iaffaldano, M.T., & Muchinsky, P.M. (1985). Job satisfaction and job performance: A meta-analysis. *Psychological Bulletin*, 97, 251-273.

[18] Judge,T.A., Thoresen, C.J., Bono, J.E., & Patton, G.K. (2001). The job satisfaction – job performance relationship: *A qualitative and quantitative review. Psychological Bulletin*, 127, 376-407.

[19] Keyes, C.L.M., Hysom, S.J., & Lupo, K.L. (2000). The positive organization: Leadership legitimacy, employee well-being, and the bottom line. *The Psychologist Manager Journal*, 4(2), 143-153.

[20] Keyes, C.L.M. (2007). Promoting and protecting mental health as flourishing: A complementary strategy for improving national mental health. *American Psychologist*, 62, 95–108.

[21] Kohn, M.L., & Schooler, C. (1982). Job condition and personality: A longitudinal assessment of their reciprocal effect. *American Journal of Sociology* ,87, 1257-1286.

[22] Levy, B.R., Slade, M.D., Kunkel, S.R., & Kasl, S.V. (2002). Longevity increased by positive self-perceptions of aging. *Journal of Personality and Social Psychology*, 83, 261-270.

[23] Lyubomirsky, S., King, L., & Diener, E. (2005). The benefits of frequent positive affect: Does happiness lead to success? *Psychological Bulletin*, 131, 803–855.

[24] Lyubomirsky, S. (2008). The how of happiness. New York: Penguin Press.

[25] Meier, L.L., Semmer, N.K., Elfering, A., & Jacobshagen, N. (2008). The double meaning of control: Three-way interactions between internal resources, job control, and stressors at work. *Journal of Occupational Health Psychology*, 13, 244–258.

[26] Meyer, J.P., & Allen, N.J. (1997). Commitment in the workplace: Theory, research, and application. Thousand Oaks: Sage Publications.

[27] Meyer, L., & Parton, R. (2011). How to drive value creation in the C-suite. *Corporate Wellness Magazine*, 18, 1-2.

[28] Mroczek, D.K., & Spiro, A. (2005). Change in life satisfaction during adulthood: Findings from the veterans affairs normative aging study. *Journal of Personality and Social Psychology,* 88, 189–202.

[29] Murray, C.J.L., and Lopez, A.D. (Eds.). (1996). *The Global Burden of Disease: A Comprehensive Assessment of Mrality and Disability from Diseases, Injuries and Risk Factors in 1990 and Projected to 2020.* Cambridge, MA: Harvard School of Public Health.

[30] Ostir, G.V., Markides, K.S., Peek, M.K., & Goodwin, J.S. (2001). The association between emotional well-being and the incidence of stroke in older adults. *Psychosomatic Medicine,* 63, 210–215.

[31] Quick, J.C. (1999). Occupational Health Psychology: The convergence of health and clinical psychology with public health and preventive medicine in an organizational context. *Professional Psychology: Research and Practice,* 30, 123–128.

[32] Russell, J.E.A. (2008). Promoting subjective well-being at work. *Journal of Career Assessment*, 16(1), 117-131.

[33] Snyder, C.R., Lehman, K.A., Kluck, B., & Monsson, Y. (2006). Hope for rehabilitation and vice versa. *Rehabilitation Psychology,* 51, 89–112.

[34] Schuettler, D., & Kiviniemi, M.T. (2006). Does how I feel about it matter? The role of affect in cognitive and behavioral reactions to chronic illness diagnosis. *Journal of Applied Social Psychology,* 36, 2599–2618.

[35] Spector, P.E. (1997). *Job Satisfaction: Application, Assessment, Cause and Consequences.* Thousand Oaks, CA: Sage.

[36] Warr, P.B. (2005). Work, well-being, and mental health. In J. Barling, E.K. Kelloway, & M.R. Frome (Eds.), *Handbook of Work Stress* (pp. 547-573). Thousand Oaks: Sage Publications.

[37] Williams, S., & Cooper, C.L. (1998). Measuring occupational stress: Development of the pressure management indicator. *Journal of Occupational Health Psychology, 3,*306–321.

[38] Wright, T.A. (2003). Positive organizational behavior: An idea whose time has truly come. *Journal of Organizational Behavior,* 24, 437–442.

[39] Wright, T.A., & Cropanzano, R. (2004). The role of psychological well-being in job performance: A fresh look at an age-old quest. *Organizational Dynamics*, 33(4), 338-351.

[40] Wright, T.A., & Bonett, D.G. (2007). Job satisfaction and psychological well-being as nonadditive predictors of workplace turnover. *Journal of Management*, 33(2), 141-160.

[41] Wrzesniewski, A., McCauley, C., Rozin, P., & Schwartz, B. (1997). Jobs, careers and callings: People's relations to their work. *Journal of Research in Personality*, 31, 21-33.

Opportunities and Challenges in an Inclusive Workplace: With Special Reference to Corporate Leadership

Anshu Lochab, Megha Grover and Priyanka Gautam[1]

Rukmini Devi Institute of Advanced Studies
[1]Chandraprabhu College of Higher Studies & School of Law

ABSTRACT

Equally, future prospects for social inclusion and social justice are heavily dependent on successfully accommodating this diversity in the workplace and in the wider society. An environment where everyone is treated with dignity and respect, where the talents and skills of different groups are valued, and where productivity and customer service improves because the workforce is happier, more motivated and more aware of the benefits that inclusion can bring So the business leaders have to be continuously learning and discovering new things, ideas, processes and systems for doing better for the firm. For this purpose, they need both far sight and foresight, in 2012, they should be focusing on the firm's entity in 2022 ten years hence. The leaders can themselves become competitive factors for gaining advantage over competitors. The leaders must be in learning mode all the time and this way they can create a learning organization. Leadership for learning organization has become crucial to the success of the firm, because all the management tools may not be enough. Most firms need to continuously develop means and improve ways of doing things and this requires organizational learning. Leadership, as a consequence entails huge responsibility on the shoulders of the leaders, the CEO's of any firm. Position gives power to the concerned person and he can either use it to his firm's benefit or abuse it for his own. Firms have known to reach great heights just because of their CEO's reverse is also true unfortunately.

Keywords: *Innovation, Motivation, Learning, Opportunity, Leadership, Strategies, Challenges, Employment*

Two factors distinguish top leadership organizations: Attention to the combined leadership needs of the individual and corporation, and leveraging custom training programs to accelerate key leadership talent. – *The Harvard Review,* March 2010

INTRODUCTION

An inclusive workplace is one where the human rights principles of fairness, respect, equality, dignity and autonomy are promoted and are part of the organization's everyday goals and behaviuor. To continue progress towards the society in terms of economic inclusion based on full employment, consistent economic development that is socially and environmentally sustainable. Social inclusion and a commitment to social justice, based on continuing adaptation to change. It is important to recognize that the future growth prospects are heavily dependent on successfully mobilizing, retaining and developing increasingly diverse sources of labour. The importance of business leadership is well articulated by this observation: A good leader can make a success of a weak business plan, but a poor leader can ruin even the best plan. That's why developing effective leadership by using a consistent talent management program at all levels across the organization can return significant business value. To identify, attract, fill, and retain corporate leadership talent, companies need leadership development programs focused on hiring strategies, employee development, and career and succession planning.

Companies face two major challenges in finding and developing leaders. They need to identify qualified candidates to fill current and future leadership roles, and they need to develop a comprehensive leadership program to cultivate and develop the leaders of tomorrow.

In the past, leadership development was focused on only a few individuals in the organization. First-generation systems to assist with leadership development were siloed and/ or hard to use and were not widely adopted. Companies needed a system-enabled way to unify methods of assessing and selecting leaders, executing programs to develop skills, and measuring the success of these programs.

Now technology can be deployed to extend these practices across the enterprise and down into all levels of the workforce. This white paper explores leadership challenges and highlights the elements of a successful leadership development program that uses technology to support processes and practices.

Persons who do not wield the power but are in some manner connected to the government or firm; in political or business arena usually criticize power. In politics it can be seen at the election time that incumbency factor goes against the ruling party. In business once it is understood that CEO's power has a great influence on the firm and its results, it becomes important and necessary to know about the power and how best it can be canalized for the maximum benefit of the firm.

OBJECTIVES OF THE STUDY

- To understand the meaning of corporate leadership and major challenges in recent trends.
- To study for creation of a positive work environment for employees of diverse backgrounds should include strategies for the inclusion of people with disabilities.
- To highlight how leadership influences organizational performance

- To study the role and impact of effective leadership in corporate world.
- To understand the role of leaders in CSR initiatives by the companies.

RESEARCH METHODOLOGY

This paper is purely academic and finds out some suggestive ways to handle the turbulent situations in the corporate organizations which may come without prior notice and that is the real mettle test of the leadership. Secondary data has been referred (books, journals. articles and from websites) to explore such situations and opinions have been taken from the corporate leaders either through their writings or personal interviews being reflected at various places.

LEADERSIP IN TURBULENT TIMES

Good times never remains same but suffer from some jerks time to time and that becomes the real time for leadership to prove. In this direction a survey was conducted by Business World and reported that, "When the surf is up, some just watch from the shore. Some try to ride the waves, but end up in the water. A handful succeeds, just the way some of India's business leaders did when faced with the tsunami of the global slowdown. Slowdown is for all and it depends on the leadership how it is being handled. Companies know precisely what to do when faced by these types of challenges; whether to cut costs, reduce workforce or cut the spending. But definitely in those situations leadership of the organizations is caught in the dilemma; should they prepare for the worst or to go for a turnaround? If they stop investing they would be under-prepared for the recovery from the loses from slowdowns and likely to lose market share and on the other hand if heavy investment is done with a hope that turnaround will bring heavy profit and economy doesn't improve. In these types of situations business leaders spend sleepless nights as this is never ending process and tests the mettle of a leader.

It rises so many question how a leader should handle these types of situations. How he should lead the organization? What should he communicate to the team members? Does he go for more investment or cut the costs? Whether he should advertise more or cut down advertising costs? Should he retain the workforce or ask them to leave? Should fresh hiring be done of put on hold? Should he protect market share or profitability? So these are some typical questions and situations which one leader need to handle in the times of turbulence. Let us look at some of the cases of such situations from the corporate world which was presented by Business World in the March issue of 2013.

In an Inclusive Workplace

- There is a welcoming workplace culture where everyone is treated with respect and dignity and everyone feels valued.
- Policies are in place concerning equality and human rights, working conditions, dignity at work, employee welfare and fair recruitment and procurement practices.

- Members of staff at all levels are aware of the inclusive values of the organisation and are actively consulted and involved in policy development.
- The workforce is representative of the local community or customers (or if not, under-represented groups are encouraged to apply).
- All employees are encouraged to develop and progress, and any barriers faced by specific groups are identified and action taken to address them.
- Unnecessary hierarchies and occupational segregation, where groups of employees are congregated into certain areas, are discouraged.
- The organisation is aware of any potential tensions within the workplace, and takes action to anticipate and address them.
- Inclusive strategies are fully supported and promoted by senior staff.

Some Cases of Corporate Leadership

Business World selected few top companies from the list of Top 500 companies that reported a net profit in fiscal 2011-12, and had at least Rs 1,000 crore in revenues and have grown at least 100 percent in revenue between 2008-09, the year the world was gripped by a recession, and 2011-12. The leaders of such organizations, which range from IT firm to automobiles, were interviewed by the Business World.

KM Birla, Chairman, The Aditya Birla Group Firms: India's largest cement maker UltraTech and the third largest cellphone operator Idea Cellular. The Chairman says that nearly a third of UltraTech's 53 million tonne capacity was added during 2008-11 when others were struggling with the slowdowns. If the ongoing Greenfield projects in Chhattisgarh and Karnataka are included than it will take it up to 62 million tonne per annum. Idea Cellular is the fastest growing operator in India having closed 2008 with 40 million subscribers and at the end of the Q2 2012-13; it had mopped up 115 million subscribers. It was also the biggest gainer from number portability, adding 3.7 million subscribers from rivals, added Chairman. The Chairman believes that slowdown brings in a positive sense of urgency and should stay focused on the basics: productivity, throughput, and customer service, let it be coming by decreasing the costs. He also emphasizes that one (leader) must fast forward initiatives in turbulent times instead of looking back and waiting for good time to come.

Natarajan Chandra Sekaran, MD & CEO, Tata Consultancy Services (TCS), which was founded nearly a decade and a half before Infosys was born, has continued to be India's largest IT services firm, hitting annual revenues of 10 billion dollar in 2011-12. But during the slowdown when its competitors were struggling, TCS continued to surprise investors, rivals and analysts alike, reporting a top line growth of 113 percent. The leadership of TCS attributes this to a new nimble-footed organization structure that was, coincidentally, already being put in place in 2008 with 23 strategic independent units with complete charge of deal management, marketing and delivery. It's a model that's being replicated by all its rivals now.

The MD says that, "If the strategy is right, it's very important to stay committed and stay the course in a slowdown. Continue to make investments. You can't cut down."

The following are the three areas, which cover the organizational learning:

1. Need for leadership in organizational learning
2. Elements of organizational learning
3. Leadership activities required for building a learning organization.

ORGANIZATIONAL LEARNING NEED

Leaders need special traits for being successful in today's business environment. Leaders should be INSTRUMENTAL in changing the firm for success else they would not succeed.

In the history there have been born leaders like Nehru, Napoleon. They carried the masses through their charisma. Now, it has changed to leaders becoming instrument of change for the firm's success.

Leaders must get into the double loop learning process as can be seen in Fig.1(a).

Single Loop:

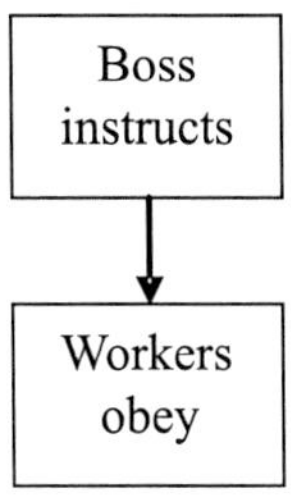

Fig. 1(a)

In double loop learning while the workers perform mechanical functions they also question the processes, methods and policies and adjust for the best fit for achieving the goals, objectives and the targets. The learning, therefore, becomes two ways, from the leader to the worker and from the worker to the leader.

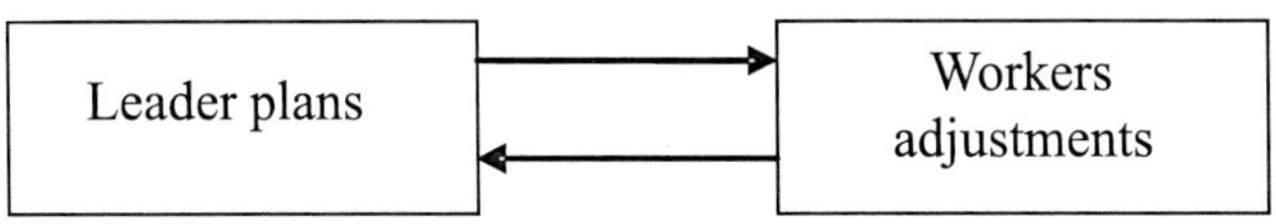

Fig. 1(b)

The definition of leadership, which is instrumental in the firm's success, is given below:

Firstly, the leaders develop and articulate exactly what the firm is trying to accomplish. Secondly, they create an environment in which the employees can figure out what needs to be done and then do it well. Employees participate in creating the plans and processes of the firm. In traditional management, the boss decided what is to be done and who would do it. In organizational learning, leaders with intellect, vision and wisdom show the ultimate goal and the followers find their own path towards success.

Leaders are, therefore, found at all the levels of the firm. A worker, through his TQM can change a process for the better, which gets known up the ladder and then it becomes the accepted norm. in this way the worker has contributed as a leader as other are following his process. Leadership covers a wide range of actions that are instrumental in bringing about a change in the firm for success. Leaders should possess a high degree of creativity, should be strategists to crate organizational synergy to increase the firm's output. the leadership mindset is defined below and illustrated in Fig.1(c).

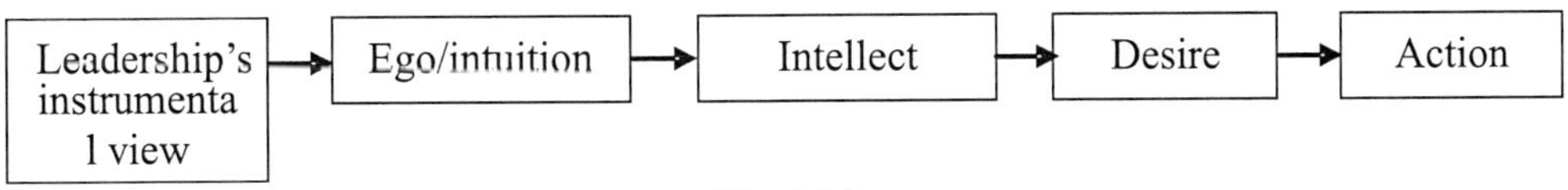

Fig. 1(c)

Leaders and the followers are supposed to achieve what is required but at times it does not happen. This gives the organizational learning a bad name. the cause is the basic distrust of the workers. Results can come when the workers are empowered to take decisions in their small areas to promote the firm wide synergy.

A leader can be described as follows:

- A leader is the innocent mirror of the collective consciousness of his followers.
- The only way towards success as a leader is to develop leadership qualities in his followers.
- If you are a follower you can lead and if you are a leader you can follow.
- Leadership must be supportive in nature, as leaders must support their followers. Leaders are found in the entire hierarchy of the learning organization. Followers (workers) should be encouraged to learn leadership qualities, as they have to lead as well.

ELEMENTS OF ORGANIZATIONAL LEARNING

In the organizational learning mode the firms use the scientific method of discovering new methods, processes by experimentation. The scientific method follows the steps given below:

Start with a theory

- Convert it into a hypothesis
- Conduct experiments to confirm the hypothesis
- Compare the results of the experiments with the hypothesis
- Conclude or draw inferences (in science these become laws or principles)

SPECIFICS OF BUSINESS LEADERSHIP

Leadership for organizational learning constitute the following elements:

1. Develop a sound understanding of the following:
    - (a) Technical knowledge and skills. Technical knowledge enables the leader to ask the right probing questions in case of any technical problem. These questions, when answered give an idea of the solution.
    - (b) Personal values that ennoble and inspire the followers, like integrity and ethics. These can be considered on the following levels-i. the first in which the leader is judged alone. Ii. Leader base their ethics on the laws of the land and social norms. Iii. Leaders have their inner source of ethical behavior.
    - (c) Moral, emotional and functional support to the followers.
    - (d) Ability to get into the psyche of the followers, to inspire them.
    - (e) Have a personality of prime mover, of a man with a purpose and urgency for the right action.
    - (f) Have high values which motivate the followers.
    - (g) Have total social acceptance.

    Leaders must be able to arrange the following specific activities:
    - (a) Establish a shared vision with which the followers indentify themselves totally.
    - (b) Instill a sense of urgency in the followers, as happy talk that all is well is just not right.
    - (c) Gain commitment of the followers about the shared vision, mission, goals and objectives of the firm.
    - (d) Identify the current mental model of the followers; understand if it explains the cause and effect of what is happening in the firm, right or wrong.
    - (e) Understand the interpersonal relationships between teams and within team members to abort conflicts before they appear. If conflicts do occur, the interpersonal knowledge would be useful in solving the same, which is one of the basic tasks of a leader.

ACTIVITIES OF LEADERS IN ORGANIZATIONAL LEARNING

The leaders have to approach their role in a practical manner, which they can arrange as follows:

- Leaders must encourage experimentation by the followers.
- Must develop tolerance for mistakes. The best way is to provide for small losses during experiments. With on successful experiment, however, no fresh idea can be generated. The successes must be rewarded and used in the firm's operations and failures must be just ignored. (It is not right to rub the mistake in as it would discourage further experimentation by the whole lot of workers).

- Leaders should have the guts to admit their own mistakes as well; it proves they are humans too and it would do a lot of good to the morale of workers who have erred.
- Apply the middle path method-if the middle management carries out the experiments, it would bring sufficiently valuable results, if successful, unlike the results of experiments by the low down workers, whose results would bring only small improvements, if successful and of course would not cause much damage if they fail. On the other hand, experiments at the top could be risky, as they would involve large sums of money at stake. It does not, however, preclude anyone from carrying out the experiments. The middle management success can then be spread horizontally as also vertically to cover the entire organization.
- Act on the results of successful experiments, as it would be the biggest motivation for others to do one better than the winner.
- Back winners – it could be rewards in cash or promotions, better salary or perks.
- Discuss failures, not to put people on the mat, but to ensure they do not occur again. In fact, a good leader would discuss his own failures too to generate warm fellow felling among followers. At this stage it is a good idea to set boundaries for future experimentation to avoid failures to the extent possible. Clear guidelines to avoid fruitless experiments, to reduce wastages in experimentation must be made.
- It must be understood that people learn from making mistakes only and if they do not experiment, make no mistakes, the firm does not gain any benefits of successful experiments either.

Leaders who encourage experimentation and act on the results influence learning organizations. Therefore, the leaders need to do the following:

- Encourage leadership among followers to motivate them.
- Leaders have a broad range of actions, which are instrumental in bringing about the needed change in the organization.
- Learning organizations differ from the traditional rational planning organizations as shown in Table 1.

In exploring to find the challenges and opportunities of the coming year, as we do at the start of every year, we search for authoritative research on where our clients may want to focus their energy, and by default where we might aid them.

In considering 2012 we once again looked at the **Ken Blanchard Companies annual Corporate Issues Survey** which has been done for several years now to pinpoint the needs and issues of organizations seeking to develop their people to their fullest potential. These are excellent reports and we recommend you explore the **Ken Blanchard Companies website.**

Table 1

Issues	*Rational Planning Organization*	*Learning Organization*
Status on change	Do not change if you are successful	You fail if you do not change
Management worries	Mistakes	Rigidity
New ideas acceptance	Do not include outside ideas	Pick up all from outside
Innovation plans	With engineers/managers	All the members
Experiments by	R&D engineers	All involved in the work
Major or minor changes	Only minor changes	Continuous changes with drastic changes in between
Competitive advantage from	Products and services	Knowledge, skills and expertise
Management control	Through budgets and daily reports	Empowering the workers
Level of assistance to workers	Minimal or none at all	Daily motivation through leadership counseling

The findings in 2011 represent the feedback from 1,300 executives, line managers, and training and HR leaders from a range of organizations, industries, and countries. Since 2003, approximately 9,800 leaders have participated in this ongoing study, and these survey reports always provide valuable information on key business issues, such as:

- The organization's outlook for the coming year.
- What will be happening with training and development expenditure?
- The top organisational challenges
- The organisation's effectiveness in addressing key issues and challenges
- The top leadership gaps
- The top management challenges
- The top employee development challenges

I'll leave you to look at the whole report, as I cannot do it justice here. But I wanted to highlight the Top Leadership Gaps the survey identified and address myself to just some of these. My reasoning is that effective leadership is paramount to every aspect of an organization's success, and perhaps we need to aim at closing these gaps in the coming year in order to achieve greater success. The chart from the survey is as in Fig. 2.

As we look at these self-identified leadership skill gaps we draw from it that major corporates are acknowledging they need to improve the calibre of their leaders in some very important areas, including:

- Being more strategic and tactical in their thinking
- Passionately inspiring others
- Driving innovation with vision and communication

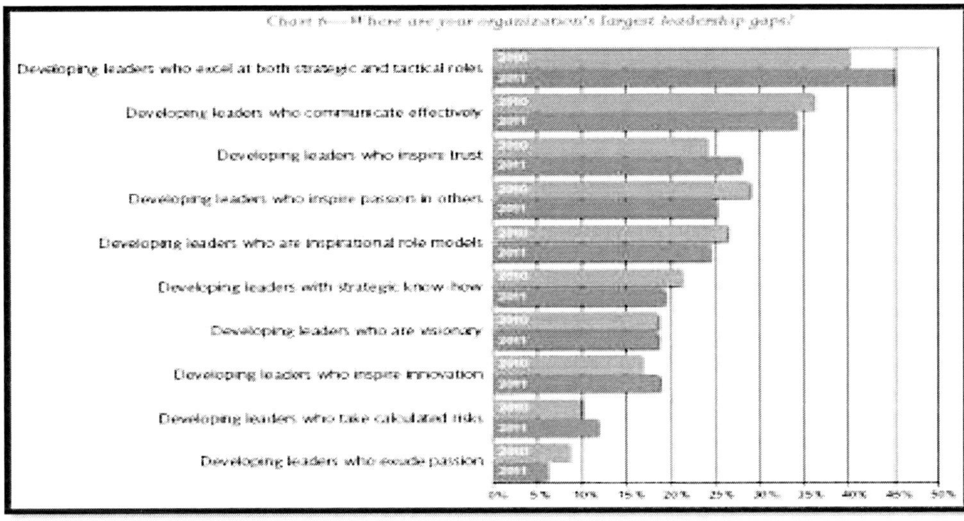

Fig. 2

Of course these are not new leadership skills, and their importance is generally well understood by organizational leaders. But what is being done to close these gaps? What tangible steps are being taken in the organization's leadership development areas? The answer here of course is mixed - from little to a lot, and those organizations taking leadership development seriously will ultimately be more successful.

And what about small and medium sized businesses, government departments, not for profits, schools, and even volunteer groups? Is anything being done there to create the passionate, visionary, inspirational, strategic thinking, and innovative supervisors and managers needed to grow and succeed?

These are questions you may want to ask and explore to make 2012 a fantastic year full of success.

There are many theories about and techniques for determining the right leadership styles for an organization. The situational leadership theory, for example, argues that the best type of leadership is determined by situational variables and that no one style of leadership pertains to all given workplace situations.6Identifying the leadership style for an organization by using this approach includes identification of the type of work, the complexity of the organization, and the qualifications of the followers.

The leadership style, for instance, that is required by a head of corporate security would obviously be vastly different from the leadership style of an art museum director: authoritative versus creative or charismatic.

Additional leadership styles include pluralistic leadership that revolves around group decision-making, a style that values the opinions of others. Whatever style is best suited for the

CEO of an organization, a variety of leadership styles may be required to lead different groups such as manufacturing operations, marketing, finance, and creative services within a company.

One of the main reasons for the high failure rate of new CEOs—more than half never make it past the four-year mark—is poor organizational fit. Ability can take leaders only so far if they are not compatible with the company culture. Here are two ways to assess leaders' fit.

- **Get to know them better. Psychological and behavioral assessments** that are typically offered via assessment center exercises have been statistically linked to current and future success in leadership roles.
- **Understand the culture better**. Ask your board, employees, vendors, consultants, and others with connections to the organization for insight into what makes an effective leader in the company.

Use both sets of information to find alignments or disparities. If there is a glaring cultural conflict, be ready to find a better candidate who possesses the unique skills for organization requires.

Actively Involve All Groups of Employees

In order to create a working culture of inclusion, respect and opportunity for all, it is essential that everyone in the organisation, from senior management to the most junior staff, is engaged with and involved in the process of creating this culture, and feels that their opinions and experiences are valued. Measures to promote inclusive working need to be thought of positively among employees, not as something that is 'done' to them. There are several things to think about in this respect.

CONCLUSION

In order to create a working culture of inclusion, respect and opportunity for all, it is essential that everyone in the organisation, from senior management to the most junior staff, is engaged with and involved in the process of creating this culture, and feels that their opinions and experiences are valued. Measures to promote inclusive working need to be thought of positively among employees, not as something that is 'done' to them. There are several things to think about in this respect. The traditional corporate philosophy that leaders are born no longer applies, given the vast amount of research data on the issue of behaviour and its role in business leadership. As these research studies point out, any prospective leadership candidate can be trained to work through their employees as a way to become a highly effective corporate leader. Firms must keep improving methods of doing things for which they need organizational learning. The best learning comes when it is a two-way communication, leader to worker and worker to the leader. Leadership can beat all the levels of the organization and it is the role of the leader to encourage others to take leadership positions. Leaders can become change triggers, or instrumental in making changes in the firm, through charisma plus their own efforts of understanding the firm and its workers. Empowering workers to conduct experiments and including the successful experiments in the firms schedule is a sure way of improving the system as also of motivating the workers. The leader must have sound technical knowledge, ethical and moral values and the latest on the firm's front. A shared vision developed in consultation with the members of the firm gets commitment of the workers in an inclusive workplace.

REFERENCES

[1] "Mellon Financial Corporate Learning Curve Research Study".

[2] "Best in Class Talent Management Metrics," Aberdeen Group, 2008.

[3] CEO survey, Booz Allen Hamilton, 2009.

[4] Daniel J. Sinnott, "Leadership Turnover: The Health Care Crisis Nobody Talks About," Trustee Magazine, July 2008.

[5] "In Challenging Times, Leadership Skills and Leader Development Matter," Workforce Management Magazine, February 24, 2009.

[6] The Battle for Brainpower," in "The Search for Talent: Why It's Getting Harder to Find" (special report in *The Economist*, October 7, 2006).

[7] "High-Impact Succession Management: Best Practices, Models and Case Studies in Organizational Talent Mobility," Bersin & Associates.

[8] 15 "Taking the Pulse—Succession Planning," i4cp, July 2008.

[9] "Whirlpool Focuses on Innovation to Attract Talent," Taleo Case Study, 2010.

Creating an Inclusive Environment for Expatriates: Challenges and Initiatives

Vijita Singh Aggarwal and Shefali

Guru Govind Singh Indraprastha University, Dwarka, New Delhi

ABSTRACT

Due to globalization Multinational Corporations (MNCs) has increased in number, hence the role of expatriates in those MNCs grows in significance. But the expatriates are continuously facing difficulties related to adjustment in the host country. This study analyzed the kind of challenges they are facing in Indian workplace which prevent them to integrate in workplace environment and second, to explore what HR initiatives are taken to create inclusive environment for expatriates. Semi structured interviews of 20 expatriates were conducted who were working in Multinational corporations situated in Gurgaon region .The results showed that language ,culture, workplace issues etc are the major problems expats are facing in the workplace which affects their work performance and acting as barriers in the integration of expats in the workplace. Finally, measures used by expatriate managers and multinational corporations to overcome the existing problems such as cross cultural training etc are presented in the paper.

Keywords: *Expatriates, Foreign National, Expatriate Adjustment, Cross Cultural Training, Inclusive Korkplace*

INTRODUCTION

With the liberalisation and globalisation of international trade, world is getting smaller and markets are getting bigger. The creation of borderless marketplace not only increased flow of investment but also increased the transfer of human capital across the globe. This increase in the international trade determines the success of globalisation. So, multinational companies seeks talented and competent people to nurture their organisations that follow from putting the right person into the right job at the right place at the right time to compete in world marketplace and to generate profit (D.Daniels et al, 2010).

To achieve these motives multinational corporations use “Expatriates” to run their foreign business operations in order to retain their core competencies related to product,services,pro cess,technology etc abroad .The term expatriate can be used to describe any person living in another country than the country where they hold a citizenship. The word expatriate comes from the Latin ex (out of) and patria (country, fatherland) (Wikipedia).Many companies send their employees in foreign nations to meet the standard requirements, to command and control so as to have familiarity with the decisions of home country, to corporate their policies and procedures, to fill the gaps in local talent and for the development of management.

According to the report of PricewaterhouseCoopers (PWC) *Talent Mobility 2020,* the number of international assignments will raise to 50% by 2020, to nearly 400 per large organization. (Lowandowski, 2011). (Esarey & Haselberger) In this changing landscape optimization of human and intellectual capital is the major challenge for all organizations (Shrivastava & Shrivastava, 2012).A research shows that MNC's should staff expatriate as an CEO on the basis of eclectic theory given by Dunning i.e. by considering the perspective of ownership specific ,location specific and international specific advantages of subsidiaries (Tseng & Liao, 2009)

LITERATURE REVIEW

Challenges Faced by Expatriates

Those persons who move far away from their origin country to achieve their professional, financial and personal goals. Expatriates are classified into three types.

Home country national –executives in MNE are sent away from country of origin to other countries. Third country nationals-a citizen of neither the host country nor the home country but a third country national and the third is Impetrates-employees work at company headquarters and belong to other countries (Gupta, Dasari, & Dasari, 2012).

India is an attractive destination for foreign direct investment and thus attracting huge number of expats.According tio the survey by The Economic times,expats number in India has risen by 15-20%since 2011. An estimate showed that approx 40,000 expats are now the part of Indian workforce (The M group, 2012). Hence expatriates must be having affective, cognitive and behavioural competencies to sustain in Indian workplace. He concluded that adaptation to the cultural values of Indian workplace are very important for expatriates to live in India and classified Indian culture as a collectivistic people oriented society whereas Germans as Individualistic task oriented society (Messner, 2011).

According to the report of Economist intelligence unit the most emerging destinations for expatriates are Asian countries especially China (35%) and India (16%). (The Economist Intelligence Unit Limited, 2010). Cultural sensitivity, foreign language and conflict with the local managers are the reasons for the failure of expatriate assignments. To cope with these issues effective training are provided to them but still is a major challenge for the workforce. A report of global mobility 2012 also presented the same results that cultural differences posed more challenges (59%), Personal security reasons came at second (42%), language conflict (35%) are the major problems occurring in the way of expatriates in getting integrate in workplace (Global mobility survey report, 2012).

This study investigated the factors influencing the performance of emigrant employee in host country; challenges faced by them along with practical approach to deal with expats. Adaptation, Adjustment, lack of cross cultural management experience, etc., are some of the problems faced by expatriates in foreign country (Esarey & Haselberger). This is explained with special reference to India in a report by (Khosla & Mukerjee, 2007) regarding the challenges concerning International mobility such as cultural adaptation, tax issues,immigration issues, payroll reporting, compensation packaging and need to stick to local laws. Dual career issues and lack of technical expertise are also the main reasons for the failure of international assignments (Vojinic, Matic, & Becic).

A study has been done in Malaysia which examined 20 female and male expatriates to find out the challenges faced by them. Gender issues, difficulty in understanding the behavior of Malaysians, custom and religion etc influenced the expatriates to survive in the host country (Tahir & Ismail, 2007).

(Liisa Makela, 2011) This research presented the experiences of 20 female expatriates regarding Work-Life balance. Female expatriates have to face many challenges to balance her personal and professional life. International assignment creates some problems for them such as adjustment to new culture, wider responsibilities, glass ceiling effect, family reasons which obstruct female employees to complete their assignments.Inspite of all these challenges females has some special features of self transcendence and work adjustment which are the reasons for expatriate success but these are opposite in case of males.

Chinese expatriates are more prone to the problem of language difficulty to adjust in the country and research on them showed the positive relationship with interaction adjustment and negative with work adjustment because of lack of proficiency in English by Chinese. (Selmer, 2006)A one more study found Guanxi as a major challenge in Chinese market i.e. maintaining strong relationship by offering gifts and giving priority etc which is very difficult for foreign nationals (Wu, 2008).

(Sakho) studied the job responsibility of senior expatriate managers of 20 multinational corporations that not only technical expertise but also adherence to the company's core values are important for them to manage global relations. Liu & Lee (2008) the use of same selection process for both domestic as well as international expatriates is the major limitation in International Human resource management. Failure in adjustment such as work adjustment, interaction adjustment and general adjustment leads to the greater dissatisfaction of expatriates in the host country .A study has been done to find out the effect of gender and employment status on expatriate spouse work adjustment and reached at the result that there is no difference in males and females in general adjustment but in interaction adjustment females scored higher than males, i.e. faster interaction of females in Swiss working environment (Ravasi, Salamin, & Davoine, 2013).

HR Initiatives to Create Inclusive Workplace

Organisations are working towards developing and positioning true *global citizens* in the workplace to have greater return on investment. To achieve these objectives various initiatives are taken by companies to overcome the challenges of Expatriates in workplace.

The most important of them is selection of expatriates. An individual who are going for expatriate assignment should posses certain personality traits which determines the success of assignment such as agreeableness, conscientiousness ,openness, language skills prior international experience etc These traits are positively correlated with the work performance and cross cultural adjustment of employees in foreign country (Caligiuri & Tarique, 2006).

A research done by (Harvey & Novicevic, 2001) also includes the above traits and also three more traits such as extroversion, intellect and emotional stability in an individual during selection to adapt and compete in the global environment. A competency based strategic process has been used to select expatriates which is divided into three types-Input competencies, managerial competencies and transformational competencies to manage global diversity in the workplace.

Similarly a competency based model also determines the different types of intelligence required in global workforce, i.e. analytical, practical and creative intelligence to solve the handle business problems effectively and efficiently. Training and development have been used by companies since many years to develop cross cultural competencies in the personnel so as to integrate the particular person with the domestic work place but it varies from company to company and person to person. Cross cultural training, Diversity training, mentoring, orientations are the techniques used by human resource department to develop competencies to adjust and to reduce the cultural shock (Caligiuri & Tarique, 2006) & (Tahir & Ismail, 2007). Organisations can construct competencies to cultivate inclusive and harmonious workplaces by embedding them in formal HR practices such as recruitment, selection ,learning and performance management.

To avoid these socio-cultural barriers universalism and benevolence should be included in the training of expatriates (Cole & McNulty, 2011). Research on Croatian expatriates explained that during training period skill development opportunities and career development programs leads to job satisfaction and positive work performance (Vojinic, Matic, & Becic). Localisation of expats is an approach used by companies to reduce the cost of expats i.e. conversion of expats into local rules and regulations as followed by domestic workforce regarding salary, etc. (Heaps, 2010).

Pre-departure training, Language training and career counselling of spouses of expats to solve the problems of cultural and language conflict along with dual career dilemma (Chew, 2004). Mendenhall et al. (1987) proposed a model of pre departure training for expatriate assignments. This model follows cross cultural training approach which is classified into Immersion, affective and information giving approach .The training lasts for about 1-2 months and has a considerable impact on degree of integration of Expats with the workplace.

OBJECTIVES OF THE STUDY

- To examine the challenges faced by expatriates in getting integrated in Indian workplace environment.
- To study human resource initiatives to deal with these challenges so as to create an inclusive workplace

RESEARCH METHODOLOGY

A total of twenty interviews were carried out to explore the problems which are being faced by working foreign nationals in host country (India) and efforts which the companies are putting in to cope with these challenges. The qualitative research design method based on semi structured interviews of 20 expatriates who are working in OEM multinational corporations has been used to complete the research. The interviews which we took in New Delhi few of the organizations were set up specifically in Gurgaon. Convenient sampling method was used to draw sample.

Challenges Faced by Expatriates	*Responses of 20 Respondents*	*Critical Comments (Verbatim)*
Cultural(cultural sensitivity, cultural shock)	Major issue-16 ,Can deal with it-2,Minor issue-2	One of the respondent quoted "Cultural problems are the key, especially with in Indian culture"
Language	Major issue-18 ,Minor issue-2	"Language is a biggest issue"
Work place etiquettes	Major issue-10,Can deal with it-6,Minor issue-4	"I asked my junior to do left over job ,he suddenly replied me in NO"
Gender discrimination	Major issue-08 ,Can deal with it-8,Minor issue-4	"Because I am a women, I could not work at night because of Indian men teasing me"
Adjustment at workplace	Major issue-18 ,Can deal with it-3,Minor issue-1	"I have travelled almost whole world before coming here ,I find difficult to adjust here"
Family maladjustment	Major issue-12 ,Can deal with it-4,Minor issue-2	"Overseas ,we need the support of family to work better ,it is not easy as we assume"
Spouse career issues	Major issue-07 ,Can deal with it-9,Minor issue-4	Respondent told us that his wife said "You are spoiling my carrier by prioritizing own career"
loneliness	Major issue-11 ,Can deal with it-9,Minor issue-0	"I miss my family and had to care myself"
Environmental(Pollution,Traffic, congestion, water quality, etc.)	Major issue-16 ,Can deal with it-2,Minor issue-2	"Health care and protection of environment remain two of our top challenges"

The interviews lasted between 20-30 minutes and conducted in English language with the help of interpreters. To check validity and reliability, the study reviewed from experts in the field and peer consultation was also incorporated. These experiences shared by expatriates are very important to gain further insights in the research .Personal bias should put aside to avoid errors in the research. Secondary research has also been applied as a research methodology for this study in order to support the information collected through interview. Responses collected during the interview session of 20 expats in an organisation to examine the challenges faced by them in getting integrated in Indian workplace environment.

FINDINGS OF THE RESEARCH

Expatriation involves a lot of adjustments in the personal and corporate front. However expatriates often face more challenges in both personal lives as well as at the corporate level.

Cultural Differences

Expat view of life in India: "Be prepared for cultural differences, but try to embrace the culture, and not fight it (HSBC, 2012). It is the deeper cultural differences in mindset, customs and interpersonal interaction that trigger this phenomenon and turn cultural transition into a struggle (Internations connecting globalminds).The research showed that Indian culture is very different from their culture and they found it hard to adjust. India has an unorganised workplace culture than Japanese as told by an expat during the interview .It is evident from the research that Indian employees are not targeted to the results and are not good team players (Sharma, 2005)so it is very hard to rely on them. As per the findings, the way of thinking of expatriates and Indians also vary from each other. High power distance, cultural differences and lack of soft skills such as communication hampers the expatriates to mingle into Indian culture (Dezan Shera and Associates, 2010).

Language: According to the research findings expats found the Indian language difficult to understand. They are not able to interact with the local employees as they do not know local language which affects the work performance. To prove this study has been done that which concludes that the Language is acting as serious barrier to integration for expats living in India. A report of HSBC, 2012 surveyed that 40% of expats found difficult to learn the language, 37% face health problems while 53% found it difficult to fit into new culture (HSBC, 2012).

Challenges Faced by Expatriates	*HR Initiatives*
Cultural(cultural sensitivity, cultural shock)	Cross cultural training programme, Diversity training
Language	Language training, Interpreters
Work place politics	Sensitivity training and stress management courses
Gender discrimination	Cultural intelligence and training

Challenges Faced by Expatriates	*HR Initiatives*
Adjustment at workplace	Stress management courses and social network
Family maladjustment	Pre departure training
Spouse career issues	Arrangement of social network for them, Information about the new culture ,shopping, education activities etc
loneliness	Counselling of spouses
Health issues (Pollution, congestion, water quality, etc.)	Environmental awareness

Workplace etiquettes, as they think Indians are polite at the face only is also the main problem coming in the way of foreign national to adapt workplace environment. Difference in workplace etiquettes between expats and Indians hinders their adjustment which leads to failure in their assignments. (Talapatra, 2010)

Gender discrimination: Girls are not comfortable in working at night hours as per their experience in India. Gender differences, improper division of work and lack of time management are also some challenges faced by expatriates in the workplace (Lisa Makela(2011)

Family maladjustment and Spouse career issues: Family issues are posing great challenges during the adjustment of expatriates. Acc to the study by (GMAC.et.al) the main reasons for assignment failure was family concerns (47%), and also spouse's career by (10%). Spouse career issues and lack of technical expertise are also the main reasons for the failure of international assignments (Vojinic, Matic, & Becic).Some of expatriates were married and having a children who told us that their spouses felt it stressful to adapt to new culture,nurture their children in new environment,finding schools for them and dealing with such a big transition(Esarey & Haselberger)

Health issues: India is one of the most populous countries in the world (Internations.org) results into congestion, pollution which adversely affects the health of foreign nationals. Changing weather, climatic conditions, temperature etc are the main reasons of expatriate's disadjustment in India .Mosquito related diseases are commonly prevalent in India, so it is very difficult for them to adapt to the environment. Expatriates especially Japanese persons commented that Indians were not throw waste at designated Place which spreads diseases.

HR INITIATIVES TO CREATE INCLUSIVE WORKPLACE

As shared by HR managers following are some methods and strategies used by companies to overcome above challenges. Training and development sessions were organised to make expatriates familiar with host country culture which ultimately improves their work performance. Organisations should make selection criteria for expatriate while transferring to another country in such a way, so that they would find easy to adjust there. He/she should be well prepared for this role, especially when going for assignment to the country like India.

A competency based strategic process has been used to select expatriates which is divided into three types-Input competencies, managerial competencies and transformational competencies to create a culture of inclusiveness(Harvey & Novicevic, 2001).

Pre-departure training, Language training and career counselling of spouses of expats to solve the problems of cultural inclusiveness and language conflict along with dual career dilemma (Chew, 2004).Shifting of employees to different departments to avoid work conflict because they rely on rotational assignments to make expatriate familiar with workplace instead of long term assignments. Nowadays CD based and web based cross cultural training programs are organised to reduce failure rate of expatriates assignments but still this programs are not readily used .A survey conducted by (GMAC, 2004) to check the effectiveness of cross cultural programs on expatriates and found that 75% of companies are happy with its success and found it effective. Six studies has been done to support the positive correlation of cross-cultural training with expatriate's adjustment leads to job satisfaction, reduce culture shock and is an effective way to mingle with host country 's culture (Ganbat, 2012).

Cross cultural simulation, sensitivity training, role plays, stress management training to prevent their loneliness and development of specific skills of adjustment .Creation of a social network for the expatriates because they are resistant to make new friends is also one of the strategy used by Human resource managers to cope with the problem of loneliness. Buddy programmes are usually put in place to help new employees adapt into the organisation environment.

To cope with the workplace stress, organisations are using training strategies i.e. problem focused and symptom focused. Problem focused strategies are constructive in nature such as patience, stress tolerance, problem solving whereas symptom focused strategies are destructive in nature such as running from host country, etc. Generally expatriates are using problem focussed strategy to make their assignment successful (Koteswari & Bhattacharya, 2007).

To avoid the problem of communication interpreters are hired for translation within company and language training are provided to employees, to local employees also to overcome this barrier. Seminars and workshops are organised on cultural intelligence. Cultural intelligence is an important step towards cultural competence. Acquiring and developing intercultural skills can help you enjoy a more relaxed life and greater success in your career abroad. We have some useful tips on how to become a better global mind (Internations.org).Arrangement for better and secured environment to work, and giving them more facilities for night hours especially for women employees. Provisions such as, cost of living allowances, travelling allowances, contributory provident funds, maternity benefits and health insurance to retain expatriates in the organisation.

To create harmonious and inclusive workplace for Indian and foreign nationals, diversity training are provided to both foreign as well as domestic nationals. An interview with Hans F&B Pte Ltd concluded that due to this kind of training productivity of workers increased by 40% and absenteeism has been reduced (National integration working group for workplaces).

LIMITATIONS AND SCOPE OF FUTURE RESEARCH

The research has been done only on twenty expatriates with the use of convenient sampling based on self reported data .No empirical test was used to check validity of the result. The refinement of this study and the use of more experienced expatriates to explain expatriation and repatriation management are useful to carry further research. Different demographics of expats having different experiences at different times of career progression is the suitable topic for further research to know more about expatriation management .Study can be done to find more reasons or expatriate assignment failure and matter of gender may enrich our finding

CONCLUSION AND RECOMMENDATIONS

In this paper an attempt has been made to explore the challenges faced by the expatriates and HR initiatives used by organisations to retain them in the host country .The research finds that language, culture differences and environmental issues are the barriers to the adjustment of expatriates. In terms of results, the study provides many insights of managing expatriates. Hence, human resource managers operating globally should implement useful strategies and measures such as cross cultural training, language training, Diversity management programmes to have positive influence on expatriates to create an inclusive workplace. Improvement in pre-departure training which also includes the family members of foreign national and helping them with adjustment in housing, education and leisure activities .Proper handling of spouse-career issues effectively by counselling of spouses earlier to departure. Revision of selection and compensation decisions should be there as per the changing landscape .Repatriation issues are also taken into consideration to improve management of expatriates.

REFERENCES

[1] Blomstrm, M., & Kokko, A. (2003). *Human Capital and Inward FDI.* Retrieved from WORDDOC: CEPR-WP-Jan_2003.

[2] Caligiuri, P., & Tarique, I. (2006). International assignee selection and cross-cultural training and development. In G. K. Stahl, & I. Björkman, *Handbook of Research in International HR Management* (pp. 302-321). USA: Edward Elgar Publishing, Inc.

[3] Chew, J. (2004). Managing MNC Expatriates through Crises: A Challenge for International Human Resource Management. *Research and Practice in Human Resource Management,* 1-30.

[4] Cole, N., & McNulty, Y. (2011). Why do female expatriates “fit-in” better than males?An analysis of self-transcendence and socio-cultural adjustment . *Cross Cultural Management: An International Journal,* 144-164.

[5] D.Daniels, J., H. Radebaugh, L., Sullivan, D.P., & Salwan, P. (2010). *International business;Environmentsand Operations.* Pearson Prentice Hall.

[6] Dezan Shera and Associates. (2010, September). An Expatriate's manager introduction to India. *India Briefing – A Practical Application of India business.*

[7] Esarey, S., & Haselberger, A. *Moving People Abroad: A Guide to Successful Transitions.* UK: Ashridge Business School.

[8] Ganbat, K. (2012). Positive Relationship of Cross Cultural Training to Expatriate Adjustment. *International Journal of Physical and Social Sciences*, 134-146.

[9] (2012). *Global Mobility Survey Report.* www.globalmobilitysurvey.com.

[10] GMAC Global Relocation Services;National Foreign Trade Council (NFTC);SHRM Global Forum. (2004). *Global Relocation Trends 2003/2004 Survey Report.* GMAC Global Relocation Services.

[11] Gupta, N., Dasari, S., & Dasari, S. (2012). Expatriation: The Solution or the Problem? *Journal of Law, Policy and Globalization* , 7-17.

[12] Harvey, M., & Novicevic, M. M. (2001). Selecting expatriates for increasingly complex global assignments. *Career Development International* , 69-86.

[13] Heaps, W. (2010). *Localising Expats-Trap or Solution.* Retrieved from International HR Forum.

[14] HSBC. (2012). *HSBC Expat: Expat Explorer Survey* .

[15] Internations connecting globalminds. (n.d.). *What Is Culture Shock?* Retrieved from www.internations.org.

[16] Khosla, P., & Mukerjee, K. (2007). *International Assignment Perspectives – Critical Issues Facing the Globally Mobile Workforce.* PricewaterhouseCoopers.

[17] Koteswari, V. B., & Bhattacharya, M.S. (2007). Managing Expatriate success. *Delhi Business Review*, 89-98.

[18] Liisa Makela, V. S. (2011). Lives of female expatriates: work-life balance concerns. *Gender in Management: An International Journal*, 256-274.

[19] Liu, C.-H., & Le, H.-W. (2006). A proposed model of expatriates in multinational corporations. *Cross Cultural Management*, 176-193.

[20] Liu, C.-H., & Lee, H.-W. (2008). A proposed model of expatriates in multinational corporations. *Cross Cultural Management*, 176-193.

[21] Lowandowski, N. (2011, November). *Young expats will hold the majority of assignments by 2020.* Retrieved from ExpatMarketing.

[22] Messner, W. (2011). *Working in India.* Munich: Capgemini.

[23] Ravasi, C., Salamin, X., & Davoine, E. (2013, December). *The challenge of dual career expatriate management in a specific host national environment: An exploratory study of expatriate and spouse adjustment in Switzerland based MNCs1.* Retrieved from http://doc.rero.ch/collection/WORKING_PAPERS_SES.

[24] Sakho, H. (n.d.). The role of expatriate managers in global economic structuring;some key components and restructuring. *Research paper in International Business.*

[25] Selmer, J. (2006). Language ability and adjustment:Western expatriates in China. *Thunderbird International Business review*, 347-368.

[26] Sharma, D. (2005). *Foreign Multinationals in India: Adapting to India's Work Culture and Management Practices.* Retrieved from http://people.f3.htw-berlin.de/Professoren/Arora/pdf/discussionpaper/Foreign_Multinationals_in_India-Dayanand_Arora.pdf.

[27] Shrivastava, R., & Shrivastava, S. (2012). Management Practices with Indian Work Culture: Towards New Frontiers in Management Thinking. *International Journal of Interscience Management Review*, 56-62.

[28] Tahir, A. H., & Ismail, M. (2007). Cross cultural challenges and adjustment of Expatriates:Acase study in Malaysia. *Turkish journal of International Relations*, 72-89.

[29] Talapatra, D. (2010). *Expats in India: Challenges At Work.* Retrieved from http://www.womensweb.in/articles/im-going-to-work-in-india/.

[30] The Economist Intelligence Unit Limited (2010). *Next Moves for the Modern Expatriate.*

[31] The M group. (2012, December 28). *India is an Attractive Destination for Expats.* Retrieved from http://www.themigroup.com/.

[32] Tseng, C.-H., & Liao, Y.-S. (2009). Expatriate CEO assignment – A study of multinational corporations' subsidiaries in Taiwan . *International Journal of Manpower*, 853-870.

[33] Vojinić, P., Matić, M., & Bečić, M. (n.d.). Challenges of expatriation process . *Recent Advances in Business Management and Marketing*, 140-145.

[34] Wu, J. (2008). An analysis of Business challenges faced by foreign multinationals operating the chinese market. *International Journal of Business and Management*, 169-174.

Creating the Road for Inclusion of People with Mental Illness

G.B. Sitaram and Poonam Khurana

Rukmani Devi Institute of Advance Studies, Delhi

ABSTRACT

Mental illness is much like physical illness in that it can be influenced by environmental factors and events, and is often treatable with drugs. In order to have a fully inclusive workplace, a work environment must be created that is physically, technologically and attitudinally accessible. An accessible workplace will maximize productivity, by eliminating barriers that can prevent people with disabilities from working to their potential. The present paper is based on the review of literature and has made an attempt to dispel some myths related to various mental illness prevailing. At the same time, this paper aims at creating a psychological accessible workplace for such employees and throws light on the various solutions for developing fully inclusive workplace.

Keywords: *Mental Illness, Inclusive, Workplace*

INTRODUCTION

Many, if not most, of our psychological and emotional states and reactions seem to be the result of brain chemistry. Mental illness is much like physical illness in that it can be influenced by environmental factors and events, and is often treatable with drugs. In addition, there are environmental factors that are so powerful – childhood abuse, severe physical injury, terrifying events, war, etc. – which they can have lifelong psychological effects, which may or may not be the result of altered chemistry caused by exposure to them.

There are periods in almost everyone's life and personal development that present challenges that can result in acting out, or in temporary states of depression, confusion, or anxiety, all of which may look similar to the symptoms of long-term psychological disabilities. They aren't actual disabilities, however, because, in most cases, they resolve themselves relatively quickly through the natural course of living, and although they may cause emotional pain at the time, most people can continue to function as they cope. True psychological disabilities can include:

- ***Schizophrenia.*** is a mental disorder characterized by a breakdown in thinking and poor emotional responses. Common symtoms include delusions , such as the feeling that someone is out to get you, watching the things that are not there; disorganized thinking and a less motivated stage. Schizophrenia causes significant social and work problems. Symptoms begin typically in young adulthood and about 0.3–0.7% of people are affected during their lifetime. Diagnosis is based on observed behavior and the person's reportedexperiences. Schizophrenia can often be controlled to some extent by medication.

- ***Manic- depressive disorder:*** Bipolar disorder, also known as manic-depressive illness, is a brain disorder that causes unusual shifts in mood, energy, activity levels, and the ability to carry out day-to-day tasks. Symptoms of bipolar disorder are severe. They are different from the normal ups and downs that everyone goes through from time to time. Bipolar disorder symptoms can result in damaged relationships, poor job or school performance, and even suicide. But bipolar disorder can be treated, and people with this illness can lead full and productive lives.
- ***Chronic depression* or dysthymia:** A chronic form of depression, dysthymia is characterized by depressed mood on most days for at least two years. On some days individuals may feel relatively fine or even have moments of joy. But the good mood usually lasts no longer than a few weeks to a few months. Other signs include low self-esteem, plummeting energy, poor concentration, hopelessness, irritability and insomnia. Many people with depression are treated with medication.
- ***Multiple chemical sensitivity limitations***. Multiple chemical sensitivity, commonly known as environmental illness, is a chronic disease in which exposure to low levels of chemicals causes correlated symptoms of varying intensity. With the continuous introduction of new substances, people with MCS suffer significant limitations to their living environment and frequently to their workplace.
- ***Learning limitations***: learning disabilities are disorders that affect the ability to understand or use spoken or written language, do mathematical calculations, coordinate movements, or direct attention. Although learning disabilities occur in very young children, the disorders are usually not recognized until the child reaches school age. Learning disabilities are a lifelong condition; they are not outgrown or cured, though many people develop coping techniques through special education, tutoring, medication, therapy, personal development, or adaptation of learning skills.
- ***Dyslexia:*** Dyslexia is actually a term that refers to a broad range of neurologically-based learning difficulties, all of which affect an individual's ability to read and/or calculate. In addition, there are several other types of learning disabilities, some affecting only a particular area – language learning, for instance – and some affecting learning in broader ways. These are not connected to intelligence: dyslexics, in fact, tend to be somewhat above average in IQ, and many learn to read well in spite of their disability. Others – often those not diagnosed in childhood, or those with other problems unrelated to their disability – may continue to struggle.

OBJECTIVES OF THE PAPER

The main objective of the present paper is to create an awareness to create an inclusive workplace where there may be a good fit between employees' interpersonal and emotional competencies, their job skills and the position they hold. A good fit means that the employees possess the technical skills and knowledge for a particular position as well as the psychological skills and emotional intelligence (self-awareness, impulse control, persistence, self-motivation, empathy and social deftness) to do the job. The present study focuses on:

1. To educate based on evidence and dispel myths related to mental illnesses;
2. To concentrate on common mental health problems;
3. To raise awareness, tackle stigma and promote mental well-being;
4. To provide practical tools for creating an inclusive workplace for people and managers.

SOME FINDINGS RELATED TO MENTAL HEALTH PROBLEMS AT WORKPLACE

It is no surprise that policy-makers are concerned about the effects of mental disorders on society and on the economy. Globally, mental disorders are leading causes of disability. In some high-income countries, as much as 40% of disability can be attributed to mental disorders. In the WHO European Region, depression alone causes 13.7% of all years lived with disability, the leading cause. Alcohol disorders are ranked second with 6.2% and schizophrenia and bipolar disorders, much rarer but often lasting many years, rank numbers 11 and 12 respectively with just over 2% each. Associated with the level of disability, mental health problems have become one of the leading causes for absenteeism from work and early retirement all over the European Region. Mental health problems in the workplace have serious effects not only for the individual but also for the productivity and competitiveness of businesses and thus the economy and society as a whole. Employees' mental health status affects employees' performance and rates of illness, absenteeism and staff turnover. Sickness absenteeism can lead to substantial productivity losses. Early retirement and exclusion from the labour force due to work-related stress and mental health problems account for an enormous share of long-term social welfare benefits. In the United Kingdom, for example, the total cost to employers of mental health problems among their staff is estimated to be nearly £26 billion each year, equivalent to £1035 for every employee in the workforce. The business costs comprise £8.4 billion per year in sickness absence, £15.1 billion per year due to reduced productivity at work and £2.4 billon per year in replacing personnel who leave their jobs because of mental ill health (Sainsbury Centre for Mental Health, 2007).

EEO Trust research (2005) has found that disabled people believe that other people's attitudes and behaviours are the main barrier they face at work. Work is a significant and important aspect of most people's lives, a place where they build relationships, develop skills and talents, and gain personal satisfaction from their participation in society. Disabled people need to be free to pursue these goals in the workplace without having to deal with the unhelpful attitudes and behavior of other people at work, whether they are colleagues and managers or clients and customers. By developing positive alternatives, employers can create environments which support everyone to be creative, co-operative and productive at work.

A person who develops a mental disorder while employed is in a totally different – and much more favourable – position than someone trying to acquire a job who already has a history of mental disorder. Securing mainstream employment is then very difficult, especially if the symptoms are clearly or apparently still present. A feeling of unease during a job interview, subtle behavioral oddities (coming just a little too physically close or avoiding eye contact just a little too often), an odd attitude or a presentation that is not entirely adequate in terms of clothing or make-up can quickly lead an interviewer to form a negative view of candidates, even without knowing anything of their history. If the interviewer is aware of that history, they are often reluctant to take the risk. Mental problems are almost by definition problems in relation to interaction and communication. In a service economy that strongly emphasizes working in relatively informal teams, this is a major obstacle to the opportunities for people with mental disorders at work. This becomes even more of a problem when unemployment is high or rising.

In practice, people with an obvious history of mental disorder are virtually absent from the mainstream labour market. The roughly 0.5% of adults with schizophrenia are in the worst position here, because they often also fail in tertiary education. People who are plagued by severe depression or anxiety and obsessions or who have a personality structure that rapidly leads to conflicts also have few opportunities. In an increasing number of cases, however, work is available for these people outside the world of mainstream employment. This may be work in a sheltered employment setting where the productivity and quality demands are less decisive or work carried out in the context of a special social security arrangement (Van Weeghel, 2002). The employer in these cases is spared most or all of the costs of employing these workers. The work they carry out is relatively simple and takes place under expert supervision. In many cases, these are forms of supervised work that are sometimes also offered to people with learning disabilities. However, a key difference is that most people with learning disabilities are more stable and consistent in their performance than people with mental disorders.

Mental illness is often assumed to be primarily a medical problem, and successfully treating the symptoms is considered the main barrier to resuming normal activities such as returning to work. For return to normal activities, mental ill health should be conceptualized as a social problem with medical aspects rather than the other way around. Thornicroft (2006) describes stigma as an overarching term that contains three elements: problems of knowledge (ignorance) and problems of attitudes (prejudice) leading to problems of behaviour (discrimination).

RECOMMENDATIONS ON THE BASIS OF LITERATURE REVIEW

1. **For People With Disabilities Themselves:** People with disabilities have often been incredible self-advocates. They can demonstrate how lack of accessibility affects them, and speak eloquently about their experiences. As participants in planning the design and construction of new buildings and facilities, they can bring their experiences to bear to make projects as accessible and usable as possible.
2. **For Employers:** It makes sense for employers to make sure they can hire the best person available. Making their workplaces accessible allows them to do just that, without having to think about accommodation if that person happens to have a disability.
   - Mental illness is not the same as having a learning or intellectual difficulty. It is often a temporary condition and most people will recover fully.
     - People with mental illness may find everyday activities confusing, distressing or difficult. Try to be kind, non-judgmental and patient.
     - Give the person plenty of time if there are decisions to be made.
     - According to the Americans With Disabilities Act (ADA), "the term 'disability' means an individual has a physical or mental impairment that substantially limits one or more of his/her major life activities or there is a record of such an impairment or an individual is regarded as having such an impairment." Caused by injury, disease or medical condition, or neurological, chemical, or developmental factors, severe disabilities affect about 12% of the U.S. population.
     - About 18% of the population has some level of disability, a figure that expands to 72% for those 80 and older, and shrinks to 11% for children ages 6 to 14. Four percent of the population over age 6 is severely enough disabled to need personal assistance with one or more activities of daily living.
     - Improve and expand its customer base to people with disabilities by eliminating barriers that may prevent or deter them from accessing the services and products offered
     - The first concerns the strength of our commitment to provide work opportunities to the mentally (and physically) disabled, even where there are significant costs involved in reasonable accommodation. In some cases, employers may be obliged to ignore modest decrements in relevant talents and skills, decrements that would have been grounds for replacing a non disabled employee.
     - A person with mental disabilities may require modest concessions on the job -- more frequent breaks, release time for counseling, or shifting job responsibilities -- where these involve extra costs, even from the perspective of a workplace that already was structured to protect equality of opportunity. Hiring or retaining the mentally disabled worker under these conditions -as opposed to hiring or retaining the slightly more efficient non-handicapped worker might be a reasonable accommodation, but

it would seem to involve "more than equal" opportunity. Or can this case, regardless of whether it is hypothetical or rare, be accommodated within a concern about equality of opportunty?

CASE STUDY OF IBM

IBM

Company size: 433,362 employees

Key product/service items: IBM is an information technology (IT) company, engaged in providing consulting, delivery and implementation services, enterprise software, systems and financing.

Accessibility website overview: IBM's Human Ability and Accessibility Center offers a newsroom of accessibility publications and articles, a series of case studies, developer guidelines, an overview of laws, standards, and regulations, as well as a resource center of accessibility education tutorials and presentations. The Human Ability and Accessibility Center also highlights IBM's accessibility services, products, ongoing research, as well as free IBM accessibility downloads.

IBM is taking the lead in the following areas:

- providing solutions, services, and technologies that help their customers realize the benefits of accessibility
- making information technology accessible to more people, including those with disabilities
- helping define international accessibility standards to help define and provide for interoperability
- inventing technologies that help remove barriers and extend capabilities

REFERENCES

[1] Gaal E, Van Weeghel J, Van Campen M, Linszen D. (2002). The Trainee Project: Family-aided vocational rehabilitation of young people with schizophrenia. *Psychiatric Rehabilitation Journal* 26(1): 101-105.

[2] Disability and Employment – Review of literature research, May 2005.

[3] Kavka, Gregory S. 1992. "Disability and the Right to Work," Social Philosophy and Policy 9:1, 262-90.

[4] Rawls, John, 1971. A Theory of Justice. Cambridge: Harvard University Press. Sainsbury Centre for Mental Health (2007). Mental health at work: developing the business case. London, Sainsbury Centre for Mental Health.

[5] Shaw Trust (2006). Mental health – the last workplace taboo Wiltshire, Shaw Trust (http://www.shaw-trust.org.uk/files/st_mental_health_summary.pdf, accessed 15 June 2010).

[6] Singleton N et al. (2001). Psychiatric morbidity among adultsliving in private households London, Office for National Statistics.

[7] Thornicroft G (2006). Shunned – discrimination against people with mental illness. Oxford, Oxford University Press.

[8] Thornicroft G et al. (2009). Global pattern of experienced and anticipated discrimination against people with schizophrenia: a cross-sectional survey. Lancet,373:408–415.

Websites

[9] *www.*centreformentalhealth.*org.uk/.../*Sainsbury_Centre_*Annual_Review...*

[10] http://www-03.ibm.com/able

[11] *en.wikipedia.org/wiki/*Americans_with_Disabilities_Act_*of*_1990

Reservations in India: An Inclusive Perspective

S. Sanjay Kumar

Guru Gobind Singh Indraprastha University, Dwarka, New Delhi

Abstract

Reservation policy in India has been a tool for upliftment of the marginalized sections of the society such as Scheduled Castes and Scheduled Tribes. However the policy is limited only to the public sector employment. With the rise of market capitalism the employment opportunities in public sector have started shrinking and demands to extend the policy of reservations to private sector have been rising. Government of India has responded to the demands and urged corporate India to assist it in extending the benefits of growth to the marginalized sections. Corporate India is averse to such policies being imposed on them by the government. But it responded to the call and agreed to implement affirmative action voluntarily. This paper argues that the understanding of reservation policy of government of India and the affirmative action of corporates is missing on the perspective that such policies contribute to the work force diversity and promote inclusive growth. Appreciation of this perspective enables policy makers and corporate heads to realise the business sense involved.

INTRODUCTION

Globalization has brought to forefront the issues related to diversity in work force. Managing work force diversity has become integral to human resource strategy. This signifies the recognition of potential benefits of diversity in the work force and its contribution to the success of business organizations. Reservation policy in matters related to employment in public sector has been constitutionally sanctioned and implemented for ensuring adequate representation to the backward classes of the society in India. However private sector is not subjected to such policy. It is only of late that private sector business organizations in India have started realizing the benefits of making their work force more diverse and started creating employment opportunities to the socially and economically disadvantaged sections of the Indian society. Even though it is argued that these initiatives of the private sector enterprises in India are essentially aimed at stalling the efforts of the Government of India to extend the protective discrimination policies to the private sector, one cannot undermine the fact that the approach of few private sector organizations towards creating employment opportunities to the disadvantaged groups has changed. While the corporate world predominantly is of the view that any intervention of government by prescribing "quotas" will be a compromise of principle of merit, it is heartening to find voices from corporate class, though few, which acknowledge the merits of creating inclusive work places by providing access to employment for people with diverse backgrounds. It may not endorse the reservation policy in private sector but certainly demonstrates a new perspective that is emerging within the corporate world – a perspective that inclusive policies do not necessarily militate against the virtues of "meritocracy".

In the above context this paper tries to discuss the protective discrimination policies adopted by the Indian State within the frame work of the Constitution of India, approaches used for ensuring representation to the disadvantaged groups in public employment, attempts being made to extend the protective discrimination policies to private sector employment and the need to look at inclusive policies from a new perspective.

CONSTITUTIONAL STATUS OF RESERVATIONS

Right to equality enshrined in Article 14 of the Indian Constitution provides for equality before law or the equal protection of laws. Article 15 prohibits discrimination on grounds of race, religion, caste, sex or place of birth and Article 16 provides for equality of opportunities in matters related to public employment. Through the Constitution (First Amendment) Act, 1951 an enabling provision in the form of sub clause (4) to Article 15 was inserted which empowers the State to make any special provisions for the advancement of any socially and educationally backward classes of citizens or for the Scheduled Castes (SC's) and the Scheduled Tribes (ST's). Sub-clause (4) of Article 16 also empowers the State from making any provision for the reservation of appointments or posts in favour of any backward class of citizens which, in the opinion of the State, is not adequately represented in the services under the State.

The Union government has been implementing the policy of reservation for Scheduled Castes and Scheduled Tribes through executive orders under which 15% and 7.5% of posts are reserved for Scheduled Castes and Scheduled Tribes respectively. Similar policies have been implemented by State governments in their respective States for SC's, ST's and Backward Classes (BC's). Consequent to the acceptance of Mandal Commission's Report by the Union government and the decision of Supreme Court of India in Indira Sawhney & Ors *Vs* Union of India reservations for Other Backward Classes (OBC's) are being implemented in central services since 1994.

LEGAL APPROACH TO THE POLICY OF RESERVATIONS

The journey towards social justice along the path of reservations was not without road blocks. Numerous cases came up before the Supreme Court of India during the post-independence period challenging the constitutional validity of the reservation policies pursued by the State. Reservations on the basis of social and educational backwardness where caste is a predominant criterion for determination of backwardness were contested on the grounds that they are infringement of fundamental right to equality. The courts in India have rejected these contentions and affirmed the right of the State to provide for protective discrimination to the backward classes. There was heavy reliance placed on the notion of "substantive equality" than "formal equality" in matters related to reservations. It was emphasised that creating a level playing field is a "compelling interest" of the State without which unequal outcomes will be produced and existing inequalities will be perpetuated.

The rationale and reasons articulated to legitimize the policy of reservations may be summarised as follows:

1. Historical deprivations suffered by lower castes due to the hierarchical and oppressive social structures existing for centuries coupled with the social privileges enjoined by upper castes have created natural disadvantages to the lower castes and natural advantages to the upper castes. In such context formal equality will produce unfair outcomes for the lower castes and therefore substantive equality which produces fair outcomes need to be applied.
2. Positive discrimination is meant to compensate for the historical wrongs committed against lower castes and the price paid in terms of compromises made with merit is justifiable.
3. Communities that were ghettoised for centuries need the special protection of the State without which it is impossible for them to become part of main stream society.
4. Right to equality envisages equal treatment of equals but not equal treatment of unequal. Therefore treating unequals equally is as much discriminatory as treating equals unequally.
5. Special protection extended to backward classes is not arbitrary but based on intelligible criteria having nexus with the objective of social justice.

POLICIES BEYOND PUBLIC EMPLOYMENT

In the recent past Government of India has taken decisions with respect to the procurement policies of the government under which preferential treatment is accorded to the trading and manufacturing enterprises owned by members of SC/ST communities. It mandates that a specified percentage out of total purchase expenditure has to be incurred on purchases sourced from SC/ST entrepreneurs. This marks recognition of the need to extend protective discrimination policies to spheres other than public employment. In an economy dominated by market where public sector role is gradually diminishing it is imperative to find market oriented approaches to realise the objectives of social and economic justice. The initiatives are to be viewed from the perspective of creating opportunities for growth to SC/ST communities by integrating them into the supply chain.

CORPORATE INDIA AND AFFIRMATIVE ACTION

The limitations of confining positive discrimination policies to the public sector are too striking for any government to ignore. Realising such limitations, the Prime Minister of India in the year 2006 had appealed to the Corporate India to implement affirmative action policies and programmes and assist government in addressing problems that surfaced in the course of implementing neo-liberal reforms. Post liberalization period not only witnessed growth but also glaring inequalities in distribution of benefits of growth and marginalization of under privileged sections of society. Corporate India which is averse to accept any kind of legislative measures that requires them to implement the policy of reservation in the manner akin to the reservation policy in public sector had reacted sharply and condemned the contemplated actions as regressive. However it had agreed to certain voluntary initiatives. CII, ASSOCHAM and FICCI had developed Code of Conduct for Affirmative Action and Voluntary CSR Guidelines and persuaded their members to become signatories to the Code of Conduct for implementation of Affirmative Action in their respective organizations.

A report published by Partners In Change – a non-profit organization working in the area of Corporate Social Responsibility – in December 2012 highlights the status of implementation of Affirmative Action (for SC/ST) in BSE- Listed Companies. This report states that only 39 of the targeted 145 companies participated in the study aimed at analysing the Affirmative Action initiatives in the work place, market place, supply chain and community level. This by itself indicates that majority of the private sector corporates are not deeply committed to share their achievements on Affirmative Action initiatives. It reveals that most of the organizations expressed positive opinion on Affirmative Action but very few have actually taken up initiatives under it. Tata Group companies followed by Godrej and Crompton Greaves are found to be responsive to Affirmative Action. Affirmative action for most of the organizations is reduced to philanthropic/charity initiatives at community level. Reasons cited for lacking commitment to pursue affirmative action included, 'does not want to be seen as promoting interests of certain communities', 'backlash from employees', 'initiatives focussed on economically weaker sections will suffice to take care of the needs of SC/ST's', 'leads to compromising merit which can't be afforded', etc. It reflects lack of appreciation of the business sense involved in the affirmative action initiatives at the top management level.

ACADEMIC AND PUBLIC DISCOURSES

Management literature is replete with research findings from studies related to diversity. Diversity exists at two levels – surface-level and deep-level. Demographics such as gender, race, religion, ethnicity, caste, disability etc; only reflect surface-level diversity. Distinction is also made between unfair discrimination and fair discrimination. If surface-level diversity is reckoned without any regard to the deep-level diversity we may end up judging individuals through stereotypes. This leads to unfair discrimination which is harmful to organizations and employees. On the other hand discrimination on the basis of deep-level diversity without any regard to surface-level diversity is fair discrimination. This contributes to the work force diversity and pro-diversity culture in the organizations which is conducive to innovation and helps in building capacities to serve diverse markets.

The public discourse on the subject of reservations/protective discrimination/affirmative action in Indian context is on two extreme positions. Proponents often tend to over emphasize surface-level diversity (social or caste/administrative category) which is implicit in the position that it is justifiable to provide "quotas" in proportion to the population of each administrative category viz; SC, ST, OBC. Those who oppose tend to lay emphasis on deep-level diversity (attributes of merit) implicit in the position that "quotas" violate merit and adversely affect performance of organizations. Interestingly, real experience represents neither of these extreme positions. It would be naïve to believe that employment opportunities in India, be it in public sector or private sector, are solely based on social or caste/administrative category or merit. Historically, opportunities are contingent on combination of both social or caste status and merit.

Merit in Indian context is invariably associated with social/caste status. This is evident from rigid hierarchical social structures operating for centuries. The society was divided into priestly class, warrior class, trading class and labouring class with specific roles and privileges attached to each class which were regarded as divinely ordained. This division was characterised as *"varna"* system. Those who were within the fold of *varna* system are called as *"savarnas"* and outside it were called as *"avarnas"* which literally means "out castes" (later administratively classified as Scheduled Castes). They were subjected to inhuman practice of untouchability and were assigned degrading and menial work.

The reservation policy based on "quotas" in practice has not completely eliminated the influence of social or caste status. All that it could achieve is to include hitherto excluded castes to be considered for appointments under the so called merit based system. Enabling provision under Article 16 (4) of the Constitution is unambiguous when it empowers State to reserve posts in favour of backward classes of citizens which, in the opinion of the State, are not adequately represented. Merit continues to be a relevant factor for selection within an administrative group. Policy of reservation in India is not blind to individual differences. It takes into consideration both surface-level and deep-level characteristics.

NEW PERSPECTIVE

For those who distinguish between quota system followed in India and affirmative action followed in United States of America, it would be interesting to know the decision of United States Supreme Court in a land mark case **Grutter v. Bollinger.** While upholding the admissions policy of University of Michigan Law School, United States Supreme Court by a majority judgement ruled that the University of Michigan Law School had a compelling interest in promoting class diversity. A race-conscious admissions process that may favour "underrepresented minority groups," but that also took into account many other factors evaluated on an individual basis for every applicant, did not amount to a quota system that would have been unconstitutional.

CONCLUSION

The basis of upholding the policy that favour underrepresented minority groups without completely ignoring other individual factors is stated to be the compelling interest in promoting class diversity. The "compelling interest" no longer is only correcting historical wrongs. It now includes benefits that flow from diversity. This decision brings a new perspective and reduces the differences in understanding reservation policy in India and affirmative action in US. Policy makers and corporate bosses will do well if they can appreciate this perspective lest they fail themselves. If not, those who are not included into the benefits of the Indian growth story will fail them.

REFERENCES

[1] Grutter v. Bollinger, 539 U.S. 306 (2003)

[2] Indira Sawhney & Ors v. Union of India. AIR 1993 SC 477

[3] http://en.wikipedia.org/wiki/Grutter_v._Bollinger

[4] http://www.picindia.org/publication/status_action.pdf

Author Index

Aggarwal, Vijita S. 115
Aggarwal, Vijita Singh 166, 200

Bhargava. Somya 122

Dabas, Deepali 177

Garg, Shalini 15, 52, 93
Gautam, Priyanka 88
Grover, Megha 88
Gupta. Puneet Kumar 52

Handa, Meenakshi 157

Jain, Prachi 166

Khurana, Poonam 211
Kukreja, Jyoti 157
Kumar, Ashish 102
Kumar, S. Sanjay 218

Lather, Anu Singh 15
Lochab, Anshu 88

Mathur, Gunjan 177
Mishra, Rekha 93
Mittal, Rupa 48
Nain, Bhavya 84

Philip, Justin J. 66
Prabha, Y. Lakshmi 108
Prakash, Pranava 122
Pyngavil. Rajesh S. 73

Rajendran, Thilakam 3

Sanchita 52
Sareen, Puja 140
Sargam, Shruti 38
Shefali 200
Sinha, Neena 9
Sitaram, G.B. 211
Swarna, Ramani 30

Thomas, Bino 66

Vaksha, Anuj 24
Vijayran, Manisha 131
Vikas, Sona 15